Women of Scotland

Women of Scotland

fishwives to scientists

Helen Susan Swift

Copyright (C) 2013 Helen Susan Swift
Layout design and Copyright (C) 2016 Creativia
Published 2016 by Creativia
Paperback design by Creativia (www.creativia.org)
ISBN: 978-1534937918
Cover art by http://www.thecovercollection.com/
All rights reserved. No part of this book may be reproduced or transmitted in any form or by any means, electronic or mechanical, including photocopying, recording, or by any information storage and retrieval system, without the author's permission.

Acknowledgements

I would like to thank all those people who have helped me in my research including the staff at Aberdeen University Library, Dundee University Archives and the National Archives of Scotland.

Contents

1	Saints and Warrior Women of the Celts: Folklore and Legend	2
2	The Pious and the Patriots	13
3	'God Be Thanked, I am Pregnant by the King'	31
4	Rascall Women of the Covenant	45
5	Wise Women, Witches and Seers	58
6	Jacobite Women	67
7	Victims and Avengers	80
8	Class and Culture	89
9	The Countess and the Clearances	104
10	Press Gangs and Powder Monkeys	114
11	Only Weavers Wore Hats: Industrial Women	128
12	All at Sea	140
13	The Fisherwomen	148

14	High Adventure	157
15	Scotswomen and Drink	168
16	Local Girl Done Good	177
17	The Suffragettes	187
18	Political Women	199
19	Women and War	208
20	Women in Medicine and Education	221
21	Women of Literature	233
22	L'envoi	246
23	Selected Bibliography	249

Introduction

A small country at the western fringe of Europe, Scotland has produced more than her quota of outstanding personalities. The exploits of Scottish men such as William Wallace, David Livingstone and John Logie Baird are well known. However, Scotland has also produced an amazing number of outstanding women. From mediaeval warriors such as Black Agnes of Dunbar to Betsy Miller, Britain's first female ship master, from Williamina Fleming, the leading female astronomer of the 19th century to Victoria Drummond, Britain's first female chief engineer, Scotswomen have faced tribulation and emerged triumphant. Scotland has also produced politicians such as Flora Drummond and Katherine Marjory, and literary women such as Mary MacLeod and Alison Cockburn.

Nevertheless, despite such a gathering of genius and grit, it is perhaps the ordinary, unsung women of Scotland who deserve more praise, for they have held the nation together. From fisherwomen to mill workers, temperance workers to smugglers, this book introduces some of Scotland's women.

Chapter 1

Saints and Warrior Women of the Celts: Folklore and Legend

'Where there's a cow there's a woman, and where there's a woman there's mischief.' Saint Columba

When the Romans invaded what was to become Scotland they had to contend with a ferocious enemy who fought with courage, skill and a mastery of guerrilla tactics that caused the legions many problems. Although they won a significant victory at Mons Graupius in 83 AD, the Romans could not conquer this northern land and eventually withdrew behind Hadrian's Wall. Few eyewitness account relate the type of persons the Romans encountered in the glens and straths, but when Ammianus Marcellinus, a Roman of the fourth century AD met the Gauls, a Celtic people similar to the Picts of Scotland, he said that they were 'terrible from the sternness of their eyes, very quarrelsome and of great pride and insolence.' It is a description that may still be apt to many Scots today. Yet, while the Romans considered that Celtic men were dangerous opponents, they seemed to hold their women in even greater awe.

Marcellinius claimed that 'a whole troop of foreigners would not be able to withstand a single Gaul if he called his wife to his assistance.' It seems that these women were 'very strong... especially when, swelling her neck, gnashing her teeth and brandishing her sallow arms of enormous size, she begins to strike blows mingled with kicks.' As the Romans eventually defeated the Gauls, but failed to defeat the Picts, it is conceivable that the latter were even more formidable.

The morals of the Pictish women, at least, seem to have scandalised the visitors for, according to Roman accounts, they were free to make love with whomsoever they wished. Marriage among the Celts was easy, and divorce so simple that weddings may have been an annual event. However there were also legal concubines, a second wife who lived beside the first or principal wife. The law permitted a jealous principal wife to beat the concubine, which must have created some uneasy relationships. Yet concubinage appears to have been quite a common practice, despite the second wife's title of 'adultrach': the adulteress.

There were as many as ten different forms of marriage in the Celtic world, from a conveniently casual sexual bond to permanent union. An echo of these arrangements was apparent as late as the 18th century when Handfasting, a form of trial marriage, was common in Scotland, despite the disapproval of the kirk. There is an interesting legend that a Pictish woman made love to the father of Pontius Pilate while he was on a mission north of the Roman Frontier. Between them they created the young Pilate who later became governor of Jerusalem. Although the story is probably apocryphal, it does illustrate the idea of sexual freedom that Scotswomen enjoyed.

But who would marry one of these dominant, ferocious women? Many, for Celtic women echoed society; warfare and quarrelling were major pleasures so a docile, humble wife would have been no fun, no challenge. A woman of might and assertion was an equal partner in life's adventures.

When not fighting or loving, Celtic women took pride in their appearance. The Celtic women known to the Romans seemed to have lived short lives, with many dying in their early twenties, but they made the most of the time that they had. They married young, at about twelve years old and apparently flirted outrageously. They used dye from berries to tint their eyebrows and paint their lips, and also rouged their cheeks. They seem to have been immensely proud of their braided hair, and kept their combs in personal bags.

Celtic women wore plaid skirts and gold or silver anklets, necklaces and bracelets, they had rings on their fingers and in their ears and thrust decorated pins through their hair. The noblewomen wore elaborate torques around their neck and decorated the brooches that held their clothes. They even washed in warm water, a habit that many of their urban descendants forgot, and were very careful of their fingernails. It is possible that Celtic women wore sandals, so they could display the rings in their toes.

Indeed, Celtic women were so vain of their appearance that the law demanded a fine from anybody who insulted their looks, clothes or make up. Celtic law also forbade anybody from lying about a woman's reputation or insulting her. If her husband had slept with another woman, a Celtic wife could legally kill her love rival provided she committed the deed in hot blood. The wife was allowed three days between discovering the adultery and despatching the culprit; after that her anger was supposed to have abated. There does not seem to be anything written about subsequent relations with her husband; presumably they kissed and made up once she had proved her love.

Men, however, enjoyed the beauty and appearance of their women. 'Her upper arms were as white as the snow of a single night and they were soft and straight; and her clear and lovely cheeks were as red as the foxglove.' So says the 8th century saga of Etain, the most attractive woman in Ireland. The description praised her eyebrows, teeth and eyes, smooth shoulders, long hands, slender sides and warm thighs.

It concluded, 'all are lovely till compared with Etain. All are fair till compared with Etain.'

So these assertive women did not overawe their men, nor did they adopt masculine habits to prove their capability; both genders accepted and joyed in the differences of the other. Women enjoyed equal legal standing with men; they possessed property and in widowhood they became owners of their husband's goods. Women could lead the tribe as Queen or even war leader. Although there are no remaining records of Pictish Queens, leaders such as Boudicca of the Iceni, Cartimandua of the Brigantes and Medb of Connacht were powerful Celtic queens. There is no reason to doubt that their Pictish contemporaries were any different.

Women appear to have been extremely important in Dark Age Scotland. Celtic mythology awards women with skills, powers and prestige that were sadly lacking in many other peoples. Women were deeply involved in the spiritual cult of rebirth, and goddesses such as the Morrigan, or Great Queen, and Danann, the queen of other gods were at the apex of the Celtic pantheon. It is tragic that the Picts have not left us a literary legacy, but the Gaels told tales of the great Queen Medb of Connacht, while Cu Cuchlainn, the hero of Dark Age Ireland, was trained in the Isle of Skye. His trainers, Scatach and Aife were both women, while Welsh legends also tell of training schools where females instructed male warriors. Women seemed equally important in religion, where black-clad female Druids resisted the Roman assault on Anglesey.

Ancient tradition maintains that the name Hebrides evolved from the name Ey-brides or Isles of Saint Brigit, who looked after the outer isles. The original Saint Brigit was a Gaelic goddess, daughter of the Dagda, patroness of poets. Legend says that Brigit was also the goddess of fire, and only women of noble birth could attend the holy fires at her temples. These women were known as the 'daughters of fire.' With the advent of Christianity, Saint Bride replaced the goddess Brigit and a new set of legends began in the Isles of Saint Bride. The oystercatcher became Bride's especial bird, the First of February became St Bride's Day and Bride, who was also known as 'Mary of the Gael' was thought to have been midwife to the Virgin Mary. A charming folk tale relates how Saint Bride lit a crown of candles on her head, to distract Herod's searchers from the Christ. Such a colourful and resourceful woman was the natural choice for a Celtic saint, so the Christian Church established the order of the nuns of St Bride to eradicate memories of the pagan goddess Brigit. These island nuns were possibly the first community of Christian women in Western Europe. In time Christian women settled in other parts of what became Scotland, with, for instance, Abbess Aebbe ruling at Coldingham, southeast of the Forth.

Scotland seemed to produce a clutch of unique female saints. One of the earliest came from what is now East Lothian, which according to legend, was ruled by a pagan king named Loth. The king was unhappy when his daughter, Thenew, embraced the new Christian religion, and even more unhappy when she embraced a lover who was not only Christian but also from a lower social class. It was almost inevitable that she became pregnant, and that her father should notice. In those days of the 6th century, a king's wrath could be explosive, and Loth ordered his warriors to throw Thenew over the sheer cliffs of Traprain Law. Perhaps it was because she was persecuted for the sake of righteousness that Thenew landed safely, and a cool spring gushed from the spot where she had fallen. Unabashed, King Loth remained determined to execute his daughter, so placed her in a coracle and pushed her without food, water or paddle into the Firth of Forth.

Secure in her faith, Thenew waited for the next miracle. The tide carried her to the Isle of May, then over toward Culross in Fife. When Thenew saw a fire on the shore, she took it for a message of hope from the Lord, and approached closely. She knew that her time was close, and gave birth to her son in the gentle warmth of the flames. The monks that tended the fire took Thenew to St Serf, who adopted the infant boy. The saint named the youngster Kentigern, which meant

Chief Lord, or Mungo, which translates into Loveable Man, and when Kentigern grew up he created the religious foundation that became Glasgow Cathedral. Kentigern's mother, Thenew was also sainted, and is remembered as Saint Enoch.

Another of Scotland's early saints was Saint Triduana, who, according to legend, landed at Kilrymont in the company of St Rule. Kilrymont was an important Pictish community that is better known as St Andrews, but Triduana eventually settled at Restenneth near Forfar in the Pictish kingdom of Circinn. Unfortunately, Nechtan, the local king, was a passionate man with an eye for the ladies, while Triduana was young, shapely and beautiful.

When Nechtan's attentions became too offensive, Triduana fled from Circinn and settled in Dynfallandy, in the hill country near Pitlochry. However, Nechtan was as persistent as he was amorous, and sent his men to scour the country for the eastern beauty. Naturally, a woman as exotic as Triduana could not remain undetected for long, and the king's men found her.

'Come back to Circinn,' they pleaded, 'for King Nechtan desires your company.'

Triduana listened to their requests then asked 'What does so great a prince desire of me, a poor virgin dedicated to God?'

'The king desires the most excellent beauty of thine eyes,' answered the ambassadors, 'which if he obtains not, he will assuredly die.'

'Ah,' said Triduana, 'then that which he seeketh he shall assuredly have.' Plucking out her eyes with a thorn, she handed them to the ambassadors, who carried them back to Nechtan.

Strangely, once he had her eyes, the king seemed to lose interest in the saint, who moved south to Lothian and settled in a cell near Edinburgh. Restalrig Church now stands where Triduana lived out her life, and because of her sacrifice, she is known as a saint for the blind.

These harbingers of Christianity were not always welcome. One monastic community was established on the island of Eigg, seven miles west of the Scottish mainland. At one time St Donan ruled over more than fifty monks here, white robed, peaceful and devout as they pastured their animals and prayed to the Lord. Unfortunately they had not reckoned with their neighbours. In 618 AD the *Martyrology of Donegal* relates: 'there came robbers of the sea on a certain time to the island, when he, Donan, was celebrating Mass. He requested of them not to kill him until he should have the Mass said, and they gave him this respite, and he was afterwards beheaded and 52 of his monks along with him.'

Massacres of monks were virtually unknown in those pre-Viking days, and this particular act of butchery was highly unusual in that a woman sanctioned it. A Pictish queen from nearby Moidart grazed her sheep on Eigg and so resented the monk's intrusion that she told her warriors to remove them. If the chronicles are correct, the reaction of this Moidart queen is an early example of what became a recurring theme of history: it is always better not to anger a Scotswoman. It was no real wonder that Eigg was also known as the 'island of the big women.'

In these days before Scotland was formed, the country was a confusion of small kingdoms, each ruled by a petty sub-king. Interestingly, some historians, such as Nora Chadwick, believe that the Picts, whose kingdoms covered a great deal of the north and east of the land, followed laws of matrilineal succession. That meant that the kingship was decided on the bloodline of the mother, rather than the father, which highlights the importance of women in old Scotland. Other historians, namely Alfred Smyth[1], dispute this unique manner of selecting a monarch, and explain that the Picts may have been a subject people, ruled by foreign kings who may, or may not, have had a Pictish mother.

---

1. Smyth, Alfred, *Warlords and Holy Men: Scotland AD80 – 1000* (Edinburgh 1989)

There is no doubt that within the Celtic world, kings and princes married outside their own kingdom. It also happened that a non-Celtic noble married an indigenous Celtic woman, thus easing the process of integration. Some of these incomers were extremely tough warriors, with the redoubtable Norsemen probably the most ferocious fighting men in Europe. Perhaps some of these marriages were by mutual consent, but the Viking poetry of Bjorn Cripplehand presents another picture.

> 'The men of Mull were tired of flight;
> The Scottish foemen would not fight
> And many an island-girl's wail
> Was heard as through the Isles we sail.'

Contemporary chronicles confirm that Norsemen carried off Scotswomen as slaves, so that rape and brutality marked the Norse incursions, but once the dust had settled, the Norse found that Celtic women were eminently capable of looking after themselves.

With her husband often absent on his Viking forays, it was natural that the Celtic wife and mother would bring up the offspring of any union. It was equally natural that the mother would teach the child her own culture in her own tongue, so that within a couple of generations, many Norse settlements were Gaelic speaking, with a fusion of Norse and Celtic lore and culture. A recent DNA study of Iceland has produced the surprising result that a majority of the inhabitants have Gaelic ancestry, indicating that the influence of Scottish mothers was extremely powerful as well as enduring.

Perhaps Norse women were loath to travel far from their homes, for the Norsemen certainly delighted in Celtic wives. Olaf of Dublin married at least twice; his first queen was the daughter of Aed Findliath, High King of Ireland. His second was Scottish, perhaps the daughter of Kenneth Mac Alpin, reputedly the first king of a united Scotland. The combination of Norse and Celt created a hybrid woman who seemed as adventurous as any Viking.

One such was Aud, the Deep Minded, daughter of Ketil Flatnose, king of the Hebrides. Aud may also have been a wife of Olaf of Dublin, but when the mainland Scots killed her son Thorstein in battle, she decided to emigrate. The *Laxdaela Saga* claims that she left because 'she did not have much chance of recovering her position' in Scotland. By building a ship in Caithness, Aud became Scotland's first recorded female ship builder. She then loaded her valuables and led her family, followers and slaves out to sea. Not only servants and slaves followed her, but noblemen such as Koli and Hord who were to make their mark in Norse history. Aud sailed north, first to Orkney, where she married off one of her granddaughters, then to the Faeroe Islands and finally Iceland, where she became a major landowner.

Celtic mothers were not prone to mollycoddle their Norse sons. On one occasion, when Earl Sigurd of Orkney asked his Gaelic mother if he should attack a rival king on the Scottish mainland, she replied:

'I would have reared you in my wool basket if I had known you expected to live forever. It is fate that governs a man's life, not his comings and goings, and it is better to die with honour than live in shame.'

This trait in Scottish mothers was to be repeated for many generations. Tough love may be a relatively new phrase, but as a concept it was accepted in pre-mediaeval Scotland. Sigurd's son, Thorfinn, bore a Norse name, but he was the product of a Scottish mother and a Gaelic, possibly Irish, grandmother. The Norse may have believed that they ruled the Isles, but generations of Gaelic women were gradually winning the race game. In time the Outer Isles, among the most densely settled by the Norse, were to become a bastion of Gaeldom, surely due to the influence of hundreds of Gaelic speaking wives and mothers. Perhaps the Norse were ferocious warriors with sword and axe, but

Scotswomen won the longer war with patience, endurance, culture and guile.

The descendants of the Pictish women who had extended such a friendly welcome to the emissaries of Rome fought the Vikings with terrible stubbornness. History has recorded few of their names, but a woman named Frakok in what is now Sutherland organised a guerrilla war against the Norse that only ended when they surrounded her Kildonan headquarters and put it, and her, to the torch. The fact that women were prepared to fight the invaders proved their sheer bloody-mindedness, for a century and more had passed since a law had declared that women and children were non-combatants. It was in 697 that Adomnan, the Abbott of Iona, passed his 'Law of Innocents.' This law was no casual decision, but a carefully considered agreement that had been negotiated with 40 prominent clergymen and over fifty chiefs and kings including Bridei, King of the Picts and Eochaid, King of Scots.

Probably created at Iona, the most single holy site in all of Britain, Adomnan's Law was intended to protect non-combatants, such as children, the clergy and women from suffering in the constant flow and ebb of Dark Age warfare. There is a tradition that the Law also stated that women should not be forced to participate in tribal warfare, or even that it banned them from fighting completely. It may be a pointer to the influence of Celtic women that, although the clergy created the Law, a woman may have initiated it.

According to an Irish account, Ronait, the mother of Adomnan, witnessed one of the frantic tribal battles of the period. The mediaeval writer related that 'men and women went equally to battle at that time' and a woman in one of the armies hauled her opponent out of the enemy's ranks by thrusting a reaping hook through her breast. This sight distressed Ronait, who staged a one-woman sit-down strike and said to her son, 'you shall not move me from this spot until you exempt women from being in this condition.' Unwilling to argue with his mother, Adomnan negotiated his Law with the surrounding kings.

    The merging of the imposing Picts, warrior Gaels, Anglo-Saxons and finally the Norse created a strong, virulent line of women in Scotland. Women such as Aud, Frakok and Thenew were willing to meet any challenge on their own terms. Their descendants were joined in time by a strain of Normans who added to the cultural alloy that fused Scotland into the distinct nation it became. If the Scotswomen of today require a model, they may look to their distant ancestors in the Dark Ages.

Chapter 2

The Pious and the Patriots

> Came I early, came I late
> I found Black Agnes at the gate. – Traditional

In the middle of the Eleventh century, Malcolm III, known as Canmore, was King of Scots. Although he was a native Gael, his mother was an Anglo-Dane, the daughter of Earl Siward of Northumbria. Malcolm was a learned man, with the ability to speak a handful of languages and the guile to rule for thirty-six years a kingdom that was still raw, with ill-defined borders and enemies pounding at the gates by sea and land. King by virtue of his Gaelic blood, it was perhaps the memory of his mother that urged him to seek a wife from beyond the orbit of Alba.

Not long after Malcolm became king, Knut of Denmark conquered England and drove many nobles into exile. One such family was Edgar Atheling and his sisters Margaret and Christina, descendants of Edmund Ironside. They fled to Hungary, from where Agatha, Margaret's mother had come. Margaret's grandfather had been Stephen, the king who had been sainted after he Christianised the country. In 1068, after a brief stay in England, Margaret again fled, this time seeking sanctu-

13

ary from the Normans. Her ship landed in the Firth of Forth and it is said that she at once captivated the Scottish king.

Margaret and Malcolm were married in 1072 in Dunfermline, where the site of Malcolm's Tower still survives in a glen cut by the linn or stream from which the town takes its name. Margaret was said to be both intelligent and beautiful, a fitting match for the capable King of Scots.

The Scots and Norman English skirmished along the Border, but Margaret seemed content with Malcolm. She appeared a gentle woman, but her love of luxury sat ill with her supposed humility and reverence for her church. Her children were born in Dunfermline, where she founded an abbey church in honour of her marriage. Margaret perhaps laid foundations for the Roman Catholic Church in Scotland, replacing the old Celtic Church of Columba and Adomnan. She also gave Dunfermline Abbey gifts of her husband's lands as well as gold and silver ornaments. One of the most significant sacred relics was the Black Rood of Saint Margaret, said to be a piece of the True Cross. This relic was held in a reliquary studded with gems until the rampaging armies of Edward Longshanks looted it in 1296 and it disappeared into the maw of acquisitive England.

Margaret's court was said to be very gracious, with Norman customs and clothing replacing the Gaelic culture of the Scots. The queen is also said to have been kind to the poor, feeding them and even bathing their feet with her own hands. She is also credited with erecting the first inns in Scotland, which were intended for pilgrims crossing the Forth to visit Dunfermline. It was a significant step toward dragging Scotland into the European mainstream where hospitality was a branch of commerce rather than an extension of common courtesy.

There is one well-known story where Queen Margaret's book of the Gospels, hand written and illuminated with miniatures of the Evangelists, was dropped into the water of the Forth. When it was recovered without a stain, people knew that they had witnessed a miracle. Margaret was well on her way to becoming as sainted as her grandfather. Margaret died in Edinburgh Castle in 1093, not long after her husband's death in battle. Her body was taken out of the castle during a fog, carried over the Firth and buried in Dunfermline. She is still remembered as a saint-queen, despite her Anglicisation of Scotland and the damage she was reported to have done to the Celtic Church.

Saints were uncommon in mediaeval Scotland, but good women were not. Mediaeval Scotland was overwhelmingly rural. The major towns, Edinburgh, Perth, Dundee and Aberdeen, were tiny by today's standards, so that most people lived country lives. But country or town, most people's lives could be brutal and short. Warfare, terrible working conditions, famine and disease waited constantly to claim even the wealthy, while the poor were lucky if they saw their fortieth birthday. Plague was always dreaded, particularly because the reasons for its spread were not understood. As well as bubonic plague, spread by fleas living on rats that thrived in the unhygienic conditions, there was pneumonic plague, helped by the cold and rain that hit Europe in the thirteenth century.

Added to these horrors was typhus and typhoid, carried by marching armies, smallpox, tuberculosis, dysentery, roundworm and tape worm, augmented by the ubiquitous skin diseases that were all too common amongst a population whose cleanliness was not always of the highest.

Women, of course, suffered as much as the men, and were often unfairly blamed
for spreading the various venereal diseases that were worst in the coastal towns frequented by visiting seamen. Prostitution was always an option for the poorest, but women were more empowered than many people realise. One career was the church, for a woman could become a nun and rise to become prioress, with control over a large establishment that included lands and revenues.

Although there were schools in the burghs, it is unknown if girls were allowed to attend such establishments, yet there were a sufficient number of businesswomen to reveal that some women possessed an education. A single woman had to have some means of support, for the law leaned heavily in favour of men. The twelfth century *Leges Burgorum* stated that once married, women lost all her rights to moveable property, with rentals of all lands that she possessed and interest on loans she had made moving to her husband. She was however allowed to retain her personal jewellery and a receptacle known as paraphernalia in which to store them. If her husband sold lands that she had once owned, he had to hand her a gown or other gift, which a generous law allowed her to keep.

Women, however, were not completely disempowered. A married woman could own property in her own right, while in some places the daughter of a first marriage took legal precedence in property rights over the son of a second. In the absence of a husband on business, war or personal affairs, the wife controlled the lands, property and servants. Women then, were often secondary to their husbands, but had some rights and could often assume authority. As always in every society, the wealthy had more power than the poor did. There were some women who struggled through the mire to prejudice to become burgesses of a town, and even a few who became sisters in a trade guild. Most remained as mere spectators to the world of business.

Naturally, women were not so docile within their own house. With men often absent at work or war, it was the women who organised the servants, both male and female. Women also were solely responsible for childcare. Traditionally, women were also midwives, using the cumulative knowledge and experience of centuries to overcome often-appalling health and hygiene problems. The Lowland midwife was known as a 'granny-woman' or 'howdie,' while the Highland midwife was a *bean ghluin*, or knee woman. Their work was a mixture of sound practical sense and superstition, for they placed iron or twigs of the rowan tree to protect their charges from the fairies and malignant spirits that were known to haunt the birthing bed. Once they had helped with the delivery, the midwife bathed the wriggling new baby in salt water and quickly wrapped her in her mother's shift or in a shirt of his father if he was a boy. In a nation of small communities, the midwife would probably be well known to the mother, and might well be a relative. She would remain with the mother for a day or so, giving advice and helping with household chores, for which she was often paid in kind. There was seldom a cash economy among the mediaeval Scottish poor. The midwife could also recommend a wet nurse if required. It was not until the seventeenth century that midwifery was taught in hospitals and medical schools.

Even at that early date Scotland was a trading nation and widows who lived in the coastal towns often became ship owners. Some became factors or even acted as procurators in court, although it was more usual for women to enter business as innkeepers, ale sellers or dealing with food. In Aberdeen, women worked as shore porters in sweaty equality with men, while others washed clothes for their supposed betters.

Women then, could become involved in a number of occupations but few made such an enduring impression on the mediaeval world as Devorguila, the Lady of Galloway. Devorguila, which is a Latinised version of her real, Gaelic name *Derbhorgail*, was the daughter of Alan, Lord of Galloway and Margaret of Huntingdon, who was the great-granddaughter of King David I. This distinguished bloodline made Devorguila one of the elite of Scottish nobility, and when she married John Balliol in 1233 she netted one of the wealthiest of the Scotto-Norman knights.

At that time the Balliols were an established family with lands in Yorkshire and Picardy as well as Scotland, and John Balliol, at 25 was about ten years older than his bride was. When they married, the young Balliols were in more than comfortable circumstances. Their combined income of perhaps £500 a year placed them in the upper bracket of Scottish, or indeed European, nobility. However, their financial situation improved year by year as first Devorguila's father, and then other relatives died, leaving lands and possessions to the young couple. As Devorguila's father had no male heir, she inherited both the title of Lady of Galloway and a broad sweep of land in the south west of Scotland. John also became influential in his own right, acting as Guardian to the infant King Alexander III, lending money to the King of England as well as performing all the duties of a major landowner.

The mid and late 13th century was remembered as a golden age in Scottish history, as King Alexander maintained peace with an England that was not yet considered an unrelenting enemy. He also defeated the Norse at the Battle of Largs to ensure that the Hebrides were Scottish and not Norwegian. Devorguila and John made the most of the peace, with eight of their children, four boys and four girls, surviving to adulthood, which was remarkable in an age when infant mortality was shocking. They seem to have worked happily as a married couple as they jointly endowed Franciscan friaries in Dumfries and Oxford as well as a house of Black Friars in Wigtown in Devorguila's own province of Galloway.

In 1268 John died, leaving Devorguila as Lady of Galloway and administrator of the vast Balliol estates. It was in her protracted widowhood that Devorguila made her name for her constant love for her late husband and her generosity to the poor. Although she had gentler lands in England, Devorguila spent much of her time at Buittle in Galloway, her ancestral homeland, where she is credited with founding the church. She also said founded the Franciscan monastery of Greyfriars in Dundee, which apparently had a fine church and convent. It is unfortunate that these buildings no longer stand, for in 1310 the Scottish clergy gathered here to announce their support of Robert Bruce, and the orchards and lands were quite considerable.

Nevertheless Devorguila is better remembered for more southern works. The most enduring has been her foundation of Balliol College in Oxford, which still prays for the soul of Devorguila and her beloved husband. The college rules reflected the piety of its founder, while a

18

condition of the foundation ensured that any food left uneaten at the table was donated to the poorer students. Devorguila had a definite interest in helping the poor, for she also created a charity to benefit these same students, while always giving food from her own table to those less fortunate than herself.

If Balliol College is her best-remembered monument, the most endearing was Sweetheart Abbey, south of Dumfries. In this period, the bereaved could offer payment to a priest to say mass for the soul of their loved one. The wealthier may splash out on a chantry in their local church, with enough money to pay a priest to pray on a more regular basis. Never a woman to think small, Devorguila founded an entire abbey, and granted two parishes from her lands to ensure that the monks were never short of funds. Although the foundation charter stated that the abbey was also dedicated to the souls of the Scottish kings and other of Devorguila's ancestors, there seems no doubt that the soul of her husband was her primary concern. She may well have ridden across from Buittle to supervise the building work as the rich red sandstone structure rose, block after carved block to glorify God and bless her husband's memory.

In 1273 the buildings were complete and already the abbey was known as *Douz Coeur*, Sweetheart. There is another legend that highlights the love between Devorguila and John. It was said that she had her husband's heart removed and embalmed, then placed in a casket that sat at her side whenever she ate dinner. It was the poet Wynton who put Devorguila in context when he wrote 'a bettyr Lady was ther nane in al the ile of Mare Bretagne.' However, although she is remembered for her charity and love, it should never be forgotten that Devorguila was also a sound businesswoman who ran her vast estates at a profit.

Fortunate in so many aspects of her life, Devorguila was also blessed in the timing of her death. She died in 1290, having experienced only peace in her lands in Scotland and England. Only a few years later, Edward I of England began the terrible series of wars that were to devastate the country and blight international relations for centuries. If she had lived, Devorguila would have witnessed the fall of her family as her son John Balliol ascended to the throne then fell from power and grace. The Scots named him Toom Tabbard, empty coat, and remember him with a contempt that may not be entirely deserved.

The Wars of Independence tore Scotland apart, with much of the social structure seriously damaged. In many cases men disobeyed their liege lords to fight for freedom, and women often followed a cause in which they believed rather than obeyed the word of their male kin. In 1299, Margaret, Lady of Penicuik, helped the Scottish resistance forces raid in English-held Midlothian but she was only one of many Scotswomen who made their mark. Few people realise that when King Robert Bruce was little more than a hunted outlaw, his followers a ragged band of hungry swordsmen and his chances of success so slender that they were near invisible, it was the women of Scotland that helped him. The fourteenth century chronicler John Fordun wrote:

'He suffered these (hardships) alone for nearly a year, and at last, through God's mercy, with the help and by the power of Christiana of the Isles, a noble lady who wished him well, he returned to the earldom of Carrick, after much journeying in different directions, and after an infinity of toil, grief and adversity.'

Christiana of the Isles was also known as Christiana of Mar. She was the daughter and heir of Alan Macruarie, Lord of Garmoran and when he died she became Lady of Knoydart, Moidart, Arisaig, Rum, Eigg, Uist, Barra and Gigha. This heritage was a sizeable chunk of land on the western seaboard and a collection of islands stretching from the outer to the Inner Hebrides. Christiana was a powerful woman and her part in restoring Scotland to independence has surely been understated. In time she married Duncan of Mar, brother of Bruce's first wife, so she became kin to the crown.

Even on the mainland Bruce needed female help. After landing in what is now Ayrshire, he was under severe pressure, short of men and hemmed in by English and pro-English forces. Again a woman came to help, this time Christian of Carrick, who sent forty fighting men to his side. Not a lot in a war between nations, but all she had and a great deal more than the major earls and lords of Scotland were prepared to spare.

Sometimes Scotswomen revealed a bloody-minded obstinacy that matched that of Wallace, combined with cold courage that is nearly unfathomable. One such was Isabel MacDuff, Countess of Buchan. In 1306 Isabel was still in her very early twenties, but when she heard that Robert Bruce intended to be crowned king at Scone, she immediately rode to attend the ceremony. Her decision was brave on three counts. Firstly, Scotland was in the middle of a brutal war and such a journey was extremely dangerous. Secondly, her husband supported the enemy and would surely disapprove and thirdly the personal repercussions would be immense.

However, it was the duty of a MacDuff to place the new king on the Stone of Destiny or on a substitute if the Stone was unavailable. Isabel performed this ceremony, and suffered accordingly. When King Edward I, renowned throughout Christendom as a paragon of Chivalry, learned of Isabel's actions, he took a terrible revenge. He had the young Countess imprisoned in a cage of wood and iron that legend states hung outside the walls of Berwick Castle. Here, caged like an exhibit in a zoo, Isabel was subjected to the ridicule of onlookers and forbidden any communication. Other women, including Bruce's sister, wife and two-year-old daughter, were treated in a similar manner. There they remained for years, until the death of Edward and the victories of Bruce ensured first a lessening of their punishment, then an eventual release. Chivalry, it seemed, was a flexible commodity.

While Scotswomen could be intensely patriotic, some were also capable of acting against the king. For instance there was Countess Effie of Ross who joined the pro-English forces in opposing Andrew Murray in the early fourteenth century, although she may only have been attempting to help her husband, whom the English held prisoner. Among the conspirators to murder King Robert in 1320 was the Countess of Strathearn, who was sentenced to life imprisonment for her treason. Seventy years later Annabella Drummond, Queen of Robert III, was a powerful influence in court intrigues, helping to place the Duke of Rothesay as governor of the land in place of the king, while ensuring personal benefit in the form of a large annual pension.

While their Lords rode off to the wars, the Ladies ran the estates, ensured the land was farmed, maintained the buildings and, where necessary, defended the castle from predators. There were many heroic women, with few better than Black Agnes of Dunbar. Border warfare was commonplace, the army of one nation raiding its neighbour and bringing death, rape and terror to the fields of the Merse and the green valleys of Cheviot and Cumbria. After Robert Bruce reasserted Scottish independence, there was a brief respite north of Tweed, but by 1335 there was again war between the two nations, with English armies triumphant as the Scots forgot the lessons that Bruce had taught them. That year Lady Christian Bruce, sister of the king, held Kildrummie Castle in deepest Aberdeenshire against English and pro-English armies. Her stand has been virtually forgotten, but another Scotswoman made her name in a more southern siege.

In 1337 King Edward III sent William Montague, Earl of Salisbury with four thousand men to attack Dunbar Castle, which was the lynchpin of Scottish resistance in the southeast. Perhaps Montague believed that the castle would fall easily, as the owner, Earl Patrick of March, was away in the Highlands. Only his wife, the 26-year-old Countess Agnes was in charge of the 40 strong Scottish garrison. Agnes, however, came of good stock, for she was the daughter of Thomas Randolph, Earl of Moray, who had been one of Robert Bruce's chief lieutenants. She was also the second cousin of David II, King of Scots. History has recorded her as Black Agnes, presumably because she had black hair. Salisbury was to find her a difficult opponent.

Dunbar Castle was a massive, red walled fortress situated on an East Lothian peninsula that thrust into the North Sea. Its position was its main strength, for Salisbury could only attack along a narrow neck of land, giving him a front of only fifty yards. Where other castles stood amidst fields, Dunbar was built on solid rock, nearly impossible to mine. Well aware of the defensive strengths of her home, Agnes seemed to have concentrated her men on the front wall, overlooking the besiegers. Salisbury had only two choices: starve out Dunbar or take it by frontal assault. Warlike by nature, he decided on the direct approach.

The mediaeval English army was one of the most effective in Christendom, so Salisbury was well served by professional soldiers. He had the best archers in Europe, experienced knights and men at arms and access to heavy artillery that had pounded half a hundred castles into surrender. He must have felt confident when he looked to the far end of the peninsula and saw the bright colours and flowing dress of Lady Agnes and her ladies as they stood on the battlements, watching. Salisbury's first attack came when catapults hurled their fifty-pound missiles against the sandstone walls. According to legend, Agnes, having exchanged her dress for chain mail and helmet, calmly appeared on the battlements, flourished a cloth and contemptuously dusted away the marks left by the English missiles.

With the catapults useless against Dunbar's massive walls, Salisbury next tried a sow, which was the mediaeval equivalent of a tank. Mounted on wheels, this vehicle contained a number of soldiers, who were protected from the defender's arrows and boiling oil by a wide fireproof canopy. Agnes, however, had the answer. As soon as the sow moved close to the wall, she had a massive boulder dropped on top. The weight of rock crushed the canopy, and when the surviving English scattered for safety, Scots spears and arrows mowed them down.

'Salisbury!' Agnes is said to have jeered, 'your sow has farrowed!'

Among the English dead were many knights, including William of Spens and Lawrence of Preston. Brave as any of their men, both Agnes and Salisbury were in the forefront of the battle. Mediaeval English armies were famous for their archery, although at this period many of the archers were Welsh, but on this occasion the Scots archery seems to have been at least equal to their opponents. When one Scottish ar-row killed a man standing right next to Salisbury, he noted that the missile had slammed through the man's chain mail. 'Aye,' he is said to have said, with a suspiciously Scottish brand of sardonic humour, 'Agnes's love shafts go straight to the heart.'

With both his direct assaults beaten back, Salisbury resorted to more ugly tactics. Sending for Agnes's brother John, Salisbury threatened to hang him in full sight of the garrison if Agnes did not surrender. Agnes only laughed, reminding Salisbury that if her brother were hanged, she would fall heir to his Earldom of Moray. Frustrated, but obviously more humane than many of his contemporaries, Salisbury returned John to his prison.

Instead he tried bribery. When one of his agents located a porter who agreed to leave the main gate of Dunbar unlocked, Salisbury thought that victory was assured. Paying the man an agreed amount, Salisbury waited for dusk and sent a picked force toward the castle. There must have been a tense period as the soldiers slipped, one by one, under the raised portcullis and into the castle. As usual, Salisbury advanced with his men and was pushing toward the front when a shout rang out and the portcullis clattered down. Many of the English were trapped within the castle and fell victim to the exultant Scots, but while Agnes had hoped to capture Salisbury; she only succeeded in taking Sir John Copeland. Once she had heard of the English spy, Agnes had set a double trap for the attackers.

'Adieu, Montague,' Agnes is reported to have shouted, 'I intended you should have supped with us tonight and then assisted us in defending this fortress against the English robbers!'

There was one final option open to a mediaeval besieger: starvation. Salisbury settled down before Dunbar and cut off all supplies coming by land to the castle. He also hired two Genoese galleys to sit offshore in case the Scots should send provisions by sea. However, starvation was time consuming and costly, for a mediaeval that sat in one place for long soon finished the local food stocks, and was always open to loss by disease. A static English army in Scotland was also vulnerable to guerrilla attacks. The local Scottish commander, Sir Alexander Ramsay of Dalhousie, took full advantage. Operating from Hawthornden in his home territory of Midlothian, he harassed the English supply convoys, hit stragglers and defeated small English units. The English knew these Scots guerrillas as 'grey wolves.'

Frustrated by this delay, and probably requiring Salisbury's men, Edward III came north in person to demand that Dunbar be taken. Salisbury, assisted by the Earl of Arundel, increased his efforts, but without success. By now the English army was weakening, their supplies were running low and morale was failing. Their situation deteriorated when Alexander Ramsay fitted out a boat, took it to the Bass Rock and slipped through the Genoese blockade with enough food to re-supply the castle. Once again Agnes mocked the besiegers, sending Salisbury a gift of bread and wine.

At last Salisbury and King Edward realised that he would never defeat Black Agnes. On the 13th of June the English abandoned their five month long siege and withdrew south. It is said that in leaving Salisbury mouthed the words:

> 'Came I early, came I late
> I found Black Agnes at the gate.'

In time Agnes became Countess of Mar and lived to a fine age for the time. She remains one of Scotland's most renowned military heroines.

Other women could be just as heroic, but did not always fight on the side of the patriots. One such was Katherine de Beaumont, the daughter of Henry Beaumont and widow of David de Strathbogie, claimant to the Earldom of Atholl and a lifelong supporter of King John Balliol, so an enemy of King Robert. Katherine's mother had been Alice Comyn, and she defended the remote castle of Lochindorb throughout the winter of 1335 and into 1336. Her defence should be recorded as one of the most gallant in Scotland's history, and one with significance as it created an excuse for Edward III of England to disguise a plundering raid as an act of chivalry. The English king advanced in person, relieved the beleaguered Katherine just before she was starved into surrender and withdrew. Having made her mark and proved her valour, Katherine, in common with so many mediaeval women, retired into obscurity.

Other Scotswomen were not content to be so relegated. According to the *Scalacronica*, King David II married Dame Margaret Logie 'by force of love which conquers everything.' He certainly treated her as his queen of love, as well as Queen of Scots, by giving her lands and possessions. Unfortunately it seems that she did not return the gifts with an heir. David divorced her to court Agnes Dunbar, assuming that 'Lady Margaret Logie, onetime Queen', would disappear quietly with her £100 pension.

However, Margaret had no intention of sliding quietly into the shadows. Taking a ship to Europe, she travelled to Avignon disputed her divorce with Pope Gregory XI. There was no doubt about her beauty, or her persuasiveness, for the hierarchy of the Church contemplated placing Scotland under a papal interdict. Margaret's unexpected death saved them the trouble. Other Scotswomen were similarly quick to appeal to the Church, as Elizabeth Livingston, the neglected wife of MacDonald of Islay, complained to the Pope that her husband was attempting to poison her.

Lady Margaret's travels are a reminder that unaccompanied Scottish noblewomen were not bound within the realm, but could freely travel abroad. Many journeys were for pilgrimage, such as that of Countess Beatrix Douglas and Countess Margaret Douglas who in 1454 obtained safe conducts to travel on pilgrimage inside England.

Despite such freedom, on many occasions Scotswomen were mere pawns in the game of dowry and lands, so that marriages were less for love and more for policy. For instance in 1453 the marriage between Earl James Douglas and his sister-in-law, the Fair Maid of Galloway was intended to end 'wars etc between their respective families and friends.' The feelings of the couple for each other were not taken into consideration.

There were also attempts at marriage where the woman had even less choice. In 1299 Herbert Morham took time off from his siege of Stirling Castle to abduct Joan de Clare as she journeyed between Stirling and Edinburgh. Taking her to Castlerankine, Morham tried to persuade Joan to marry him, but she rebuffed his efforts. Most mediaeval marriages at this level were about property and power. Marriages for lands could involve women of frighteningly low age. For instance when William Douglas married his cousin Margaret in the early 1440s, she had just attained her twelfth birthday

After marriage, women retained their own name, partly as a reminder that marriage tied two families together in dynastic and often military alliance. A marriage was not merely between two individuals, but between two kindred groups. While there must have been some marriages in which love was an important factor, the songs of minstrels make it clear that sexual love was often sought away from the marriage bed. Wives and husbands bedded for heirs rather than pleasure.

Some lords hoped for an heir that would raise the social level of the family. At the end of the fourteenth century Archibald the Grim, Earl of Douglas bribed King Robert III to gain the marriage of his daughter to the Duke of Rothesay. The Duke had already agreed to marry Elizabeth, daughter of George Dunbar, Earl of March. Not surprisingly, Dunbar was unhappy at this insult to his daughter, or perhaps to the loss of a marriage with such political potential He appealed to the English king, who used the opportunity of such a split in the Scottish nobility to invade the country. Only his admiration for Queen Annabella of Scotland, with whom he had exchanged courtly letters, prevented him from putting the countryside to the torch.

In 1401 Queen Annabella died, to be recalled by Wyntoun as

> 'faire, honorabil and pleasand,
> cunnand, curtas in hir effortis,
> lovand, and large to strangeris'

(Fair, honourable and pleasant
Courteous in her efforts
Loved and generous to strangers.')

While few Scottish queens have been remembered, Annabella was regarded as a pillar of decency within the nation. Few of her contemporaries even approached her high standards. However, these women seemed to live well. In 1473 the royal treasurer handed over £757 9/10d to Queen Margaret, mainly for her new clothes.

On a lower social level, mediaeval women were always busy. In the towns, women brewed ale and ran inns and alehouses. In Dundee, Marjorie Schireham held the responsible position of custumar, or collector of customs, while doubtless matriarchal rule was common in many Scottish households. Women also continued to hold property without the supposed benefit of a male's guiding hand.

Although in some ways mediaeval women had more freedom than their descendants did, they were still strictly regulated, as were their men. In 1430 an Act of the Scottish parliament categorised the clothes that people could wear. Those of the highest rank had the most choice, while the further down the social scale one was, the more limited was the choice. In general a wife could only dress to suit her husband's position in life. Later laws also specified what food people could eat.

While the Romans commented on the free morals of the Pictish women, Aeneas Sylvius, who visited in 1435, had similar views. 'The women,' he said, were 'fair in complexion, comely and pleasing, but not distinguished for their chastity, giving their kisses more readily than Italian women their hands.' Sometimes this loose application of morality could rebound.

There is a story that a MacFarlane chief caught his wife in bed with the chief of the Colquhouns. The woman watched in fear as her husband lifted his sword and chased away Colquhoun, but, to her surprise, he did not even raise his voice to her. If anything he treated her with more affection than usual. A few days later he insisted on making her a meal, and even served the food himself. Noticing that the MacFarlane was watching her closely, the wife asked why, and he motioned to the dish that had just been served. Curious, she lifted the lid and screamed in horror. MacFarlane's men had killed Colquhoun, and he had castrated the body and now served the genitals to his wife as a meal.

Often, of course, men welcomed the free sexuality of women. Cardinal Beaton, the Archbishop of St Andrews and Chancellor of Scotland, was said to have had relationships with a number of women. His 'chief lewd' was Marion Ogilvy, who mothered seven children. Despite the disparaging epithet, Marion Ogilvie was more of a wife than a mistress, spending over twenty years as the companion of the cardinal. She seems to have been a confident, independently minded woman who managed his affairs in a thoroughly efficient manner when he was working on State and Church business. The liking was mutual and not only sexual, for in 1543 the Cardinal built her Melgund Castle, which still bears her initials, M.O. above the main stair. Cardinal Beaton spent the night with her just before the extreme Protestants arrested and murdered him at St Andrews.

Scottish kings were also notorious for sharing their sexual favours. James IV had a succession of royal mistresses, including Marion Boyd, whose son became Archbishop of St Andrews, and Margaret Drummond, who died alongside two of her sisters, possibly from food poisoning. Margaret Drummond was reputedly the king's favourite mistress even though he had executed her brother for murdering 120 Murrays in a clan feud.

In common with every other European nation, Scottish towns possessed brothels. In 1426 parliament claimed that they were particularly prone to fire and ordered them to move to the outskirts. Brothels created other dangers too, as Aberdeen found in 1497. The seamen of Columbus had returned from the New World carrying tales of white-sanded islands, exotic natives and gold. They also carried syphilis, or *grand gore*, and when that reached Aberdeen, the magistrates closed down all the brothels in town.

On a higher level, women contributed to the cultural side of life far more than may be realised. When MacNeill of Gigha, Constable of Castle Sween, died in 1455, his widow composed one of the most beautiful laments of the age. The poem delves into the anguish of the bereaved wife, until the sixteenth and final verse 'my heart is broken within my body and will be so until my death' reveals not only the poetical talent of an educated Gaelic lady, but also the depth of her marital attachment. Isobel Stewart was another widow who lauded her late husband with touching and skilful verse. Perhaps the world is now ready to be exposed to poetry of such feeling and skill.

History does not record where these Highland widows were educated, but a number of women were now being educated at schools, which previously had been almost exclusively for males destined to become clerks or clergy. As early as 1493 Katherine Bra, who was merely of the middling class, signed the Burgh Court book in Dunfermline.

However, for most mediaeval women, life was just a daily grind of work and controlling her family. It is natural that comparatively few women, as comparatively few men, were mentioned on the pages of history books, but those that did proved the enduring spirit of Scottish womanhood.

Chapter 3

'God Be Thanked, I am Pregnant by the King'

En ma fin git mon commencement (In my end is my beginning)
- Mary Queen of Scots

In the romantic perception of Scotland, one woman outshines all. She has been seen as the tragic queen, the brave heroine who rode half way across the Borders to see her lover and the defender of Catholicism against the new Protestant religion. Such was her mystique that as late as the 1970s, tourists who came to Edinburgh asked if she still lived in Edinburgh Castle.

There have been many books written about Mary, Queen of Scots, some of them fine pieces of scholarship, others sycophantic to the point of absurdity, but she is such an enigmatic figure that it would be impossible to write about Scotswomen without including her. Queen Mary was undoubtedly a woman of character. She played golf against men and owned a billiards table. She rode through some of the wildest parts of the country alone to see her lover. She led armies in battle yet was devout in her faith. She was tall, redheaded and beautiful. She was a typical Scotswoman, enigmatic, brave and hot blooded.

Mary was born in Linlithgow Palace in 1542, and the news reached her father, the womanising King James V when he was in shock and dying after hearing of the defeat at Solway Moss. 'It cam wi a lass,' he is said to have groaned, referring, one supposes, to the Stuart dynasty, for Walter the Steward had gained the throne by marrying Marjory, daughter of Robert Bruce, 'and it will gang wi a lass.' In the event he was wrong, but not through any virtue of Mary's. She may be seen as a pawn in power and religious struggles, but her unfortunate taste in men certainly added to her troubles.

Right from her birth, men quarrelled over her. The homicidal Henry VIII, king of England decided that the baby Scottish queen would be a suitable bride for his son, Edward. There was some logic in his proposal, for Mary had a strong claim to the English throne so a marriage union with an English prince would tie both kingdoms together under English authority. With King James dead, the Earl of Arran, Scotland's vacilating Regent, agreed to Henry's demands, but the Scots parliament was cannier. Perhaps they believed that Edward might follow his father's example of serial wife-disposal, or maybe they just did not trust the English. For whatever reason, they refused the match.

Where it was commonplace for bridegrooms to woo the bride with soft words and presents, Henry chose a more direct approach. He sent his armies north with orders to 'put all to fire and sword, burn Edinburgh town, so razed and defaced when you have sacked and gotten what ye can of it, as there may remain forever a perpetual memory of the vengeance of God...putting man, woman and child to fire and sword without exception...' It was Henry's method of securing a bride for his son. Once again, Scotswomen suffered along with their men, and records speak of the 'wailing and lamentation of poor women.' The Scottish Borders was turned into a charnel house as armies marched and fought and women grabbed their children and fled to the hills.

Not all the women fled. One Scotswoman has been remembered during Henry's Rough Wooing. On the road from Carter Bar to Edinburgh, near a place named Ancrum, a small memorial stone marked the site of the Battle of Ancrum Moor. On the stone was a simple verse:

'Fair Maiden Lilliard lies under this stane
Little was her stature but muckle was her fame
Upon the English loons she laid mony thumps
And when her legs were cuttid off, she fought upon her stumps.'

Exactly who Maid Lilliard was is a mystery, but in a way she typifies the women of the Border who had to endure the constant threat of warfare or reiving. She was only one of thousands who suffered during those campaigns, but it is gratifying to know that her efforts were successful and Scotland won the battle of Ancrum Moor and the war of the Rough Wooing. Henry did not succeed in marrying his prince to Scotland's queen, and in time his armies were beaten back, but at shocking cost.

After being carried from palace to stronghold around Scotland, Mary was whisked away from English clutches and onto a galley that carried her off to France. It was a sensible move, for her mother was Mary of Lorraine, one of the great Guise clan, and France was safer than contemporary Scotland. There was, of course, an ulterior motive, for once in France the infant queen was to be groomed for marriage to Francis, the eldest son of Henri II and Catherine de Medici.

Her French couriers claimed that Mary was the only woman not seasick on the voyage and on arrival in France she was promptly separated her from her Scottish contingent of Lords and Maries. Lauded for her health and beauty, Mary was pampered and groomed as a future queen of France, untainted by any uncouth Scots. By 1558 Mary was more French than Scots, she had changed the spelling of her surname from Stewart to the more French Stuart, and that year she married young Francis, the Dauphin of France. Despite all their efforts, however, Mary retained her Scots accent; they could take the Queen out of Scotland, but could not take Scotland out of the Queen.

In November of that year, perhaps prompted by her advisors, Mary announced that she was the rightful heir to the English throne in place of Elizabeth. There was a reason for her claim, for Europe was suffering from the split between the Catholic and the Reformed Church; Henry VIII's divorce and remarriages had not been sanctioned by Rome, so many Catholics saw Elizabeth as illegitimate. To further Mary's point, the English arms were added to the heraldry of Mary and Francis, but that was the high point of her claim to the double crown of France and England. Her mother, father-in-law and husband all died in a shocking two year spell and Mary found herself no longer queen of rich France, but a 19 year old widow who could be queen of cold, war-ravaged and now Protestant Scotland.

Possibly in the spirit that any queendom was better than none, Mary took ship for her barely remembered homeland. There was a chilling North Sea haar that August day of 1561 when she arrived in Leith and was immediately met by Protestant protests. Devoutly Catholic, Mary must have experienced mixed anger and despair at the riot that disfigured her first Mass. Surely it was in a spirit of reconciliation that Mary kept quiet when the Privy Council, controlled by the Protestant Lords of the Congregation, banned the Mass to all but the Queen and her household. These early months in Scotland showed Mary at her best as she diplomatically dealt with the new order while still managing to promenade around the country to show her authority. When the Earl of Huntly led a Catholic rebellion in the Highlands, Mary placed statecraft above religion and allowed her half brother, James Stewart, the Earl of Moray to defeat and quells Huntly's Gordons.

Relations between the Catholic Queen and John Knox, the dynamic head of the Protestant Reformation were often strained, but on at least one occasion they came close to friendship. In the early summer of 1563, diplomatic Mary asked Knox to intercede between the Earl of Argyll and his wife, Mary's half-sister Jean Stewart. Lady Argyll seems to have adopted the old Scottish habit of finding her pleasures outside the marriage bed, for even Mary said she was 'not so circumspect in all things as she might be.' Obligingly, Knox wrote a brisk letter to the pair.

Once again, Europe was a-clamour to find a bride for the tall, beautiful, auburn haired Scottish queen. Prospective bridegrooms included the Archduke Charles of Austria and the Earl of Leicester, while at one time Mary tipped her cap toward Don Carlos of Spain before settling for her cousin, Henry Stewart, Lord Darnley. It was not perhaps the most sensible of choices. Henry Stewart was the son of Lady Margaret Douglas, who herself was granddaughter of Henry VII of England. While contemporary opinion stated he was a 'fair, jolly young man,' their Catholic marriage fomented a civil war.

This time the Earl of Moray led his Protestants against the Earl of Bothwell and the Queen's army. Again Mary's men won, with Moray running to a cold welcome and foul words from Elizabeth of England. With her throne secured by force of arms, Mary settled down with her husband. Perhaps strangely, the marriage worked for a while; Mary became part of the Lennox-Stewart family, but Darnley was himself a schemer.

When Darnley demanded more power than Mary was inclined to devolve, he chose her loyal Italian secretary, David Rizzio as focus for his displeasure. In 1566 a mob of Protestant lords hacked Rizzio to death in the palace of Holyroodhouse, mostly as a demonstration against what they viewed as growing Catholicism. Most history books seem to sympathise with the secretary, but Rizzio seems to have been a thoroughly arrogant man, given to saying that the Scots were boasters, which was not likely to endear him to the volatile Scottish nobility. At a time when Mary herself seemed in danger, Lady Huntly, another of the Gordon clan suggested various methods of escape, such as climbing through a window and down a rope ladder. In the event Lady Huntly contented herself by smuggling a letter out to her son, ordering him to make ready to help the queen.

Perhaps Darnley supposed that the murder of Rizzio had shocked the queen, but Mary was tougher than women were supposed to be. Judicial violence was no stranger to a woman who had witnessed scores

'God Be Thanked, I am Pregnant by the King'

of executions when she was Queen of France. Mary certainly believed that Darnley might have been involved in Rizzio's murder, but at that time remained loyal to her husband. After all, she was carrying his child. On the 19th June 1566, their son, Charles James was born. The birth was difficult, even though Margaret. Countess of Atholl used her witchcraft in a vain attempt to transfer the queen's pain to Margaret, Lady Reres, who was also conveniently with child. In time the prince would be James VI of Scots and First of England, but there was marital discord when Darnley refused to attend the Catholic baptism at Stirling.

As the marriage between Mary and Darnley withered, the Queen spent more time with James Hepburn, the Earl of Bothwell. On one notable occasion that reveals that the queen's strong character was balanced by weak judgement, Bothwell came across the Border badman Little Jock Elliot of the Park and engaged him in single combat. Elliot had a hard reputation and is remembered in verse: 'my name it is Little Jock Elliot, and wha daur meddle wi' me,' but Bothwell was never backward in a fight and, although wounded, triumphed. It was when Bothwell was lying injured in Hermitage Castle, deep in the wild land of Liddesdale that Queen Mary made her epic ride across the Borderland to visit him.

As always in old Scotland, disease lurked in the wings and in January 1567 smallpox thrust its ugly talons deep into Darnley. With her man sick, Mary became the loving wife and brought him from his home in Glasgow to the Kirk o' Field, a mansion that lay outside the walls of Edinburgh. Despite the contagious nature of the disease, Mary visited Darnley every day. Perhaps it was because of her now intimate experience of illness that Mary, that same year, announced that Scottish surgeons were exempt from bearing arms, on condition that during warfare they treated the wounded on both sides.

In the evening of 9th February, Mary left Darnley in his sick bed at Kirk o' Field to attend a masque in Holyrood, and three hours later someone set a torch to three barrels of gunpowder in the cellar of the house. By some quirk of fate, Darnley escaped the explosion, but his body was found in the garden, strangled to death. Bothwell was the prime suspect, but he survived a peremptory trial and on the 24th April ambushed the queen as she rode from Linlithgow to Edinburgh. Mary proved willing, and allowed herself to be carried to Dunbar. The next step was marriage, once Bothwell's current wife, Jean Gordon, divorced him on account of adultery with a blacksmith's daughter. Jean Gordon was probably glad to see the back of him, for Bothwell was a serial adulterer.

The marriage of Mary and Bothwell in the middle of May scandalised the country and a scant month later the Royal army refused to fight the opposition forces. At Carberry Hill, overlooking the Firth of Forth where she had arrived in Scotland a scant six years earlier, Mary surrendered, to be taken to Edinburgh where the mob jeered at their fallen queen.

Once Mary knew the gay chateaux of France, now she was shuttled to a grey castle that squats on its island in Loch Leven. Surrounded by chill lapping water and the forbidding faces of Protestants, Mary signed away her crown to her infant son. As the Lords of Congregation gave a collective sigh of relief, Mary escaped. It is one of the most enduring images of Scottish history, the beautiful queen sitting in the stern of a small boat that slid across the dark loch in a small boat, but tragedy was to follow. Moray's men defeated her 6000 loyal followers at Langside, where the opposing pikes were so dense that a thrown pistol would clatter across the poles. Running again, Mary crossed the Solway and sought sanctuary from the English queen, who promptly threw her in prison. She was still only 26 years old, three times married and had been queen of two countries.

Mary remained a prisoner for the nineteen years that remained of her life, constantly plotting to take Elizabeth's place on the English throne. There were so many conspiracies to rescue her, or to invade England with various Catholic armies that the English authorities kept her constantly on the move. Mary came to know the inside of English prisons, but the Tower of London was like an unwelcome second home. The infamous Babington Plot was the final straw and on the 1st

'God Be Thanked, I am Pregnant by the King'

February 1587, Elizabeth put her sputtering quill to the death warrant of the Queen of Scots. Mary died with no sign of weakness, despite the blundering stroke of the headsman and it said that as she died, Mary's pet dog ran under her skirts.

Whatever the defects of her character, there can be no denying Mary's courage. She was born at an unfortunate time, but played her own hand in a complex game of religious and dynastic intrigue. Her beauty was legendary, her strength undoubted and perhaps she deserves to be Scotland's best-remembered queen. She was also one of the world's first known woman golfers, and owned a billiard table, which highlights the fun-loving side of her character that most history books forget.

Mary, however, was only one woman at a time that Scotland had a plethora of feminine character. It is unfortunate that, save for kirk and criminal trials, the lives of ordinary people were very seldom recorded, so that the upper classes fill a disproportionate number of pages in any volume of history, but sometimes these nobles were indeed fascinating. Janet Beaton certainly falls into this category. At a time when most women were old before their fortieth birthday, Janet Beaton married her fifth and final husband at the age of sixty-one. With the retention of her beauty accredited to magic, she enjoyed as many lovers as any lustful man, sometimes, as in the case of the Earl of Bothwell, men many years her junior. A superstitious commonality also accused Beaton of using her witchcraft to murder Darnley, despite the obvious marks of strangulation on his throat.

Mary MacLeod of Dunvegan was another woman who made free with a selection of men. For the early part of her life she was used as bait to entice men, with Queen Marie, mother of Queen Mary, handing her over to Gordon, Earl of Huntly. From there, Mary's affections were transferred to MacNeil of Barra, an island chieftain who fathered her son. Her next man was a Campbell, who gave her another son, while the Mackenzies of Kintail contrived to hold her person, if never her heart. In her own time Mary became the 10th chief of Dunvegan, a matriarchal and energetic Lady of Skye.

Janet Mackenzie, a daughter of Mackenzie of Kintail also had definite ideas about her sexual partners. Although she was married to Ruaridh MacLeod of Lewis, she much preferred the company of Morrison, the Brieve from the same island. The Brieve was quite proud to claim paternity of their son Torquil. Husband Ruaridh could not really complain of her infidelity as he fathered five sons by other women. It is quite ironic that the six boys grew up as close friends, even to the extent of attacking the castle of MacLeod of Lewis.

Lowland women were as adept as Hebrideans at getting their own way. Janet Stewart, Lady Fleming, who accompanied the infant Queen Mary to France as her governess, was an illegitimate daughter of James IV and the Countess of Bothwell. Well known for her good looks, she also had the quick temper common to many Scots. The Venetian ambassador thought her 'a very pretty little woman,' but although she demanded that the captain of the galley that was taking her to France put her ashore, he was immune to her charm.

Other people, however, were not. Duchess Antoinette of Guise, Queen Mary's grandmother, had little time for the unwashed and uncouth Scots that accompanied their queen to France. Her only exception was Lady Fleming. The king, Henry II was even more attracted, and promptly added the Scotswoman to his list of lovers; or perhaps Lady Fleming made the running. She certainly boasted of her accomplishment in having intimate relations with Henry, while keeping her Scottish temper, and accent, intact. 'I have done all that I can,' she once loudly proclaimed, 'and God be thanked, I am pregnant by the king.' The result of Lady Fleming's relations was also named Henry, and in later life he became a noted Scottish dancer. But by that time his mother was back in Scotland.

On other occasions, young women could be as reckless as any man. Three miles west of Perth sits the house of Huntingtower. In the sixteenth century the house was composed of two 60-foot high rectangular towers standing close by, but with a nine-foot gap in between. Perhaps it was no accident that the chamber of the daughter of the house and that of her lover were in separate towers. Despite the disapproval of her parents, the girl habitually visited her man, until on one occasion a friendly maid warned her that her mother was ascending the steps to her room. Discovery would be disaster, so the girl ran to the top of the tower, gathered up her skirt and leaped across the gap. When her mother arrived in the chamber, the girl was waiting innocently in her own bed, but next morning the couple eloped.

Elizabeth, Countess of Huntly, was another of these vibrant and powerful women that filled Scotland in the sixteenth century. Decisive in character, she was quite capable of arguing with the queen, as she did on the occasion of Huntly's rebellion in 1562. She hoped for leniency for her Gordon family, but when Mary refused her request, Elizabeth promptly persuaded Huntly to attack the queen's army. He lost the subsequent battle at Corrichie.

Throughout the 16th century, upper class Scotswomen seemed to be at least a match for their men. They possessed the same spirit, were practical, intelligent and sexually independent. Antonia Fraser in her splendid biography, *Mary Queen of Scots*, noted that Lady Huntly and Lady Errol were also more literate than their husbands were.

Why should Scotswomen apparently outshine their men at this time? Perhaps the answer lies in the wars of the period. The century began with the tragic battle of Flodden, where the cream of Scotland's nobility fell, while 1547 saw the battle of Pinkie, with equally disastrous consequences for the manhood of the country. After these calamities, noblewomen would assume the leadership of their families, while extremely young and immature noblemen would be forced to accept responsibilities for which they were clearly neither ready nor educated.

Although some single women became involved in business, such as Dame Margaret Balfour who worked the saltpans in her Pittenweem lands, in theory, men were still in charge in the household. The marriage service of the 1560s contained the words and the reminder that the wife was 'in subjection and under governance of her husband, so long as both continue alive.' In practice, then and now, the character and personalities of the couple determined whom, if anybody, dominated.

For most Scotswomen of the 16th and 17th centuries, however, life was merely humdrum. Scotland was still a rural community, with life revolving around farm tasks and domestic duties. Women worked alongside their men, brought up their families and hoped to avoid the more serious scourges of disease, famine or war. Widowed women seem to have had tenant's rights on some cottages, with 'grasswomen' or small cottars in parts of Aberdeenshire. They might have a modicum of independence, but life was basic. Christopher Lowther visited Langholm in 1629 and described a Scottish rural house:

A poor thatched house, the wall of it being one course of stones, another of sods of earth, it had a door of wicker rods and the spiders webs hung over our heads as thick as might be.

Good housekeeping, it seems, was not yet a common virtue of Scotswomen.

Except for Edinburgh, the burghs were small enough to also be regulated by rural matters, while two bodies ran them: the burgesses and the Kirk. In our secular age it is difficult to imagine the power of the church in old Scotland. Men, women and children were expected to attend services regularly, or have a very good excuse for their absence. The Minister and Kirk Elders constantly scrutinised the affairs and particularly the sexual morals of their parishioners, closely questioning those they thought failed to meet sometimes impossibly high standards. With Elders and burgesses often the same people, the Kirk's care crept through every corner of the burgh.

Adulterers were forced to stand bareheaded, barefoot and dressed in sackcloth at the door of the parish kirk, or on the Stool of Repentance. Sometimes they were also fined. If they refused the Kirk's discipline they could be executed; the iron fist behind the iron glove. Fornication, where the culprits were unmarried, was less serious. The man would be stood on the stool and the woman ducked in some foul pond or loch. Sometimes an outraged community could take matters into their own hand and meet out brutal punishment such as riding the stang.

A stang was simply a pole, across which the offender, male or female was straddled and carried through the jeering multitude. Nonetheless, casual sex between consenting adults was probably as common then as now. The Englishman, Sir Antony Weldon, known for his Scotophobia, declared that the Scots held fornication as 'but a pastime, wherein man's ability is approved and a woman's fertility is discovered.'

It was when the fertility became obvious that the trouble began. The Kirk Elders were always alert for unmarried pregnant women, whom they would interrogate with terrible rigour. Sometimes the Elders sat at the bedside of women actually in labour, probing to find the father of the child. Once discovered, the errant man was forced to marry the woman, and then both faced the sackcloth and public penance.

Nearly inevitably, such persecution forced frantic women to desperate acts. In 1659 Margaret Bannatyne of Peebles confessed to infanticide, so the Kirk Session passed her onto the civil authorities. Peebles, on the fringes of the Borders, was a typical burgh of the period. There was a population of 1000, with around 120 burgesses. Where now Peebles is an attractive town bisected by the Tweed and sitting in the cusp of green hills, in the late 16th century it was unprepossessing, mainly single story whinstone buildings with thick walls and heather thatch. A few of the better houses had two stories, with a forestair leading to the timber framed upper apartment. A wall 'four and a half ells high' surrounded the town, with access by four ports or gates, and a toll bell rang every night to ensure that everyone was inside the burgh before the ports were locked to keep out undesirables. The men and women who disobeyed the burgh laws were subject to various disciplines, such as imprisonment. Christian Robeson, who lied to the council, was imprisoned and fined £1, while two women accused of witchcraft suffered six months in jail until the council relented and released them into a form of house arrest. More common were the stocks and jougs in which an offender, male or female, was exposed to public ridicule.

Another minor witch was Janet Henderson from Blyth, who had 'turned the riddle', or told fortunes, in 1626. She was made to stand at the door of the kirk at Linton for six consecutive Sabbaths, dressed only in sackcloth and with her feet bare. However, the burgh also had power over other, arguably more serious offences. In 1637 Isabell Stensone, a thief, was sentenced to two hours in the jougs before being scourged through the town and banished, with the promise of drowning if she returned. Perhaps she was fortunate, for in 1623 Thomas Patersone, another thief, was drowned without any previous warning.

Larger burghs had similar laws. Betty Trot, a hawker from the Lawnmarket of Edinburgh was another thief, so in 1635 the authorities ordered her ducked four times in the Nor' Loch 'to ken the differ between what was her ain gear and ither folks.' Betty, however, did not agree that she should suffer, so retaliated. As soon as the public hangman began to tie her into the stool, she pushed him into the loch, hitched up her skirt and ran for a nearby boat. Two boatloads of city officials followed, but Betty rocked her craft from side to side to dislodge their grasping hands. The watching crowd laughed as some of the self-important officials fell into the loch, but Betty was outmanoeuvred. She put up her hands in surrender as the officials boarded, and then capsized her boat and everybody was ducked.

It was not until 1663 that ducking stopped as a punishment, mainly because one unfortunate woman drowned during the procedure. Despite their reputation for sexual licence, most Scotswomen had more concrete worries. The end of the 16th century saw a decline in the climate, with cold winters and wet summers, along with a general rise in the population. Poor harvests naturally led to food shortages, and so to an increase of violence as Border reiver and Highland clansman sought food for his family. As the population grew, some rural areas became crowded in a manner that would be inconceivable today, with even the remote Manor Valley in Peeblesshire holding ten tower houses and an unknown number of cottages. There were many people who sought at explanation for this rise in numbers. Sir Thomas Craig of Riccarton near Edinburgh had his own, slightly smug answer, that showed his high regards for the women of Scotland: 'Our women do not indulge themselves with wine, exotic foodstuffs and spices from distant lands, so harmful to the womb, hence the more readily do they conceive.'

Throughout the sixteenth and seventeenth centuries, the assertive Scotswomen in high positions were well able to create life as they wished. Those lower down the social scale were more subject to the law, as were their menfolk. Many history books tell of the wild clans of the Border, whose men indulged in reiving and bloodshed all their lives. But these men too, married Scotswomen, and one, possibly apocryphal tale, reveals that the women were quite capable of handling even the most lawless of the men.

Auld Wat Scott of Harden was a Border Reiver of repute. His name was known from the walls of Berwick to the shifting sands of Solway and from the Debatable Land to Lauderdale. His wife was Mary and people knew her as the Flower of Yarrow, but Mary was no shy primrose. If Wat had been backward in reiving and the family's herds were thin on the ground, Mary would remind him of his duty. Putting a large covered dish on the table, Mary would flick off the cover to reveal a pair of spurs; a clear reminder that it was time to refill the beef larder. Whatever their station in life, Scotswomen had a knack of controlling their own environment.

Chapter 4

Rascall Women of the Covenant

> The yettis of Hell ar brokin with a crak
> The signe triumphall is of the Croce
> William Dunbar

'Beastly Belly God,' they cried, 'Wolf!' and 'Crafty fox!' Then they began to hurl their stools and Bibles at the head of the Dean of Edinburgh. Dean Hannay stopped in dismay, staring at the riotous mob of women who had interrupted his sermon. When the bishop stepped up to the pulpit, he was subjected to the same barrage of abuse, as was the Archbishop of St Andrews.

It was the 23rd of July 1637 and the Dean had attempted to read the new Service Book to the congregation of St Giles in Edinburgh. For the past thirty-four years Scotland had shared her king with England, but separate parliaments and distinctive religions divided the two nations. King Charles I was a small man with a large opinion of himself. He took the divine right of kings for granted, and he believed that he should ordain the religion of his subjects. Unfortunately, he also thought that the Episcopal Church of his English subjects should replace the Presbyterian Church of the Scots. Anybody, Scots or English, who objected to the King's word on religious matters could be excommunicated, which was a serious matter in the 17th century.

Used to the austerity of Presbyterianism, the Scots viewed the trappings of High Anglicanism with distrust. They did not want altars with candles. They did not want the king at the head of their Kirk. They did not want priests and bishops and Prayer Books. Above all, the Scots worried that the Anglican Church was only a step toward creeping Catholicism.

When Dean Hannay of Edinburgh stepped forward that July day, he would know that there was disquiet among the Scots churchgoers. However, he would also see the High Kirk of St Giles, now renamed the Cathedral of St Giles, packed with parishioners perched meekly on their creepie stools as they assiduously read their Bibles. Women made up the majority of the congregation; their dark clothing contrasting the spotless white mutches that covered their heads, as was right and proper in kirk. Any whispering would end in a respectful hush as Dean Hannay appeared. As he began to read, a solitary woman stood up from the mass. Folklore claims that she was Janet or Jenny Geddes, a kailwife who worked in the herb market at the Tron. In 1661 Sydserf termed her 'the immortal Jenet Geddes' who burned 'her leather chair of state.' Tradition, backed by Sir Walter Scott, also asserts that she screamed 'Out! Out! Does the false loon daur say mass at my lug?' but other versions claim she screamed 'Will ye say that book in my lug?' before she hurled her stool at the good Dean's head. If it was Jenny who shouted any of these things, she could be blamed for putting in the first blow in the Civil Wars that were to spread havoc across four countries.

The congregation of St Giles could not know what repercussions their actions would bring, but they did know that they had upset the authorities of the church. After their barrage of bibles, the women hissed and booed as the service was read, clapped their work-hardened hands and shouted imprecations and insults until the city magistrates used brawny arms to bundle them out of the kirk. Undefeated, the women clustered at the tall windows of St Giles, shouting their belief that 'Popery was now brought in' as they smashed the glass with stones and battered at the iron-studded door with fists and feet.

They were still there when the Bishop of Edinburgh retreated from the Church, dodging the clattering stones that the women flung at him. 'Rascall women!' he retaliated as he scrambled into the Earl of Roxburgh's coach that waited at the door. As the coachman whipped up the horses the coach careered down the High Street with a mob of screaming women taunting the bodyguard of footmen, who responded with wild sweeps of their swords. All the while the stones rattled down, bouncing off the coach as it disappeared through the turreted Netherbow Port. With their usual dry humour, the good citizens of Edinburgh termed this day the 'Stony Sabbath,' and laughed quietly at the discomfiture of the bishops and the defeat of the king.

Even the most casual student of Scottish history will know something of the Covenanters. They will have heard of the Conventicles, where devout Presbyterians gathered in lonely fields and hills to hear the word of the Lord, and of the fierce guerrilla wars fought by the Muirmen. They might be able to quote some of the names, such as the Prophet Peden, Wallace who fought at Rullion Green, Richard Cameron of the Cameronians and Cleland who defended Dunkeld. Few, however, will know of the vital part that the women of the Covenant played, not always quietly, not always unobtrusively, but always with courage and determination. Jenny Geddes was only the first of a long list of women who became involved in the struggle between king, Covenant and Cromwell.

In 1638, much of Scotland rose against the king's interference in the Kirk. They signed a wordy document that declared loyalty to the king while denying him any power over the Church of Scotland. It may seem a very conservative document, but it raised the people of Scotland in a way not seen since the fourteenth century. It was said that, in the staunchly Presbyterian southwest, some signed this National

Covenant with their own blood. If so, it was an omen of the horrors to come. When a General Assembly of the Kirk met in Glasgow, it abolished Episcopacy throughout the nation. Correctly acknowledging this decision as a direct challenge to his authority, Charles raised an army and a fleet and sent them north to attack Scotland.

Meanwhile, the Covenanters had been busy. They called back the Scots mercenaries who were fighting in the Thirty Years War that burned across Europe, formed a Scottish army and repaired the walls of Edinburgh and Leith that had crumbled during the long peace. According to reports, the walls were rebuilt by 'not only mercenaries but an incredible number of volunteers, gentry, nobility, nay the ladies themselves surmounting the delicacy of their sex, and the reserve so becoming to them' as they 'put their hand to the work.' In the event, there was no immediate emergency, for while the king's fleet hovered offshore, picking off Scots merchant ships, his English army was outfaced by the Scots at Dunse Law and the First Bishop's War petered out.

The Second Bishop's War was more serious. It erupted the following year, with a Scots army marching its Blue Bonnets over the Border as a Covenanter force besieged the Royalist General Ruthven in Edinburgh Castle. There was consternation and carnage in the capital; cannonballs crashing down the Lawnmarket and eventually Ruthven surrendered. The siege had taken its toll, with 180 men, women and children dying in the city, and a further 160 in the castle, 'through a sickness contracted by eating of salt meat.' As the 70 surviving soldiers marched through the castle gates, 32 of their women accompanied them, their names, characters and thoughts hidden to history.

The ensuing wars followed their customary sequence of battles and sieges, victories and defeats, all to the background of mourning wives and wailing mothers, but often the fighting men came across the steely fibre that underlay the acceptant exterior of Scotswomen. The great Montrose, victor of half a dozen battles, was unfortunate to run across a woman who lacked the capacity to forgive. He was on the run after his final defeat, and sought refuge at the Castle of Ardvreck, by Loch

Assynt. MacLeod of Assynt has carried the blame for handing him over to the Covenanters, but there is a strong tradition that his wife did the actual deed. Her maiden name was Munro, which clan Montrose had damaged when he switched allegiance from Covenant to king.

Fate, however, often evens things out and when the Marquis was held prisoner within the Leslie stronghold of Pitcaple Castle, another woman tried to help him. The Lady of Pitcaple, aware that she was putting herself in danger, showed him a secret passage that ran through the wall. Montrose took one look and shook his head. 'Rather than be smothered in that hole,' he is said to have exclaimed, 'I'll take my chance in Edinburgh.' Perhaps he regretted refusing the Lady's help as he stood before the crowd in Edinburgh, waiting for the swing of the headsman's axe.

The tide of war turned against the Covenant as Cromwell's armies marched north. Victorious at the battles of Dunbar, Dalnaspidal and Inverkeithing, their steel-breasted troopers overran the country, imposing martial law as they occupied every stronghold that they could. Sometimes there was resistance, as at Fyvie Castle, where the ladies of Seton fought back until they could fight no more. At other times the women fled, only for Cromwell's men to follow.

After the collapse of Glencairn's rising in 1653, the people of the southern Highlands took to the heather. Many clans had specific safe areas in which they left their women while the men marched to fight; one such was the island in Loch Katrine, now known as Ellen's Isle. When a party of Cromwell's men marched around the loch, the local women hastily clambered into a boat and rowed to the island. Cromwell's soldiers, temporarily baulked of their prey, roared revenge at the women and promised rapine and murder if they could only reach the island.

Without a boat, however, the soldiers could only threaten, until a volunteer swam to capture the women's boat. He was a young man; a strong swimmer and he cleaved to the island, encouraged by his friends and watched by the anxious women. However, highland women were not inclined to sit and be victims, so one lifted her husband's sword and, rushing forward, sliced off the soldier's head. Not surprisingly, the remaining soldiers hurriedly retreated, leaving the women in peace.

Sometimes women revealed a more cold-blooded courage, as when Lord Ogilvie was incarcerated in Edinburgh Castle. His sister came to visit him, smiled nicely to the guard and closed the dungeon door firmly behind her. Changing her clothes for those of her brother, she remained behind when His Lordship calmly walked out, with his skirts rustling at his ankles. Such women took a great risk for despite their proclaimed Puritanism, Cromwell's soldiers were not known for their chivalry. They had butchered their way through four nations, sneered at Scottish beer and the garrison of Leith set a dozen plump women onto horses and cheered as they raced for a prize of cheese.

There were few tears when Charles II was restored to his throne, until he ignored his promise to uphold the Covenant. Where once the Covenanters had held power, now they were a persecuted minority, hiding in the damp muirs of the West and holding secret Conventicles amidst the hills. Again the king imposed the Episcopal Church on the people, but this time there was less support for the Kirk. There was resistance to the new clergy, with mobs of women howling abuse as the new priests took their positions. Women were also in the forefront of the stone-throwing mobs that could drive back the Episcopalians, and devout women encouraged their men to attend the Conventicles. One major riot occurred when the Church authorities of Perth sent a delegation to stop the preaching of the minister of Dunning. A mob of 120 women, led by the wife of the Auchterarder minister, met the men at Dunning Kirk. The women chased away the horses, dragged the cloaks from the men and beat the Synod Clerk with sticks 'until he foreswore his office.' When the men recovered, they announced that since woman had attacked them, 'now the whole sex should be esteemed wicked.'

Nevertheless, women were victims as well as aggressors. Women endured as the authorities billeted soldiers on those who refused to conform. They suffered more when their men marched to fight.

After the battle of Rullion Green, Tam Dalyell's victorious Government troops left the bodies of their defeated Covenanter foe on the frosted grass of the Pentland Hills. It was the women of Edinburgh who came out to tend the wounded and bury the dead and the women of the west who mourned the loss of husband, brother and son. Women also took part in the battle of Drumclog in 1679, and were extensively used as spies. During the Killing Times of the 1680s, the Covenanting women's intelligence network spread the news when the dragoons were coming. Suspicious of armed men, the dragoons virtually ignored the long-skirted, shy women who were obviously going about their own business. The women, however, were watching everything that the soldiers did, and Claverhouse, one of the main persecutors of the Covenant, suggested a mercenary streak in Scotswomen, as they seem to have charged households for information about troop movements.

This mean streak however, was not only apparent in the women. In the 1670s the Earl of Queensberry was acting as Sheriff of Dumfriesshire. The Covenanters knew him as the 'De'il o' Drumlanrig', while his wife no doubt called him something similar, for he was reputedly very loath to part with his money. The Deil's parsimonious nature seems to have been a family trait, for his sister, the exceptionally wealthy Lady Margaret Jardine, had her own methods for adding to her fortune. At a time when bridges were few, she used to wait on the banks of the River Annan during the local fairs and ferry people across for a halfpenny a trip. She was not the only woman to supply this service, for many women kilted up their skirts, hoisted travellers onto their backs and carried them across the Scottish rivers. Known as Fordswomen in the south, these women were engaged in a recognised occupation.

Sometimes women were persecuted merely for their choice of husband. Such was the case with Barbara Mure, generally known as Lady Caldwell, who was forcibly hustled from her home at Caldwell Castle near Uplawmoor and thrown into the dungeons of Blackness. She was guilty only because she had married William Mure, a Covenanter. During her three years in prison, her husband died in exile and government troops looted her home.

It is never easy to force an unwanted religion on a stubborn people, but the Restoration government tried everything they knew. They even hoped that husbands would keep their wives under control, but in the 1670s some landowners complained bitterly that their wives would not listen to reason and hastened away to the Conventicles. People who refused to conform to the Episcopal religion were either fined, or had troops quartered in their homes. Both penalties were severe for people not naturally wealthy, and doubly so for the women who had to find the wherewithal to feed unwelcome soldiers in addition to their own family. It must also be remembered that seventeenth century soldiers were often uncouth, uneducated and prone to drink and violence. They would not be the easiest of houseguests.

The more recalcitrant of the Presbyterians, those men and women who attended Conventicles or refused to take the oath of allegiance to the King were imprisoned, and some were executed. Tollbooths, castle dungeons and other prisons overflowed with men and women, who suffered privation and disease, so that an order to transport many to the Colonies may have seemed a mixed blessing.

When there was no more space in Scotland's prison, the government decided to use the dungeons of Dunottar to hold them. This castle climbs skyward on the Eastern coast, exposed to the bite of the wind while the North Sea sucks and thunders at the cliff below. There were 67 women among the 189 Presbyterian prisoners that were thrust into two underground vaults. Conditions were so horrific that the wives of two of the prisoners petitioned the government for leniency, saying that 110 prisoners were in a single dungeon with little daylight and:

'contrarie to all modestie, men and women promiscuouslie together…' They were fed on 'such bread and drink as scarce any rationall creature can live upon…at extraordinary rates…twenty pennies each pynt of ale…and the peck of sandie dustie meal…at eighteen shillings the peck…they are not only in a starving condition, but must inevitably incurr a plague…'

Many of the sufferers were packed onto ships and transported to the Americas as bonded servants. The voyage was long and often fatal with the promise of near slavery at the other side of the Atlantic. Life was not easy for the stubborn women and men of the Covenant.

Sometime threats to women could be much more personal than religion or government. For instance there was the case of Andrew Scott of Peebles who in 1678 sold his wife to John Wood for £40 Scots. The Church promptly hauled Scott in for questioning and he said that he had been drunk at the time. Anyway, he claimed, she was 'cheap at the money.' There is no record of his un-named wife's feelings on the matter, but perhaps she would have been pleased to rid herself of an obviously obnoxious man.

Although most of the executed martyrs of the Killing Time were men, women were involved in some notable events. While Isobel Alison and Marion Harvey were hanged for their faith in 1681, the Wigtown Martyrs are better remembered. These women, the 63 year old Margaret Maclaughlan and the teenager, Margaret Wilson were thrown into the Tolbooth in Wigtown in 1685. Alongside them were Margaret Wilson's sister, the 13-year-old Agnes, and Margaret Maxwell, Maclauchlan's servant. Although there seems to be a scarcity of evidence about what occurred, folklore gives a strong account.

Margaret Wilson and Maclaughlan had been arrested either for failing to drink the king's health or, more likely, for attending Conventicles. It seems that they were also accused of participation in the battles of Airds Moss and Bothwell Brig. When Bothwell was fought, Margaret Wilson would have been thirteen and her sister only seven. On the 13th April 1685 a court consisting of Sir Robert Grierson of Lag, Captain-Lieutenant Thomas Windram, Captain John Strachan and David Fraham, the Sheriff of Galloway found them guilty.

On the 13th January 1685 the Privy Council had issued orders that the only women its commissioners could examine were those known to be active Presbyterians, and 'these are to be drowned.' Accordingly the court sentenced Margaret Wilson and Margaret Maclaughlan to death by drowning. It may have been a guilty conscience that urged the Privy Council to reconsider its own severity, for it pushed the Secretary of State to ask for a Royal Pardon. King Charles seems not to have responded, whereupon, on the 11th May, both women were taken to the where the River Bladenoch flowed into the Solway Firth. It is a beautiful spot, with vast views and the call of sea birds, but nobody on that day would appreciate the works of the God about whose doctrine they disagreed. The two women were tied to stakes to be drowned by the tide.

The executioners positioned Margaret Maclaughlan furthest out, with the idea that young Margaret Wilson would see her struggles and take the oath of abjuration. That meant she would renounce Presbyterianism and accept Episcopalianism, thus saving her life. However, Margaret Wilson chose instead to sing the 25th Psalm as the slithering Solway choked her elderly companion to death. A town officer had been detailed to hold down Margaret Maclaughlan, and accounts, written quarter of a century after the event, say that the official held a halberd at her throat. With the first execution complete, he is said to have splashed back to the younger woman, pleading that she take the oath and save her life.

'I am one of Christ's children,' said young Margaret, 'let me go!'

Margaret Wilson seems to have been a very stubborn, or very devout, young woman. Her father, Gilbert Wilson, farmed Glenvernoch in the parish of Penninghame, near Newton Stewart, and had taken the oath, along with his wife. Both were fairly regular attendees at the Episcopal services, but their children, eighteen-year-old Margaret, her sixteen-year-old brother and thirteen-year-old sister Agnes, refused to conform. If the stories are correct, Margaret at least was sincere in her beliefs, but there is always a possibility of teenage rebellion in the children's actions, for they knowingly endangered their parents.

When they were challenged over their Presbyterianism, the Wilson children took to the heather. Rather than live rough, she moved into the house of Margaret Maclaughlan, a known Presbyterian who had already been raided by the dragoons. Young Agnes was also sentenced to death, but released when Gilbert Wilson gave his bond for £100.

Gilbert Wilson also attempted to secure the release of his elder daughter, while there was a petition to release Margaret Maclaughlan. The servant girl, Margaret Maxwell accepted the oath. Despite the desperate pleadings of the town officials, Margaret Wilson refused to deny her principles, and she was also drowned by the tide.

The Covenanting period seems to have spawned a breed of young heroines. One of the best remembered was Grisell Hume of Polwarth, the fifth child of eighteen, of whom nine survived. Grisell's father, Sir Patrick Hume, was notable for his stance in confronting the Duke of Lauderdale, who along with his wife, Lady Dysart, controlled Scotland with an iron grip. It was said that Lauderdale tyrannised the country, while Lady Dysart tyrannised him, to the extent of robbing the furniture from Holyrood Palace.

However, Patrick Hume did not enjoy the privileged position of Lady Dysart, so Lauderdale had him imprisoned, first in Edinburgh's Tolbooth, then in the Bass Rock and Dumbarton and finally in Stirling Castle. None of these prison fortresses were pleasant, but Patrick stuck to his Presbyterian religion throughout, an example of fortitude that may have been copied by his daughter Grisell. On one occasion, Sir Patrick asked Grisell to carry a letter to Robert Baillie of Jerviswood, then living in Edinburgh.

In the 17th century, a trip between Stirling and Edinburgh was not to be undertaken lightly, especially by a twelve-year-old girl. However, Grisell obeyed her father's instructions by donning 'country clothes' so she would not be recognised as a landowner's daughter, and travelling with the ordinary carrier. That meant a journey of at least twenty-four hours in a jolting cart with only a rough, unshaved and possibly foul-mouthed man for company. However, Grisell not only completed her mission successfully, but also met the son of Robert Baillie, a youth called George, whom she was later to marry.

By the early 1680s it appeared that the Covenanting cause was dead in Scotland. The Episcopalian sun was waxing, persecutions were whittling down the Presbyterian numbers and there was little cause for hope within the bounds of Scotland. However, the world was wide there were ships on the sea and freedom beckoned from across the Atlantic. Patrick Hume was one of the group who suggested founding a Covenanter settlement in the Carolina colonies in North America. At first the King agreed, for such a colony would not only rid Scotland of an unsettling opponent, it would also act as a barrier between the Spanish and English colonies.

Unfortunately, some of the supporters of the colony were implicated in a plot against the crown. Accused of complicity, Sir Patrick fled before the red coated soldiers could arrest him. With the countryside alerted, Patrick hid in the vaults of the disused Polwarth Church, on his own estate. The church was small, and the vaults had no light save a tiny grated window at ground level, and no heat. Only Sir Patrick's wife, Grisell, and one servant knew where he hid, and of the three it was Grisell who cared for him.

Polwarth Church was more than a mile from the house, but every night the eighteen-year-old Grisell carried her flickering lantern across the countryside and through the eerie churchyard with food and news. History is confused about the length of time Patrick remained hidden in his vault, but Grisell made her nightly walk, daring searching soldiers and barking dogs, for at least a month. She also had to obtain her father's meals without anybody noticing, so often hid food on her lap during the family dinner. Her brother, Alexander, is said to have complained about her greed.

During the day, Grisell and her mother attempted to dig a secret chamber beneath the floorboards of Polwarth House, so that Sir Patrick could live there, but when floods ruined their work, they decided to flee to Holland instead. It was Grisell who did much of the work on the stormy voyage into exile, and Grisell who returned to collect her sister, who had been left behind, sick, and also collect some money. After years spent in the Netherlands, Grisell accompanied Princess Mary to Britain, as the Glorious Revolution brought a measure of religious freedom, at least for Protestants and in time Grisell Hume became Grisell Baillie.

Apart from the stubborn heroism that helped found a national Kirk, the struggle of the Covenanters produced at least one more tangible benefit. Scottish cheese had not been known for its quality, possibly because the cream was removed from the milk to make butter, so the resulting cheese was ill to taste and quick to sour. However, things changed when the Glorious Revolution encouraged young Barbara Gilmour to return home from Ulster to Scotland. She had not wasted her time in exile, but had learned a recipe for cheeses making. Barbara married a man named Dunlop in 1688, settled at the Hill Farm at Dunlop and became quite famous for her cheese. By using full cream milk from Ayrshire cows and pressing firmly, the resulting Dunlop cheese was better-flavoured and longer lasting than previous Scottish cheese; perhaps it should be known as Gilmour cheese?

With the present climate of religious freedom, there is no need for men and women to run to the hills to worship. There was no fear of a sudden knock at the door, or a descent of dragoons onto a conventicle. Instead, as the Reverent Christine Sime reminded when she preached at Skeoch Hill in July 1996, there are other threats: 'apathy, mockery, the couldn't-care-less attitude of so many,' but as the Reverent Sime also said, if we stand against them, 'then we are following those men and women we admire.'

Chapter 5

Wise Women, Witches and Seers

Thou shalt not suffer a witch to live – Exodus 22:18

Throughout history, wise women and spey-wives have enjoyed unusual influence in many Scottish communities. While most of these people had local significance, some attained national fame. Perhaps the most significant was the Lady of Lawers.

Nobody now knows the name of the Lady of Lawers but traditionally she was a Stewart of Appin who around 1650 settled with her new husband at Lawers on the north shore of Loch Tay. Unlike most seers, her prophecies were clear, spoken before the event and have mainly proven to be correct. It is said that her words were written down in her lifetime, and retained in the Red Book of Balloch. According to legend, this book remained for years inside Taymouth Castle, but has since disappeared. As the Highlands had a strong oral culture, it is not surprising that the Lady's words were also handed down by word of mouth, to be recorded in the nineteenth century.

The Lady appears to have had some standing, for when she was escorted from the west coast by a bodyguard, known as *Na Chombaich, Na campanachd*, which translates as The Colquhouns, the companions. These men were Colquhouns, veterans of the savage battle of Inverlochy where Montrose had defeated Argyll's Campbells. Impressed by their valour, Stewart of Appin recruited them as his personal bodyguard, and they formed a ring of broadswords around their chief. With such men as companions, the Lady of Lawers was well protected. Perhaps she had to be, for she was marrying into a cadet branch of Campbell of Lawers. Although the Campbells were major landowners, the wars of the 1640s had depleted their resources so by 1650 they were deep in debt. The Lady was not moving to a plush mansion, but to a two-storied house with a thatched roof, while her husband, Sir James, was a younger brother of the family, who lived as a tenant of Lowland merchants from Stirling. The Campbells would not regain ownership of the estate until 1693. There would, however, be a little income from the ferry that crossed the Tay to Lawers.

When the wars ended and the Highland economy revived, the little town of Lawers expanded. As workmen toiled to erect a fine new church for the growing town, and carved sandstone capping stones were transported along the loch from Kenmore, the Lady watched, and spoke her first prophesy: 'the ridging stones will never be placed on the roof. If they are then all my words are false.'

The Lady's words were proved true that same night when a storm sank the barges in the loch, losing the copingstones in deep water. As the church was completed with a different set of stones, the Lady made other predictions, some of which did not come true until long after her death. When an ash tree was planted on the north side of the church, she stated 'the tree will grow, and when it reaches the gable the church will be split asunder, and this will also happen when the red cairn on Ben Lawers falls.' In 1833, many years after her death, the tree finally reached the gable; the same year that lightning shattered the west loft of the church, which was abandoned. Ten years later, the year of the Great Disruption when the Kirk and the Free Kirk divided, a red cairn on top of Ben Lawers collapsed. Nearly the entire congregation of the Church at Lawers joined the Free Kirk, so spiritually splitting the Church.

It seems that the building of the church was the catalyst that unlocked the Lady's powers, for she made further prophecies concerning the ash tree and the church building. She said that when the ash tree reached 'the ridge of the church, the House of Balloch will be without an heir.' In 1862 the Marquis of Breadalbane, who lived on the site of the old castle at Balloch at Kenmore, died without leaving an heir. That same year the ash tree stretched to the ridge of the church. It remained there, a symbol of the Lady's powers, until 1895, when John Campbell a local tenant farmer, chopped it down. Immediately he was reminded of the third of the Lady's prophesies about the tree, 'evil will come to him who harms it.' Killed by his own bull, John Campbell was not the only victim, for a neighbour who had helped in the felling was soon committed to a lunatic asylum.

When the Lady had come to Loch Tay, the area was still shattered by the depravations of Montrose's soldiers, but she predicted prosperity in the future. 'There will be a mill on every stream,' she said, 'and a plough in every field and the two sides of Loch Tay will become a kail garden.' Such events did not occur until well into the next century, when a dozen lint mills hummed along the loch side, providing peaceful employment and economic security for the population. When the 4th Earl of Breadalbane improved the farming practices of his estate, potatoes and turnips were introduced and crop rotation became the norm, so that 700 tenant farmers ensured that both sides of the loch did indeed resemble a kail garden.

Not all change, however, benefited the local population. The Lady had warned that 'the land will first be sifted, then riddled of its people' and her prediction came terribly true during the time of the Clearances. The improvements of the 2nd Marquis involved the eviction of 55 families from the western end of Loch Tay, followed by the clearance of another sixty families from Glenquaich. The words improvements and clearances understate the horror of these years, which saw families thrust from homes that had been there for generations, blazing torches thrust into thatch and a future of poverty, city work or emigration as the only option. The population of Glenorchy slumped from nearly 2000 in 1806 to a mere handful at the end of the 20th century, while the Loch side villages and farms saw their numbers fall from over three thousand to around 100.

The Breadalbane area had been populated for centuries, enduring wars, poverty and pestilence, but what the broadswords of Clan Donald and the microbes of typhus could not remove, the legal landlord swept away by the power of the written word and the John Muir's four-footed locusts. When the Lady predicted that 'the jaw of the sheep will drive the plough from the ground', nobody could have envisaged the enormity of the change. The Clearances removed the people and the dun cattle that had kept the Highland economy alive for centuries. In their place, flocks of sheep filled the vast desolation so that another of the Lady's prophecies came true 'the homesteads on Loch Tay will be so far apart that a cock will not hear its neighbour crow.'

The Lady also predicted the end of the great estates, saying 'in time the estates of Balloch will yield only one rent and then none at all.' The once vast estates were gradually sold as revenue from agriculture declined, so that only Kinnell House and farm remained. Then, in 1948, this too was sold and the estate had no rent money coming in. When Kinnell was disposed of, the last Laird, the 9th Earl of Breadalbane, travelled in the company of a grey pony, so fulfilling the Lady's words: 'the last laird will pass over Glenogle with a grey pony, leaving nothing behind.'

Although local events occupied most of her attention, the Lady could sometimes be chillingly accurate on a wider scale. Speaking long before the invention of steam power, she said that 'when a ship driven by smoke comes to an end on Loch Tay, there will be great loss of life.' The last steam vessel on the Loch ceased operations in September 1939, the same year as the Second World War began. With so many of her predictions proving accurate, her warning that 'the time will come when Ben Lawers will become so cold that it will chill and waste the land around for seven miles' is a worrying puzzle. Did the Lady foresee a future ice age?

The Lady of Lawers was only one of many whose powers could alarm the authorities. Sometimes these women were known as hen wives or spae wives, sometimes as wise women and often as witches. Although a fear of, or at least a belief in, witches had prevailed throughout the middle ages, it was not until the late 16th and 17th century that the mania of witch-hunts contaminated the country.

Two Dominican friars, Heinrich Kramer and Jakob Sprenger were the originators of the European anti-witch movement, when in 1486 they published their *Malleus Malefucarum*. This book became the Bible of the witch-hunter, the font of all information and misinformation about the theory, practice and persecution of witchcraft. The friars had a simple philosophy: the Bible declared that witches were to be killed; therefore anybody who disagreed was a heretic and could be executed.

Scotland was no worse than most European nations in this inane persecution, and better than some. John Knox preached a sermon against witches at St Andrews, while in 1568 there had been large-scale witch persecution in Angus. Nevertheless, when authority for witch hunting emanated from the crown, persecution became widespread. In 1597, King James VI published *Demonology*, a treatise on the Black Arts. In this book he stated that 'such assaults of Satan are most certainly practised and that the instruments thereof merit most severely to be punished.' The king also wrote that the 'sin' of witchcraft was 'most odious' and 'by God's law punishable by death.' James appears to have caught the anti-witch bug while collecting his bride in Denmark.

There is a possibility that James was only following a family tradition, for his mother, Queen Mary, had pursued witches with some vigour, as had her father, King James V, who had pointed an accusing finger at Janet Douglas, Lady Glamis. Janet Douglas was the only woman among a group of nobles who had been accused with attempting to murder the king by poison or witchcraft. Her motive was to restore the power of the Douglases of whom her brother, the Earl of Angus, was the most important. Instead she was found guilty of witchcraft, her lands forfeited to the Crown, and she was burned at Castlehill, Edinburgh. The Scottish people, however, believed that the accusation was created so that the king could remove her as a threat to the crown.

James VI was much more interested in the superstitious side of witchcraft. On his accession to the throne of England in 1603, James VI and I ordered both parliaments to move against witchcraft. His influence was paramount in Scotland, with an average of one major witch trial a year between James' return from Denmark in 1591 and his death in 1625, but only eight in the following fifteen years.

Probably the most famous Scottish witch trial occurred in 1591, when witches from all across Scotland gathered at North Berwick with the intention of killing the king. The Devil met them in the kirk, made them 'kisse his buttockes, in sign of duety to him' before launching a hysterical rant against the king. James, he said, speaking in suspiciously guid Scots, was 'the greatest enemie hee hath in the world.' Perhaps James honestly believed he was especially selected for the Devil's ire, for as a Protestant king married to a Protestant queen, and heir to the throne of England as well as Scotland, James would see himself as a natural target for witchcraft. Many Protestants of that time honestly believed that that Roman Catholics were in league with the Devil and witchcraft.

The elder witch at the North Berwick gathering was Agnes Sampson, from Haddington, while others included Agnes Tompson of Edinburgh, John Cunningham, the Saltpans schoolmaster, Gillis Duncan, Jennet Blandilands and Ephemia Macalrean. One account says there were six men and over 90 women. When later questioned, the witches confessed to many strange things, such as sailing on the Forth in sieves, dancing to the sound of a Jew's harp, listening to the king's night-time words to his wife and raising a tempest with the object of drowning the king.

Despite King James reputation as the wisest fool in Christendom, he had sense enough to say that the witches were 'all extreame lyars'. Nonetheless, he ordered John Cunningham, alias Dr Fian to be tortured, and then burned at the stake. At least three of the female witches were likewise burned but the devil, that may have been the Earl of Bothwell, escaped.

Most witch-hunts seemed to have followed periods of poverty and poor weather. Intensely superstitious people found it easier to blame witchcraft for sudden dearth than to accept the normality of climate alterations.

As so often when ignorance and religion combine, the interrogators confused witchcraft with folklore, so that in 1676 Bessie Dunlop of Lyne in Ayrshire was executed for accepting herbs from the Queen of Fairyland. She also claimed to regularly speak with Thomas Reid, who had been killed at the battle of Pinkie in 1547.

The 17th century was a time of great religious and political division as people struggled to decide the best way to administer the Church. Presbyterian fought Episcopalian, both attacked the Roman Catholics, small splinter groups formed and collapsed, while Royalty strove to exercise a claim for the Divine Right of Kings that was disputed by many. Perhaps it was because the social fabric no longer appeared secure that some turned to alternative beliefs, and others were afraid of the difference. A people of many virtues, the Scots do not always welcome diversity, and there were fingers quick to accuse anyone who stepped out of the line of conformity.

Eighty percent of those accused were women. So were many of the accusers. Once a name had been whispered to the authorities, the unfortunate woman was hauled before the kirk-session to be questioned. The interrogation would be intense, probing for witch-like practises or meetings with the Devil. The kirk-session would hand the results of their investigation to the Privy Council, which had the power to order torture or tests such as the 'floating' of witches. With her thumbs tied to her big toes, the suspected witch was thrown into a pond, or a river, or the sea, to see if she floated. If she did, she could be legally burned as a witch. If she sank, she would probably drown.

Witches, apparently, were capable of many things. They could transfer diseases, as in the case of Margaret Hutchison, who first threatened Henry Balfour then caused him to have the pains of childbirth, complete with swollen body. They could conjure up the Devil, as Alison Pearson of Fife was alleged to have done in 1588. They could make clay effigies of their enemies, as in the case of Catharine Ross, Lady Fowlis when she shot elf-arrows at effigies of her stepson and her sister-in-law. While her Ladyship was acquitted of the crime, a witch she employed, Christian Ross, was burned. Witches could also turn themselves into animals, such as Isobel Grierson, who was convicted in 1607 of changing herself into the likeness of a cat. In this shape she led a number of her feline friends to terrify Adam Clark of Prestonpans and his wife and maidservant.

Barbara Paterson and Margaret Wallace seem to have been of a different stamp, for their sorcery amounted to using herbs, plants, berries and water to cure people of various sicknesses. After a lull during Cromwell's Commonwealth, witch trials resumed when Charles II assumed the throne. The smoke and ashes of the estimated 150 people that his administration sent merrily to the stake smudged the year 1662. Year-by-year the persecutions continued.

Little is known about Grizel Jaffray of Dundee, but she must be the only witch in Scotland to have a pub named after her. It is known that she lived at Thorter Row, where the gleaming new Overgate Centre now offers retail therapy for the descendants of witches and persecutors alike. It is known that she was married to James and she was tried in November 1667, suspected of 'the horrid crime of witchcraft' and possibly of making a pact with the Devil. It is not known on what evidence she was found guilty, before being burned at the Seagate in front of a large crowd. Perhaps Edinburgh's most famous wizard was Major Weir, one of the town guard who confessed to terrible sins and was duly executed, His elderly sister, similarly accused, entertained the crowd by stripping naked at the stake.

Witchcraft was prevalent all across Scotland, but justice for those caught seems to have been a lottery. For instance there were two witch trials in Bute in 1673; one woman was executed at Gallows Craig, now the Gallowgate in Rothesay, while the other accused was allowed to live. 'Mary Campbell,' the records say, 'is ordered to leave the parish because she sometimes reads cups for amusement.' Other women were also exiled from their native parish; in Monifieth in 1629, two women were ordered away for the noxious practice of charming. Banishment may seem a mild alternative to burning, but at a time when everything centred round the parish and 'outlanders' were looked on with great suspicion, it is possible that exiles would live a short life in great poverty.

The last major episode concerning witches in Fife occurred in 1704 at Pittenweem. When a local man accused Janet Cornfoot, Beatrix Laing and other women of making him have fits; a gang of what appears to be drunken misfits grabbed the women and threw them in the tolbooth. Once locked up, the women were deprived of sleep and tortured to make them admit to witchcraft. It was said that the local minister joined in by beating Janet Cornfoot with his staff. When Cornfoot broke out of the tolbooth she was caught and dragged, struggling, back to Pittenweem.

Infuriated by her near escape, a mob attacked the supposed witch. They took her to the beach, stoned her, tied her up and swung her between the shore and a boat, until, tiring of this sport; they laid her on the beach under a door and pressed her to death. Even so, the 18th century saw a sharp decrease in the fear of witches. The last Scottish burning was in 1722 when an old woman in Loth, Sutherland was accused of hammering horseshoes into her daughter and riding her like a pony. The evidence suggests that the old woman was mentally unbalanced rather than a disciple of the devil, for while waiting to be burned, she warmed herself contentedly by the fire. Fifteen years later all statutes against witchcraft were repealed, and accusing fingers had to seek alternative victims.

Chapter 6

Jacobite Women

> It is better to break one's heart than to do nothing with it
> Margaret Kennedy

If anybody began a conversation about the Jacobites in Scotland, the name Flora MacDonald would almost certainly be mentioned. And no wonder, for she is perhaps the best known of all the women who supported the Jacobite cause, mainly because she helped Prince Charles Edward Stuart and was visited by a famous English writer. Yet the Jacobite period occupied only ten days of a life that contained many other interests, and MacDonald's husband fought for the British Crown in a far larger war.

Flora MacDonald was born in South Uist in 1722. Her father was a Tacksman, a man of some authority but he died when Flora was only two. Eleven years later, Lady Clanranald, wife of the chief, adopted Flora and gave her a more privileged life than that enjoyed by most of her contemporaries. As Clanranald supported the Jacobites, it is possible that Flora was swayed to that cause. Whatever her political beliefs, Flora was living in South Uist in 1746 when a tall, foreign sounding renegade arrived on the island. With his army broken at Culloden, Prince Charles was now a fugitive with a high price on his head. He had survived the carnage of the battlefield and hoped to escape to France and wait for better times. Unfortunately the Hanoverians were actively searching for him, with hundreds of soldiers scouring the isles and the Royal Navy active on the Hebridean seas. The government, not noted for its generosity, had even offered a reward of £30,000 for the capture of the Bonny Prince – although he may not have been so bonny after a few weeks living rough in the heather.

Possibly it was loyalty to a doomed cause that compelled her to help the beleaguered Prince, perhaps she just saw a man in distress, but she either way Flora rose to the challenge. Bringing him into her house, she disguised Charles in woman's clothing, informed him that he was now Betty Burke her maidservant and pressed the authorities for a passport in that name. History tells of a voyage by small boat between Benbecula and Portree in Skye, where Flora and Charles spent one night in Kingsburgh House, home of a MacDonald of Kingsburgh.

Folklore provides more details, with one of Flora's genuine maids commenting 'I have never seen such a tall, impudent jaud in all my life. See what long strides she takes!' Folklore also says that Flora had to keep Betty in check with the rough edge of her tongue, which hints at a less than amicable relationship between the two. Perhaps Flora's actions were necessary to convince the watchful soldiers, but while Charles eventually escaped to a drunken middle age, the authorities arrested his rescuer.

Flora spent a year as captive of the government. As she languished in a troopship in Leith Roads surrounded by the stinks and sounds of shipboard life and chilled by the bite of the Forth wind, perhaps she wondered about the fate of the Young Pretender. Her fellow prisoners certainly praised her actions, but perhaps that was little comfort as her ship battered south to London. Jacobite prisoners were not treated well, but Flora returned to Scotland and marriage to Allan of MacDonald, a son of the Kingsburgh MacDonalds.

The MacDonalds of Kingsburgh survived the immediate post-Culloden harassing of the Highlands, when red coated soldiers burned, raped and looted their way across the land, and every aspect of the Gaelic culture, from the kilt to the bagpipes, was banned. In 1773, Flora entertained the cynical, sardonic English writer Dr Samuel Johnston, who professed a liking for her. With his delight in the ironic, Johnston slept in the same bed that had once been occupied by the fleeing prince, while Boswell, his sycophantic Scottish biographer, inspected Flora. His impressions may have surprised those who expected a heroine of Amazonian proportions: 'she was a little woman of a mild and genteel appearance, mighty soft and well bred. To see Mr Samuel Johnson salute Flora Macdonald was a wonderful romantic scene to me'

The following year the mild, genteel and soft Flora, together with her husband boarded a ship in the Clyde to emigrate to North Carolina in the American colonies. It was a family affair, for Flora's stepfather and her daughter Anne with her MacLeod husband sailed on the same ship. They had joined the thousands of Highlanders who were draining out of a Scotland that no longer seemed like home. Their timing was bad, for two years later the American War of Independence broke out, and once again the Highlanders supported the losing side.

Before they were permitted to emigrate, the Highlanders had been forced to swear allegiance to the Crown. An oath was not a thing to take lightly, so they held by their allegiance even when many of their American neighbours decided to break with Great Britain. After seeing civil war in her youth, Flora must have been sick with grief to repeat the experience, but this time her husband became an officer in the British army. Allan was obeying the call of the clan, for his cousin, Alexander MacDonald; presently residing in New York had raised a company of Highlanders to fight for the Crown and enticed Allan to do the same. Flora would have fought back the tears as her husband and two of her sons paraded in their scarlet uniforms before they left for the wars.

Once again the Highlanders marched off to fight for a Crown that treated them with contempt, and once again they faced an impossible task. The Highlanders were defeated at the Battle of Moore's Creek. Allan of Kingsburgh and one of his sons were among the prisoners. There was little mercy in Civil War and the Rebels seized everything that Flora possessed. In 1779, with one son drowned at sea, another dead of the wounds he received at Moore's Creek and her husband wounded and captured, Flora returned to Kingsburgh House. Eventually her husband returned home and they remained at Kingsburgh for the remainder of their lives, the soldier who chose the wrong side and the woman who had given everything for two opposing Kings and who is remembered in history only for one selfless act.

However, Flora MacDonald was only one of many women who worked for the Jacobite cause. Some women operated behind the scenes, others were thrust into an unaccustomed limelight, but there were some to whom picturesque adventure seemed a natural part of life. Such a woman was Jenny Cameron.

The eldest daughter of Hugh Cameron of Glendesseray, a cadet of Cameron of Lochiel, Jenny Cameron was a controversial figure. A Whig minister named Archibald Arbuthnot, who was no friend of Camerons, claimed that she was sent to Edinburgh when she was eleven and lived with an elderly aunt. The aunt tried to educate her and teach her how to be a lady. At first Jenny responded well, but became friendly with a footman and household maid, who showed her the underbelly of the capital. Caught carousing in a brothel, Jenny was sent to jail. Her aunt bailed her out, but confined her to the house, where she was found in bed with the footman. The servant was sacked, Jenny had a miscarriage and her despairing family sent her to a French nunnery.

Still only sixteen, Jenny seems to have alternated between the nunnery and a Cameron relative in Paris. She continued her amorous escapades with as many men as she could. But it was an Irish soldier, Lieutenant Colonel O'Neill who persuaded her to come on campaign to Flanders with him. Dressed as a man and adopting the name of Johnson, Jenny stayed with O'Neill until he died during the Treaty of Utrecht. By 1717 she was again pregnant, but the father, an Italian Count, left her destitute and alone. Again the family stepped in, sending her back to live with her brother in Scotland, which might not have been a good idea. When her sister-in-law found Jenny sharing her brother's bed, she fainted. By 1745 Jenny's story is on slightly firmer ground. She was at Glenfinnan when the clans mustered, bringing 200 men and a herd of cattle to help the Stuart cause. Bishop Forbes described her as 'a widow nearer 50 than 40…a genteel well-look'd handsome woman with a pair of pretty eyes and hair as black as ink.' She was also described as being on a 'bay gelding decked with green furniture trimmed with gold, her hair tied behind in loose buckles, with a velvet cap and a scarlet feather, carrying a naked sword in her hand.'

There seems no doubt that she was a favourite at the court of Charles Stuart and accompanied the Jacobite army to Prestonpans and Falkirk. She wore a tartan doublet, trews and carried a sword. The Hanoverians captured her at Stirling in February 1746 and tossed her into Edinburgh Castle. She was later released, but never trusted. As late as 1753 government agents watched her, believing she was actively plotting for the Jacobites. She died at Mount Cameron, Lanarkshire in 1773.

In contrast to Jenny Cameron, many women seem to have risen to prominence on a single occasion, and then returned to their normal occupation without a qualm. Grizzel Mhor, or Big Grizzel, was such a woman. Grizzel was married to James Grant of Rothiemurchus, a supporter of the Jacobites. With her husband absent, Grizzel was in charge of Loch an Eilean Castle in the immediate aftermath of the Battle of Cromdale in 1690. After his victory, General Buchan besieged Loch an Eilean Castle, but Grizzel's defence proved too strong. After that single episode, Grizzel again slid into historical obscurity.

Of all the Jacobite Risings, that of 1715 had probably the best chance of success. The Jacobites raised a formidable army in Scotland, had considerable English support and counted on discontent with the new Hanoverian monarch to rouse the Scots. King James however, had none of the charisma of his son, while his generals, with the exception of Mackintosh of Borlum, were mediocre at best. King James came, saw and scampered back to France after the bobbing Earl of Mar had drawn a bruising encounter at Sheriffmuir with Red John of the Battles, the Earl of Argyll. When the Jacobite clans filtered back to their homes, the red coated government troops marched north. Those people who had supported the Rising generally kept low, but the redoubtable Countess of Perth burned her own Concraig Castle to ensure that the Hanoverians could not use it as a base. Her act of self-sacrifice stood out in a generally insipid year.

Lady Mackintosh, better known by her maiden name of Anne Farquharson of Invercauld was another who shone on a single occasion. In February 1746 Prince Charles Stuart was at resting at Anne Farquharson's home of Moy Hall, but the Hanoverians were pressing close. When the Hanoverian garrison in Inverness learned of the whereabouts of the Jacobites, Lord Loudon organised a force to surprise and capture the prince. However, one of the many Jacobite sympathisers in Inverness sent the fifteen-year-old Lachlan Macintosh to Moy to warn Anne Farquharson of the intended raid.

Young Lachlan arrived at five in the morning, shouting that Loudon's men were 'within five quarters of a mile' of the house. Anne, remembered to history as Colonel Anne of the Rout of Moy, had no army with which to repel the approaching redcoats, but she had her native wits and a few loyal men. Running through Moy House in her 'smock petticoat', she called on her retainers and sent Donald Fraser, the local blacksmith and four other men, to hide at the side of the road along which Lord Loudon would lead the Hanoverians. Led by a piper named Donald Ban MacCrimmon, Clan MacLeod marched in the vanguard of Lord Loudon's 1500 men. When they drew close to Moy, Donald Fraser opened fire, killing the piper.

As the Hanoverians recoiled, Fraser's companions shouted for help to imaginary Jacobite clans. 'Advance, Keppoch!' 'Clanranald! Charge!' Faced with what they supposed was an ambush by the main

Jacobite army, the Hanoverians broke and withdrew in some disorder. Colonel Anne had defeated an army of some 1500 with only five men and thus saved the Prince.

But there was another Scotswoman involved in this near forgotten drama. Nobody knows who sent the warning message to Colonel Anne, but the chief suspect is Lady Drummuir. This Lady was another strong character, who was known for her thrift and charity. On her way to church on Sunday she carried two or three shillings in small coppers, which she distributed to the poor of the town. In time people learned of this habit, so there was always a gathering of the needy sitting on creepie stools outside the church. Perhaps this controlled generosity enabled her to own one of the most desirable houses in Inverness, so that both Bonny Prince Charlie and the Duke of Cumberland used it as their headquarters. Lady Drummuir gave her pithy comment on both 'I had twa king's bairns living with me in my time and may I never see another.'

While some women were adventurers, and others had adventure thrust upon them, there were women who followed their hearts and men into war. These women sometimes proved to be amazingly resourceful. One of the best was the wife of David, Lord Ogilvy, whose adventures would not disgrace James Bond. When her husband rode off to fight for Prince Charles, she refused to meekly wave him goodbye, but joined him on campaign. She held his spare horse at the battles of Falkirk and Culloden and was imprisoned in Edinburgh Castle for her troubles, while her man slipped out of Scotland in a Dundee ship. While lesser mortals would have despaired at being abandoned in the deep, dark and dangerous dungeons of Edinburgh, Lady Ogilvie set about improving her situation. Disguising herself as a laundress, she walked past the guards and made her way to Hull. There was another flurry of excitement when a short-sighted Hanoverian mistook her for Prince Charles and tried to arrest her, but Lady Ogilvy managed to persuade him that she was, in fact, female, and escaped to the continent.

Reunited with her husband, Lady Ogilvy fell pregnant, but did not want her child to be born abroad, so slipped through the Hanoverian blockade into Scotland and gave birth to a son in Angus. In the meantime her husband was making a name for himself as a general in the French army, where he was known as *Le Bel Ecossais*. In time both man and wife were pardoned and returned to Scotland, where they rebuilt Airlie Castle.

Helping an imprisoned husband seemed to be a speciality of the Jacobite women. When the 5th Earl of Nithsdale was captured after the '15, the Hanoverian authorities sentenced him to be beheaded. Not yet ready to be a widow, Lady Nithsdale reputed to be of a delicate constitution, saddled her hose and rode south to Newcastle in the chilling cold of February. From there she took the coach to York, where she learned that snow had delayed the London stage. Despite the weather, Lady Nithsdale hired a series of horses and rode to London and, flinging aside the flunkeys, demanded an audience with King George.

Three years later, Lady Nithsdale wrote a letter to her sister in which she gave details of her endeavours. 'I threw myself at his feet,' she wrote 'and told him in French that I was the unfortunate Countess of Nithsdale.' Like many well-bred women, Lady Nithsdale spoke better French than German Geordie spoke English. When King George made to leave, Lady Nithsdale 'caught hold of the skirt of his coat...he dragged me on my knees from the middle of the room to the very door of the drawing room.' Two of the court attendants dragged Lady Nithsdale away while her petition fell, unheeded, to the ground. 'I almost fainted away from grief and disappointment.'

With no prospect of seeking grace at a graceless face, Lady Nithsdale prepared plan two. Together with her maid, a woman by the name of Evans, her landlady Mrs Mills and a Mrs Morgan, Lady Nithsdale marched to visit her husband in his cell in the Tower of London. It was the day before his execution, and the headsman would be sharpening his axe as the three women attempted to see the unhappy Earl. As only two visitors were allowed at one time, Lady Nithsdale took Mrs Morgan with her, who wore an extra set of clothing under her own. The extra clothing exactly matched that worn by Mrs Mills.

Once they entered the cell, Lady Nithsdale ordered Mrs Morgan to run and fetch the maid, who, apparently, was to hurry to the king with a last minute plea. As Mrs Morgan left, the Earl slipped on the extra clothes that she had brought. Then the pregnant Mrs Mills appeared, drying her tears with a handkerchief that conveniently concealed her face. The plan worked well, for Lady Nithsdale had noted that the guards paid far more attention to their own wives, who were in an antechamber, than to the prisoners.

'I went out leading him by the hand,' Lady Nithsdale wrote, 'whilst he held his handkerchief to his eyes.' Then, speaking of her maid, 'I said, "For the love of God, run quickly…" the guards opened the door and I went downstairs with him.' Telling her husband to walk in front, in case the guards noticed his masculine stride, Lady Nithsdale returned to the cell, picked up Mrs Mills and said farewell to her now departed husband. After a few days living near the Tower, Lady Nithsdale hitched her man a lift in the coach of the Venetian Ambassador, where he posed as a footman. The couple was reunited in Rome, where they lived for the remainder of their lives.

Another Jacobite wife was Mrs Murray of Broughton, who rode alongside her husband when Charlie's army padded into Edinburgh. While Murray of Broughton was prominent through his position as Secretary to the Prince, his wife was noted for her beauty, or perhaps because she rode with a naked sword displayed across her thighs. Jacobite poets recalled her in tantalising verse:

> 'Ride a cock horse
> To Edinbru cross
> To see a fine lady
> On a white horse.'

Many Jacobite women helped men in need and were then relegated to a footnote of history. Lady Reay, wife of the Fourth Lord and chief of the Mackays was at Durness around 1748, when government forces continued to hunt for stray Jacobites the length and breadth of the Highlands. Discipline in the army was always tough, often brutal, and when an army deserter appeared at the chief's house at Balnakil, gasping in fear, Lady Reay responded with practical help. Glancing out of the window, she saw a section of soldiers, their red coats like blood against the green hills, approaching her house. They knew that the deserter was in the vicinity, but could not be sure if he had entered the house or not. In the 18th century, the living quarters of most Scottish houses were on the first floor, rather than at ground level, and the deserter had pounded up the stairs to the sanctuary of lights and humanity. Meeting him at the landing, Lady Reay pushed the terrified man into a small, claustrophobic cupboard, ordering him to keep quiet while she distracted the soldiers.

Thinking quickly, she invited the pursuing soldiers in, escorted them pass the cupboard with its cowering occupant, and into the reception room right next door. Unused to such hospitality, and possibly in awe at the grandeur of the polished panelling when they were used to thatched cottages and the tap-room of a squalid inn, the soldiers were happy to accept liquid refreshment from Lady Reay. They were even happier when Lady Reay invited as many women as she could find and held an impromptu dance. Such hospitality would lower the soldier's guard while Lady Reay organised the escape of the deserter.

At that period, women's fashion dictated that they wore skirts so wide that it was almost impossible for two women to pass each other in a narrow street. So wide that a small man could crouch down and hide under the skirts of a woman, who could then walk slowly and elegantly past the distracted redcoats. Of course Lady Reay did not permit the deserter to hide underneath her skirts. Instead she instructed one of her maids to act as taxi, and the deserter was conveyed outside.

For many Scotswomen, the Jacobite Rising was not about high adventure and a chance to outwit the redcoats. Instead they endured an occupation by soldiers whose behaviour could be brutal. Redcoats wagered on horse races where women were forced to act as bareback jockeys in front of cheering, jeering men. With few restrictions on their power, the soldiers could loot any house that may have once harboured a Jacobite or make a wife a widow on a very flimsy excuse. Often the only defence the women had was a quiet, obstinate courage. Such a woman was Anne McKay. The rising of 1745 ended at the tragic field of Culloden, where the outnumbered and half starved Jacobite army was annihilated by artillery and massacred by musketry and bayonets. Victorious Hanoverians pursued the remnants with a savagery that owed its basis to fear rather than any sense of justice.

Many of the Jacobite prisoners were thrown into Inverness Tolbooth, a tower house that thrusts skyward near the castle Wynd, at the corner of Kirk Street and Bridge Street. As was not unusual in Scotland, an outside staircase led directly into a large stone room, into which were crammed the prisoners, some sick, some wounded, all condemned as dangerous. Whether they were Jacobites or loyalists, the people of Inverness knew that they could not help the unfortunate prisoners. This fear, or perhaps a genuine desire to be seen as loyal, kept the respectable and the good from offering succour, but some of the servant maids proved that their humanity was greater than that of their so-called betters. The local minister, the Reverend Hay, mentioned that these maids showed 'more than common courage' for they 'were sure of maltreatment.'

Inverness Tolbooth was too small to hold all the prisoners, so the government used every available space. Two men, Robert Nairn, deputy paymaster of the Duke of Perth's Regiment, and Ranald Macdonald of Bellfinlay, a Captain in Clanranald's Regiment were thrust into a damp cellar in one of the wynds of central Inverness. A dragoon had nearly hacked off Nairn's arm, while the youthful Bellfinlay had been scythed down by grapeshot. Both his legs were smashed.

Anne McKay of Skye was the tenant of the cellar. She continued to live there, while a redcoat sentry stood constantly at the door, musket in hand and bayonet at his belt. Anne acted as messenger and nurse to her uninvited guests, bringing them food and medicine and treating their suppurating wounds. The Jacobite ladies worked out a plot to help the wounded men escape, but it was Anne McKay who was to be the principal actor, and who was to take all the risks. After months of Anne's dedication, Nairn was fit enough to travel. Anne brought him clothes and, when he was ready to leave, used her femininity to decoy the sentry away from the door and into a back close. Bellfinlay did not leave the cellar. His legs refused to heal and he died in captivity. He was not yet 21 years old.

When the escape was discovered, Colonel Leighton of Blakeley's Regiment ordered the errant sentry 500 lashes of the cat-o-nine tails. Leighton then interrogated Anne. When he asked who had given food for the prisoners, she replied that 'he no' be a McLeod or McDonald or any Mac at all.' Leighton first tried kindness with Anne; he offered her a bribe of five guineas, which was a colossal sum for the time, but Anne was a loyal woman and turned the offer down. Next Leighton tried threats. Unless Anne told him who had supplied the food, he would incarcerate her in the Bridge Hole, a hellhole of a cell set just beneath the roadway of the bridge, shaped like a coffin and with barely enough space for an adult woman to stand upright. Anybody put in there would be unable to move, unable to sit or lie, and would have the constant rumble and grind of traffic and hooves a few inches above her head.

In tears, Anne begged for mercy, but Leighton refused and had Anne carried into the Hole. She remained there for days while her legs swelled with the constant pressure and her head thumped with the agony of ceaseless noise. Leighton did not release her, but instead sent an Irish woman, a soldier's wife, with bread and whisky. There was no pity in the gesture, but an attempt to make Anne drunk so she would betray the Jacobite helpers. As she proffered the whisky, the Irishwoman offered to drink the health of Prince Charlie. It was now that Anne revealed her true strength of character. Refusing the whisky, she said that she drank only milk and whey. She also refused to drink the health of the Prince, for 'I like the Duke for I be a MacLeod and MacLeods do not like Charles.' It seems that Anne was not a Jacobite, but had helped the prisoners purely out of humanity.

Leighton had produced his last card. Unable to bribe, force or drink Anne into talking, he resorted to the brutality that stained so many government soldiers in this period. Removing Anne from the Bridge Hole into the Tolbooth, he prepared to have her drummed and whipped through the town. Fortunately for Anne, Provost Fraser intervened and Anne was released. Her example of selfless courage and loyalty toward people whose cause she did not even share is surely unsurpassed. Her experience is perhaps typical of many women of Scotland during the post-Jacobite occupation.

There were some occasions when the Jacobite women more than held their own. On the occasion of Prince Charles' birthday on the 20th December, Lord Albermarle, the Commander-in-Chief in Scotland ordered that the redcoats should search through Edinburgh 'for ladies and other women dressed in tartan gowns and with ribands.' Such accessories were seen to be subversive as they hinted at support for the Jacobites. When the soldiers found any women wearing such items, they were to bring them to Lord Albermarle for interrogation.

Either the soldiers were lax in their duty, or the women were too clever, for the entire search found only one woman. Miss Jean Rollo did not seem loath to confront Lord Albermarle; indeed she argued her case so well that his Lordship released her very quickly. It seems that however effective the government army in the field, some Scotswomen still possessed superior verbal skills. The plethora of retrospective Jacobite songs that women wrote tends to reinforce this belief, for rather than the villains that they appeared in 1746; Jacobites are often seen as heroic victims. A woman's voice can never be disregarded as an effective weapon of propaganda or war.

Chapter 7

Victims and Avengers

Women and elephants never forget an injury
H. H. Munro

Rachel Chiersley, Lady Grange would have been considered a fortunate woman. Married to the eminently respectable Lord Grange, a Lord of Session known for his piety and kindness, she was mistress of the house and estate of Prestongrange in fertile East Lothian, she had money to spend and nearby Edinburgh in which to indulge herself. As she walked among the stalls and shops of the High Street that day in 1732, a party of men approached. She knew at once by their appearance and language that they were highlanders, but did not know that they were about to change her life forever.

Lady Grange may have screamed when they grabbed her, but highlanders were expert at the quick grab and kidnap and within minutes they had her gagged, bound and bundled into first a sedan chair, then a covered coach, which sped her from the familiar surroundings of the city and into the countryside beyond. She must have been terrified as the coach jolted on, north and west over the atrocious Scottish roads that took her out of the Lowlands and in the wild Highlands.

At last, with dark mountains all around, Lady Grange was taken to the sombre surrounds of Glen Coe and further north through the hills to Glen Hourn. Doubtless she screamed for mercy, or threatened dire consequences, for her husband was a powerful man, but the highlanders knew what they were about. With rough hands and rough treatment, she was thrust into a boat and carried west, across the sea, from island to island, each one seemingly more barbarous than the last, until at last she arrived in St Kilda, most distant of all the inhabited islands.

And there she was left, a gently bred lady among the ill educated, Gaelic speaking islanders who probably looked at her with as much astonishment as she at them. Yet it was in St Kilda that Lady Grange met some kindness, for the local minister fed her from his own meagre stores and clothed her with what he could not really afford.

When all this was happening, what about Lord Grange? Did he organise search parties, send for help? Have Scotland scoured by government forces? On the contrary, he announced that his poor wife had died suddenly and arranged for an elaborate funeral, during which his friends and tenants offered him sympathy as they watched an empty coffin lowered into the ground. Indeed, Lord Grange had arranged the whole thing, and although he did not have his wife killed, he had no intention of ever allowing her back into his life.

For eight years Lady Grange lived on St Kilda, watching the bleak Atlantic surge against the dramatic shores and experiencing the savage winter storms. However, she did not resign herself to perpetual exile, but attempted to send news to the outside world. In 1740 a letter written by her, maybe a solitary message, perhaps one from scores that she had sent, arrived in the hands of the Lord Advocate. When he made enquiries, Lady Grange had already been moved, first to Assynt on the mainland, and finally to Skye. She must have waited daily, hoping for release from the Gaelic Highlands, hoping for a return to her civilised life with green fields, the wide pale sky of Lothian, the shops and lights of Edinburgh. However, she was never to return to the south, for in 1745 she died in Skye and was buried in Trumpan churchyard. Her kidnapping and death were investigated, but at that period Scotland was in turmoil with Jacobites and Hanoverian armies marching back and forth. Lord Grange put all the blame on his wife and seems to have escaped without penalty.

History has often pondered on the reasons why Lord Grange treated his wife so badly. Surely his actions were prompted by more than some domestic tiff? There are however, other versions of the kidnap and isolation of Her Ladyship. It is possible that Lord Grange was a closet Jacobite, and Lady Grange, dabbling in his affairs, discovered his papers. If she intended to report him to the authorities, she might have condemned him to a traitor's death, so his reaction was one of self-preservation rather than malice, and in keeping her alive, he gave her a kinder fate than she intended for him.

There is another theory for the actions of Lord Grange. It is possible that Lady Grange was not an innocent victim but a drunken, unprincipled, often violent and probably mentally unstable woman. After suffering years of abuse from her tongue and hands, Lord Grange arranged for her kidnap. A Macleod chief had her carried to the little island of Heiskir, which was owned by MacDonald of Sleat. Lady Grange was out of the way there, but according to tradition, her drunken, violent outbursts frightened the quiet locals, who begged their chief for the mad woman to be removed. It was then that MacLeod offered the use of St Kilda, and two stalwart clansmen rowed her across miles of wild Atlantic Ocean.

Left without resources on this most outer of all the Isles, Lady Grange plotted escape, but more pragmatically, devised means of keeping alive. She learned how to spin wool, which she sent for sale to the mainland. After eight years, Lady Grange secreted a letter within a ball of wool that she sent to Inverness. Miraculously, somebody read her plea for help and arranged for a rescue ship. However, the Hebridean intelligence service was most efficient and MacLeod had her transported to his lands in Skye.

Although Lord Grange could use his power to protect himself, MacLeod was in a more precarious position. While Lady Grange remained, completely mad, on Skye, legend says that MacLeod was blackmailed for his part in the affair, which may have prevented him from taking part in the 1745 Rising.

Lady Grange was not the only Scotswoman to be kidnapped. In 1715, with Scotland torn apart by civil war, the chief of Clan Donnchaidh, the Robertsons of Struan, left his daughter Margaret a large sum of money. Her brother was unhappy at this, for he believed that the money should have come to him. He was, after all, the man of the family. Despite his desire for wealth, young Robertson was unable to actually murder his sister, so instead he arranged that he would travel with her as far as Uist, whereupon the MacLeods would kidnap her. From Uist the MacLeods would carry her to far away St Kilda, where she would remain.

Margaret, however, was a most unwilling victim. Escaping from the MacLeods, she travelled the breadth of Scotland and returned to Perthshire, where her brother eventually caught her. Their discussion was an animated as might be expected, but the upshot was that Margaret retained both her inheritance and her freedom.

Perthshire was also the setting for one of those examples of selfless heroism that occasionally illuminate the pages of Scottish history. James I was not the most popular king, for he had striven to make Scotland a peaceful place by curbing the power of the nobility. The nobles cursed and recoiled but their apparent compliance was deceptive. One, the Earl of Atholl, kept alive the memory of his own royal blood and murmured against a king who did not war on his English neighbours.

At Christmas 1436, James, his queen Joan Beaufort and a party of ladies in waiting and courtiers called in at the Dominican Priory at Perth. The king had close connections with Perth for his mother, Annabella Drummond, was born and brought up in the vicinity. In February, with the frosts of winter keeping its chill grip on the land beyond the burgh yetts, the King pursued his pleasure in Perth.

It was a happy gathering, for James was so sure that he had tamed Scotland that he placed no guards at the priory, and rather than talking war, he played chess with a young man whose nickname was the King of Love. Queen Joan would be watching her husband, commenting on his play as her ladies flirted with the King of Love and offered him the benefit of their wisdom. Perhaps it was in response to a poor move that James teased his opponent, reminding him of the prophecy that said that a king would die that year. It was a highland woman who had made that prediction, and perhaps the women in his company stirred uneasily at the memory. Behind the veneer of Christianity, Scotland was still a superstitious country. It was said that the seer followed the king to Perth and waited within the walls, holding her tartan plaid to her withered soul.

Eventually the game ended, the courtier left and the king prepared for bed, with the queen and some of the ladies fussing around him. It was then that Robert Stewart, Chamberlain to the king and son of the Earl of Atholl, opened the priory doors to a band of armed men. First to step in was Sir Robert Graham, a man once imprisoned by the king, a man who walked with violence as a friend. His son was beside him, with a handful of other resentful men and when the king's servant yelled a warning they slaughtered him on the spot. However, the servant's single cry of 'Treason!' alerted the king's party, who looked around for defence or refuge. There was none. Traitors had done their work well, removing even the bar that should have secured the king's door. James knew of a vault beneath the room and while he attacked the floorboards Katherine Douglas threw herself forward. Just as Graham reached the door, she thrust her arm through the sockets that should have held the bar and gripped as hard as she could.

Katherine Douglas was a brave woman, but she could not hold on against determined fighting men. The Grahams crashed through the door, breaking her arm in the process, and thundered into the king's chamber. There was a frantic scrimmage as the queen and her ladies attempted to defend the king, who fought with fists and feet against the armoured, sword-wielding men. As his queen staggered back, King

James fell under the busy blades. It is said that there were twenty-eight wounds in his dead body before the murderers withdrew, but they left behind a vengeful queen.

James had been a ruthless king who had cracked cheerful Latin jokes while hanging and imprisoning proud highland chiefs. He was a king who had removed all possible rivals to his throne and who had planted firm justice on Scotland's soil. However, James was much more than a king. He was a poet of note, a stubborn Catholic who was not too subservient to argue with the Pope yet who made a merry fire of heretics. The king not only removed much of the power from the nobles; he also removed much of their lands and added them to the royal domains. He seemed also to have a deep attachment for his queen, Joan Beaufort, royal English by blood but Scottish by marriage, and it was Joan who took terrible revenge on the murderers of her man.

The Earl of Atholl had been the instigator of the murder. Although he was in his mid seventies, the queen had him hideously and publicly tortured for three consecutive days. Finally, and mercifully, even Queen Joan was nearly satisfied and ordered him executed, with the bitter joke of a red-hot diadem on his head in lieu of a crown. Sir Robert Graham was treated the same way, as an example to all of the inadvisability of killing a Scottish king, or perhaps of crossing his queen.

However, not only royals, but also ordinary Scotswomen often had a way of retaliating. Highland women in particular could extract singular vengeance. In the Middle Ages Lord Walter Comyn, one of the Comyns of Ruthven Castle in Badenoch, decided to amuse himself by forcing the youngest and most attractive of his tenant women to work naked as they collected the harvest. He appointed a certain day for this amusement, and rode over the hills from Atholl especially to view the splendid sight.

The day arrived and the young women unclothed themselves and huddled in the fields, with their older sisters and mothers repelling any local man who hoped to capitalise on the warped humour of their lord. However, time passed and there was no sign of Lord Walter, so that his retainers grew worried. Sending out a search party, they scoured the hill passes, until a horse bounded toward Ruthven Castle. It was Lord Walter's horse, but was obviously terrified, with foam flecking its flanks and its eyes rolling in its head. What was worse, one of Lord Walter's boots was trailing from the stirrup, with a piece of his leg still inside.

Sick with worry, the searchers redoubled their efforts until, at the rocky gorge of *Leum na Feine*, the Fingalian's Leap, where the River Tromie thunders into the Spey, they found what remained of their lord. His body was lying shattered on the ground, with two eagles feasting on his eyes and entrails. Of course, the local women knew exactly what had happened: Lord Walter had died by witchcraft and the eagles were two of the women whose daughters he had forced to work naked in the fields.

There is a similar story in Glen Lyon in Perthshire, where the Stone of the Demon marks the spot where Governor Macnab of Carnban Castle broke his neck in a fall from his horse. According to local legend, an enraged mother had curses Macnab after he forced girls to work naked in the fields.

Highland women seemed particularly expert at laying curses when their offspring were threatened. The Clan Mackintosh had its Curse of Moy, where the Chief of Clan Chattan ordered a young man to be hanged for sheep stealing. Naturally upset, the man's mother begged for mercy, but the chief refused. The chief had the power of pit and gallows, imprisonment and death and the man was a thief. However, the mother was vengeful and had power of her own.

'If you take my son from me, then I shall take the son of Mackintosh from him. From this day forth the chieftainship of Clan Chattan shall never descend from father to son.' It is said that the curse was effective.

On other occasions, Scotswomen took more direct action to redress their wrongs. In 1446 there was a dispute between the Master of Crawford and the Ogilvies over who should be Bailie of the Regality of Arbroath Abbey. When the abbey replaced Crawford with Alexander Ogilvy of Inverquharity, they were perhaps justified, for Crawford had used the abbey's funds to pay for a body of armed men, while his general conduct made him 'uneasy to the convent.' Crawford, however, refused to surrender control. Instead he gathered the clan. While the Earl of Douglas supported the Ogilvies, the Hamiltons marched to aid Crawford.

Both armies drew up in battle formation outside Arbroath, but the Earl of Crawford, father of the Master, rode between them to try and make peace. He had his reasons, for while his son led one side, his wife was an Ogilvie and he had no desire for a battle between two sides of his family. Perhaps unaware who he was, an Ogilvie rode forward and thrust his spear through the Earl, who fell, mortally wounded.

In the ensuing battles the Crawfords were victorious and Ogilvy of Inverquharity was brought, wounded but alive to Finhaven Castle, the home of his sister. It was Inverquharity's misfortune that his sister was also the wife of the Earl, for she took revenge for her husband's murder. As her brother lay wounded and helpless on the bed, the Countess of Crawford took a pillow and smothered him until he died. Sisterly affection, it seemed, was no match for wifely love.

While royalty and noblewomen could take their own revenge, women lower down the social scale had often to seek help. In the early 17th century the MacGregors were a wild bunch. Although history has glossed their exploits with romance, there could be little but horror in an incursion by a horde of armed caterans intent on rape, plunder and slaughter. In 1603 a mob of these Children of the Mist descended on Luss and created their own brand of mayhem, killing any of the local Colquhouns who dared to oppose them.

As always, the women were left to mourn their dead, but being Scotswomen, they were not content with tears and black garments. In a traditional manner of seeking redress from the king, the Colquhoun widows stripped their dead, gathered the bloodstained shirts together and walked to Edinburgh to petition King James VI. It was said that some women, not deprived of their men, killed a sheep and dipped their husband's shirt in the blood to increase the royal sympathy, and if this is true, who can blame them? King James was not the boldest of men, and many said that he was averse to the sight of blood. When he saw the bundles that the women carried, he was quick to support their cause and granted the Colquhouns authority to assault Clan Gregor with fire and sword. In other words, King James sanctioned riot and murder in his own realm. In the event, things did not turn out as he, or the widows, had intended.

Possibly relishing the challenge, the MacGregors returned in force, fought the Colquhouns at the battle of Glenfruin and massacred many of the spectators who had gathered to watch the fun. This time the king intervened, to proscribe even the name MacGregor. The clan that proudly boasted a royal lineage was now outlawed. The Colquhoun women had gained a greater revenge than even they had sought, but their success showed that it was never wise to cross a Scotswoman.

Chapter 8

Class and Culture

> Never nod to a lady in the street, neither be satisfied with touching your hat, but take it off- it is a courtesy her sex demands
> Hints on Etiquette, 1836

Visitors to Elie in Fife often ponder at the intriguing stone structure on the coast nearby. This building sits above a rocky cove, with large windows that command panoramic views of the Firth of Forth and a fireplace set into the deep stone wall. In the second half of the 18th century, Lady Janet Anstruther, the wife of the local landowner, had this tower built. She used it as a beach hut, ensuring her privacy by sending a bellman around the area to keep away the commonality in case they saw her beauty or disturbed her privacy.

There is a down side to the story. Local legend says that she also brought a curse on Elie House. In those days the village of Balclevie was situated between Elie House and Kilconquhar Loch, and the villagers used to gather every morning and evening to hold a religious service. Their singing annoyed Lady Anstruther, as did the situation of their village, which blocked her view of the loch. Using her feminine wiles, she persuaded her husband to knock the village down, which resulted in her becoming accursed.

Lady Janet shows two sides of the upper class Scotswoman of the Georgian period: their independence and the arrogance that could disregard the wishes of others. The 18th century was a time of rational thought, when the deep religious divides of the previous century gradually eased away, but it was also a time when women were expected to be sensible, hard working, moral and conventional. Women were expected to obey a paternal or husbandly command, which is possibly one reason for many remaining unmarried.

The remaining diaries of educated upper class women reveal a life that revolved around the home and family. They also reveal that women ran even the largest houses. Grisell Baillie, who as the teenaged Grisell Hume had crossed dark countryside to feed her father, proved a more than adequate wife, able to run her house and manage her servants with a firm hand. Grisell Hume had married George Baillie in 1691 and soon took charge of the family's finances. She was already a competent bookkeeper, having learned the hard way during years of religious exile in the Netherlands, but there seems no reason to assume that she was in any way unique. Possibly upper class women were expected to manage the purse strings. Grisell Baillie, however, may have been exceptional as she also continued to look after her father's accounts, and later, those of her brother Alexander.

Hume's *Household Book* reveals a woman of meticulous accuracy, who could still indulge herself with the occasional treat. Of her six servants, the highest paid man received £24 a year, while his female counterpart was paid a surprisingly generous £36. Servants were an invaluable part of upper class living, while the position provided steady employment for both women and men. The job for a woman was no sinecure, for in 1708 a woman servant was expected to work with the farm animals, shear the sheep, brew beer, bake, wash and otherwise work outside as well as inside the house.

For all her undoubted good qualities, Grisell Baillie did not believe that her servants should be idle. She ordered that her maids should be kept spinning until nine at night, unless they were washing or doing other essential work. She also laid down strict rules for the quantity and variety of their food, and did not allow liaisons with the opposite sex. Scotswomen seemed accustomed to controlling their charges with a firm hand: in 1700 Anne, Duchess of Hamilton, employed a man 'for Scourgeing and punishing Malefactors.'

Lady Grisell also cared for her three children, seeing them all into adulthood. At a time when child mortality was at shocking levels, this success may reveal a carefulness that was unusual for the time. The children were all taught music, and the girls worked in the house and sewed clothes for the men. Like their Celtic forbears, Scotswomen of this period enjoyed bright colours, while careful housekeeping and skilful needlework ensured that the same dress could be altered to suit changing fashions. Nevertheless, Lady Grisell's household book mentions quite substantial sums being paid for clothing that was worn on special occasions.

Women of the upper classes enjoyed socialising. For instance the widow Marie Douglas, Lady Hilton, frequently visited friends in the Merse and thought little of travelling to Edinburgh. Gatherings of the gentry seem to have been quite common, with singing, dancing and music a major part of women's lives. Despite their sophistication, the women evidently enjoyed some songs that would be classed as bawdy, such as 'Show me the Lass that's True Country Bred' with its mention of town girls who 'each day make a Trade of their Sin.' Songs of courtship and relationships were popular, which reflects the genuine affection that existed between many married couples. David Home of Blackadder wrote that his wife was 'the most wise, religious, virtuous, pleasant-spirited woman and kind wife that ever man had.'

Knowing of the involvement of Scotswomen in the Covenanting and Jacobite disputes, there is no surprise to learn that they also aired their political views in song. The notion that women lacked the brain to understand serious matters had evidently not yet reached Scotland. Women could also be intensely religious. One of the most devout was Elspeth Buchan, the wife of an Ayrshire potter who in 1784 founded a fanatical religious sect known as the Buchanites. She claimed to be the woman in Revelations XII 'a woman clothed with the sun, with the moon under her feet and on her head a crown of twelve stars.' Fortunately for her 46 followers, the 'great red dragon' that Revelations XII also promises did not come forth, although Buchan did indeed 'flee into the wilderness.' But without Michael's angels and the two eagle wings, the Buchanites petered out.

As well as singing, women played the harpsichord or spinet, the virginal, viol, flute and harp. Dancing was also popular, both Scottish and imported, and women were perhaps surprisingly mobile. Women enjoyed days at the horse racing, although it seems their husband usually accompanied them. Marie Douglas was only one of the many countrywomen who visited Edinburgh for shopping or entertainment. Known to her friends as Ladykins, she rode her own horse on the terrible, unmade roads, managed a staff of five women and two men servants and gave financial assistance to her friends when asked. Other women ran much larger establishments.

When her husband died at sea, Lady Margaret Hope of Hopetoun was left in charge of the estate, as well as the mines at Leadhills. Together with her son Charles, Lady Margaret commissioned the building of the magnificent Hopetoun House. She seems to have managed a variety of business ventures, from lead mines to a windmill in Leith that was used for crushing the ore. When Charles, reached his majority, Lady Hope's sound business head had made him one of the wealthiest men in Scotland.

Upper class women in the Highlands also lived privileged lives. Elizabeth Grant, in her *Memoirs of a Highland Lady* writes of owning flocks and herds that supplied the house with food, fleece for clothing, blankets and carpets, horn and leather. They sewed lint seed for shirts and sacks, brewed beer, baked their own bread and created their own candles. 'We lived in luxury,' she claimed, 'game was so plentiful,' and there was also trout and salmon in the rivers, fruit and vegetables in the gardens and eggs and chicken from the poultry.

While women of the upper classes had a fairly comfortable lifestyle in the 18th century, existence was not so pleasant for those further down the social scale. Living in houses constructed of unmortared stone and roofed with turf or heather, countrywomen wore plaids, with white linen across their shoulders. Those travellers who visited and commented on Scotland mentioned the laziness of the men, which would further increase any burden on their wives and daughters.

Scotland was still a rural nation, with the majority of the population living off the land. Women were expected to labour alongside their men, either inside the cottages or in the fields, baking in the harvest heat of August or ploutering through the mud and sleeting rain of spring and autumn. They would work with the livestock, milking in the empty blackness of a pre-dawn winter or shearing the longhaired sheep while clegs and midges burred around their sweating faces. As well as looking after their children and men, married women carried creels of dripping peat across the sodden muirs, toiled at the lime-kilns, led the carts and spread manure while whaups cried mournfully and peewits jerked their crazed dance above the unfenced fields. Then there were byres to scrape clean and corn to winnow amidst clouds of choking dust that entered eyes and noses and hair. This list is not exhaustive, for women also worked the spinning wheels that most households would own, set up the warps if their man was a weaver and make the clothing and, frequently, the shoes for the family.

Until the advent of the steam loom, countrywomen spent much of their lives spinning. They had two spinning wheels, a small wheel for lint yarn and a larger wheel for woollen yarn. Spinning was a time consuming business, so the women would rise around dawn, or earlier in winter, to begin work. As well as spinning, the countrywoman would also be skilled in carding, boiling and bleaching wool. If she were blessed with a daughter, the countrywoman would also have to make enough woollen bedclothes for two beds, which set was known as a 'providing' when the girl left home for work or marriage. At an age when disease was misunderstood and death common, women could become widows while young, and many such unfortunate women would continue as cottars, looking after their cottage, livestock and land with the help, or hindrance, of their children.

It was usual for girls to work for their parents until they were around fourteen years old, when the household economy needed their space and they hefted their worldly belongings on their back and left. Sometimes there were tears; often there was a mingled sense of relief and excitement as they earned their own money as farm servants to a larger establishment. By that time they had learned the rudiments of domestic economy, the skill and discipline of spinning and, if lucky, a little reading. The better educated might rise to under-cook or chambermaid, suffering the daily whims of a capricious mistress for slightly better food and clothing. All the time, pragmatic young women would be on the lookout for a suitable husband, knowing that life as a wife, although punctuated by dangerous childbirth, allowed a modicum of status and self expression, while most single rural women could look forward only to a life of servility.

Worse off than either cottars or farm servants were those unfortunates who worked in the coal mining or salt industries. The life of the female mineworker is fairly well known, with young girls working half-naked in appalling conditions. Wives and daughters, classified as 'bearers,' would work together to drag huge weights of coal along narrow shafts, or carry a hundredweight or more at a time on their backs, up flight after flight of wooden ladders to the surface. Girls as young as six would carry half a hundredweight of coal for a mile, with only the yellow flicker of a candle held between their mother's teeth to hold back terrifying darkness. They could make two dozen such journeys and neither the sweating, naked men at the coalface nor the swearing men at the pithead had leisure to dry their tears.

When sixteen-year-old Ann Waugh gave evidence to the Children's Employment Commission in 1842, she mentioned 'long days' of up to sixteen hours and 'short days' of 'only eight hours.' Ann said she drew 'in harness' while her sister 'hangs on and pushes behind.' As the cart that she pulled weighed quarter of a ton, it was not surprising that she found the work 'gai hard' and mentioned getting knocked down as the cart 'descended the brae.' In an age when liberal minded people were beginning to question the practice of slavery, a few seemed concerned about the brutal conditions in which miners of all ages and both sexes worked.

Ironically, serfdom had been virtually unknown in late mediaeval Scotland. The disruption of the Wars of Independence seemed to have consigned such degradation to the past. However things deteriorated in the 17th century. Acts of Parliament suggested that men who worked as colliers or in the saltpans were serfs, so by association and tradition were their wives and children. Tradition also ensured that mines in the east of Scotland had worse conditions than mines in the west. Coal miners remained serfs until 1799. Some entered serfdom voluntarily, such as William and Helen Taits, who accepted the position in return for a pair of shoes. It is doubtful if they understood the enormity of their decision. It is equally doubtful if it was legal to buy a collier's child with a Christening present, although it was common practice for mine owners to exchange a small gift for a lifetime of bondage.

After achingly long hours underground, the miners' wife had neither the energy nor the inclination to keep a clean house. Accordingly mining cottages for their squalor, with a cramped living space shared with livestock and filth. Drinking heavily to remove accumulated coal dust from their throats, miners of both sexes were often in debt. Outsiders viewed them with a mixture of pity and horror; certainly no decent man would marry a woman from a mining family, as no respectable woman would marry a collier. Broken in body, miner's wives were aged before they reached thirty and perhaps the high incidence of miscarriages was a mercy for the child whose mother would have been too exhausted to care. Those few women who reached old age looked after the children who survived, doctoring them with watered spirits to keep them quiet and watching the great turning wheels of the pithead.

Brutal, squalid and appallingly ignorant, it was convenient for colliers to marry, for a single man had to pay a female bearer 4d for every ton and a half of coal that they carried. Wives laboured for nothing as well as producing children who would enhance the family, or the colliers' earnings. There may have been some romantic love in the coal pits, but it seems to have been a scarce commodity among the bitter blackness, the blood, sweat and toil.

The value of a good woman around the house has often been understated, but when the Earl of Dundonald stopped women working underground in 1792, the home lives and self-respect of the miners vastly improved. The lives of mining women altered beyond all recognition. It was still hard, still shadowed with the knowledge that their men and children could suffer accidents or death, but without the debilitating brutality of underground labour, women could live decent lives and civilise their men. In 1842 the Mines Regulation Act finally ended the practise of employing women and children underground. The resulting unemployment of over 2000 East of Scotland women, however, created severe financial hardship for many families.

Salters too, had terrible lives. An account of the Bo'ness saltpans speaks of 'poor miserable naked wretches' and girls with hair like snakes.' Salt workers were highly skilled, so that a long apprenticeship from childhood seems to have been essential. Like mining, it was a family occupation, with the Master Salter assisted by his wife and children. In 1770 the pans at Bo'ness employed 21 women, despite occasional attempts to lure the daughters of Salters down the coalmines as bearers. Women were sometimes paid for washing the coarse bags in which salt was carried, but often their work was part of the fee for their tied cottage. Women also found employment as 'saut wives' who bought salt directly from the pans of East Lothian and carried it in baskets to Edinburgh. Like the fisherwomen, the saut wives were reputed as practical businesswomen, so that Scotswomen of all classes were financially astute. Perhaps they had to be in a nation that clung close to the edge of poverty.

Hard in business, Scotswomen seemed to have been equally hard with their children. The attitude of a Scottish mother is well illustrated by the story of a boy being taken to school for the first time. 'Here's our

Willie,' says the mother, 'see that you lick him weel.' The tough love of Sigurd's mother continued to resonate down the ages, but perhaps their apparent inhumanity was necessary for the sort of children that they bred. Certainly the Scots of the 18th century were an able bunch who made their mark on the world.

One such was David Baird, the Scottish soldier who captured Seringapatam. His mother, Alicia Baird, did not believe in showing affection to her children. She had fourteen in total, equally divided between both genders, and proved her toughness by keeping them all alive in the teeming, disease-ridden midden of old Edinburgh. Treating any complaints with scorn, Alicia controlled her children with an iron glove. Despite this rigorous upbringing, her son David, who felt the power of his mother's arm more than most, looked back on his childhood as happy, and on his severe mother with affection. He even kept her favourite chair all his life, hardly the act of a man who had endured a troubled childhood.

There was little relenting when the children reached maturity. In 1780, an Indian prince named Hyder Ali captured David Baird and numerous other British soldiers. Keeping them in dungeons in the city of Seringapatam, Hyder Ali had them chained in pairs. When Alicia Baird heard the news, she expressed no pity at the captivity of her son, saying instead 'Lord pity the chiel that's chained to oor Davie.' In time Baird was released, returning to capture the city in which he had been a prisoner. Thirty years later he married Ann Campbell, who seems to have dominated the tough soldier with some efficiency. 'I could command ten thousand men,' he said, 'yet I cannot command one woman.' Lady Baird's powerful nature seems to have hidden genuine affection however, for on her husband's death in 1832, she erected a tall memorial in his honour, and also commissioned his biography.

Lady Anne Barnard, in her book *Lives of the Lindsays,* also spoke of the grim tyranny of her mother, Lady Balcarres. Again stern words and corporal punishment dominated the childhood of Lady Anne and her brothers, James and John, but as she wrote, Lady Balcarres taught her children 'those general rules of equity and honour, of mind and truth.'

Such an upbringing, according to Lady Anne, made 'men of boys and wise women out of silly ones.'

Sometimes women showed their strength in roles that have been regarded as very much a man's domain. One such was Maggie McConnel of Dailly in Ayrshire. She was a farmer's daughter but also helped run cargoes for the local free traders, as the smugglers were known. On one occasion the illicit cargo was on the beach when the Exciseman appeared, full of fire and fury with his cutlass and pistol ready. Without hesitation, Maggie knocked him to the ground and threw her skirt over his head. As he struggled in the sudden darkness, the smugglers removed the evidence, and when he was released, the Exciseman could only blink at the smiling Maggie. He had no chance of overpowering her, for Maggie was reputed strong enough to 'hauld up a two year old stirk.'

Some women, however, left their mark without ever straying from what was said to be their traditional role. One such was Janet Keiller. She was from a small Dundee confectionery business that had been founded at the beginning of the eighteenth century. According to tradition, John Keiller had purchased a cargo of Seville oranges from a ship in harbour, but on inspection realised that they were too bitter to eat. Folklore argues that his wife, Janet was famed in the family for her quince jelly, and she boiled the oranges with sugar in the same manner. The result was orange marmalade, which became popular throughout the world. Factory production began in Dundee in 1797 and in 1813 it became a raging success in London. Even the *Times* carried an advertisement, saying that marmalade was 'Recommended to mothers for use in the nursery, to persons of weak constitution, or such as lead sedentary lives and generally as an excellent substitute to butter at breakfast.' Indeed in France, orange marmalade was known as *Le Dundee*, and Janet Keiller had created one of the three Js that made Dundee famous. The others were journalism, which still continues, and jute, an industry that employed many thousands of women.

Cramped between Castle and Palace, Old Edinburgh was a convivial, friendly city in which to live. Middle class families lived comfortably, if not luxuriously, in a rented three-roomed 'house' in one of the tall lands that stretched a royal mile from the castle and up and down the closes and wynds. Within the house, man and wife often had separate dayrooms, while at night the children and their maid slept in their father's room, while husband and wife shared a bedroom. With tall lands and minimal sanitation, Edinburgh was not a healthy city, and one local custom has remained in public knowledge. In the evening the maidservant had the unsavoury task of emptying the contents of the chamber pot out of the window, giving a cheerful warning of 'Gardyloo!' to those unfortunate enough to be passing below. The return call of 'Haud yer haun!' was not always heard, with unfortunate results. There were many beggars, both male and female, but also a plethora of charitable foundations. One in particular, the Trades Maiden Hospital, had been created for 'the maintenance and education of the daughters of decayed merchants.'

Edinburgh had its own character, and its own characters. There were laigh houses that sold oysters caught in the Forth and water carriers who carried water up the dark stairs of the lands. There were ragged but scrupulously honest caddies that acted as city guides in the un-named and un-numbered streets and there was General Joe Smith, a cobbler who led the Edinburgh mob against dishonest landlords. He was a popular hero to most, but his wife may not have grieved when he died in a drunken fall from a stagecoach, for he believed that women were inferior to men, and made her walk behind him.

There was also the Nor' Loch, that lay, festering quietly, to the north of the city where the present day Princes Street Gardens spreads. Naturally there were social problems, which Edinburgh treated with a certain grim humour. The phrase, 'to tak a dook at the pot' referred to people who committed suicide at one particularly deep pool in the Nor Loch. On one occasion a woman leaped into the Pot, but the buoyancy of her wide hooped skirt kept her afloat as the notorious Edinburgh wind caught her. Completely forgetting her original reason for being in the loch, the woman began to scream for help as she was blown

Class and Culture

to and fro on the murky water. At last a boat pushed out to rescue her, but by then she had scrambled ashore at Lochside Farm. It is not recorded whether she was grateful for her escape or angry that her suicide bid had failed.

Women were involved in a couple of notable murders in the eighteenth century. In 1751 Lady Hume was a prominent landowner in the Merse. She was the widow of the Reverend Ninian Hume and lived at the mansion of Linthill. She also collected the rents from her tenants. Unfortunately, she relied heavily on her servant, Norman Ross, who had an eye on the rent money that Her Ladyship stored in a chest under her bed. As he entered her room, Lady Hume woke and challenged him. Although Lady Hume was elderly, she struggled with Ross, until he stabbed her, but in escaping he fell and broke his leg. In his trial in Edinburgh, Ross claimed that he only stole the money because he had fathered an illegitimate child and the mother was demanding that he help pay for its upkeep. He was hanged in Edinburgh.

An earlier murder took place in Edinburgh, when Captain John Cayley, a noted rake and womaniser, became infatuated with Catherine McFarlane, who lived near St Giles in the city centre. When the respectably married Catherine rejected his advances, Captain Cayley began to spread boasts that he had bedded her. Naturally annoyed, Catherine waited until the Captain was in the company of his friends, then burst in and told them the whole truth. By the time she left, Captain Cayley was sitting red faced, with his reputation in tatters. Perhaps in a last attempt to woo her, Cayley visited Catherine again. At first Catherine believed that he had come to apologise, and allowed him into the house, but when he made suggestive comments, Catherine turned away. She became seriously alarmed when he followed her into her bedroom. No doubt she ordered him out, but Cayley, secure in his strength, refused to leave, so Catherine lifted her husband's pistols. Cayley moved toward her, so Catherine fired, striking his left hand. He reached for his sword and Catherine shot him through the heart.

Mystery surrounds the remainder of this tragedy. Some say that Catherine caught the evening coach to London; others say that her husband built a special chamber for her and cared for her the remainder of her life. Whatever happened, Catherine McFarlane was never seen again.

Despite the very occasional murder, Edinburgh was said to be a safe city, where young ladies could walk without fear of molestation. Fashionable ladies preferred to preen themselves around the Mercat Cross, while fishwives and oyster sellers displayed the catch made by their men. Edinburgh provided other occupations for women, with dressmaking or millinery becoming more popular as the country became more prosperous. Those women who possessed some money could start a retail business, but the less fortunate might resort to prostitution, as long as their body and looks lasted. In the late 18th and early 19th century, a steady influx of countrywomen seeking better employment in the mills or as domestic servants ensured that the numbers of women rose in proportion to men in the Scottish cities.

There were occasions when the world of Lady and servant would intertwine. In the middle of the 19th century young Miss Cameron of Fassiefern admonished Mary Cameron, a kitchen maid, who promptly slapped her across the face with the warning not to speak to her mother in that fashion. Shocked and in tears, Miss Cameron ran to tell her father, Sir Duncan Cameron of Fassiefern. Although he upbraided the servant, the truth eventually prevailed. Sir Duncan had slept with Mary Cameron many years previously, and the resulting child had been brought up in ignorance of her mother's identity. Financial pressure forced Sir Duncan to secretly marry the kitchen maid, who was only named as Lady Cameron on his death.

It was more common for the two worlds to live separate lives in close proximity but total inequality. The young privileged women came to Edinburgh to shop or to be educated but also enjoyed the dance halls and flirtatious gatherings in the larger houses. Marriage may have been as much a business matter as a love match, but Scotswomen of the early 18th century were every bit as determined as their descendants to enjoy their youth before they became responsible for managing a family. There were some riots, such as the bread riots of the 1740s, where women played their part, but mostly people of all classes inhabited the common closes in rough harmony.

The building of the New Town changed the face and character of Edinburgh forever. The elegant streets, squares and crescents that developed on the north side of the Nor' Loch became home to a different type of woman. The upper and upper middle classes gradually evacuated the homes that had suited their forebears for generations, and settled instead in the neo-classical houses that offered a much grander style of living. As well as creating an Edinburgh renowned for style, this population movement altered the class balance, so for the first time rich and poor had little contact with each other.

Ensconced far south of her Highland home, Elizabeth Grant of Rothiemurchus found much about which to complain. While she thought Queen Street 'disagreeable' and 'gloomy', the grander Charlotte Square was 'most agreeable.' Settled in her Georgian house, she wrote that 'nothing could be pleasanter than our social life.' There were meetings every day between 'us young people. My mother's tea-table was, I think, the general gathering point.' As well as local walks the ladies also 'went to Rosslyn and Lasswade, a merry company.' There is no doubt that the women of the New Town would enjoy the fine architecture and the landscaped gardens. Some would be permanent residents of Edinburgh, while others would have a house in town to supplement their address in the country. This new separation of the privileged from the commonality created an unpleasant snobbery for which Edinburgh grew infamous. For instance, when Mrs Charlotte Scott, wife of the novelist Sir Walter, invited James Hogg to visit, she was both outraged and amused when he dared call her by her first name. Hogg was an apparent good friend of Sir Walter and a novelist of note, but as a shepherd he was considerably further down the social ladder.

Elizabeth Grant was many rungs further up, and her writings reveal exactly how structured social class had become to women of the period. She said of Sir Walter: 'his family were all inferior' so that his depiction of the 'ideal gentlemen and ladies' was flawed. After all, as a mere novelist 'he knew none better.' She was even more scathing of Charlotte, who she thought 'very silly and foolish,' with a mother of 'absolutely no rank'.

Such ladies would be fitting companions for Lady Janet Anstruther of the bathing folly. The 18th century witnessed a gradual change for many Scotswomen as class differences became more important than clan, religion or parish. In the past, women such as Agnes of Dunbar or Grisell Hume had been able to mingle with people from different social backgrounds, but the new emphasis on wealth and position created a huge gulf. Some upper class Scotswomen abused their position. One who has been remembered was perhaps the most powerful of them all

Chapter 9

The Countess and the Clearances

From the lone shieling of the misty island
Mountains divide us, and the waste of sea
Yet still; the blood is strong, the heart is highland
And we in dreams behold the Hebrides.
John Galt

Women in the Highlands lived different lives from those in other areas of Scotland. They did not have mines, saltpans or small spinning wheels. They did have hard work on the communal farms. James Loch, the infamous Commissioner of the Sutherland Estates, wrote that the men were 'impatient of regular and constant work' so that 'all the heavy labour was abandoned to the women.' While men would help in building the house, women did virtually everything else 'even in dragging the harrow to cover the seed.'

The writings of Hugh Miller lend support to the views of Loch. In 1823 he wrote that Highland women were 'regarded rather the drudge than the companion to the man.' While the husband dug and sowed the land, 'the wife conveys the manure to it in a creel, tends the corn, reaps it, hoes the potatoes, digs them up, carries the whole home on her back.' As if that was not enough, while carrying the creel she was also 'engaged with spinning with the distaff.' A woman's hands were always busy with something; Highland life was not a tartan rural idyll.

Not all Highland women were tied to their native glens. The young women of Rothiemurchus used to undertake long treks through the pass of the Lairig Ghru to Braemar. They walked in small groups, chattering cheerfully as they balanced on their heads baskets of eggs to sell to the gudewives of Mar. It would be interesting to see how these carefree women would react if they met a party of modern hill walkers with their expensive clothing and heavy boots who follow the same route in the belief that they are braving the Highland wilderness.

Before the time of individual family crofts, the Highlanders lived and worked in the same communal fashion as they had for centuries. They lived in small clachans of stonewalled houses, with fields for crops nearby. In the summer there was an exodus to the shielings in the hills, where cattle and children were free to roam. People worked together, herded animals together, lived in a close community and in an environment that they understood perfectly. They harvested the peat for fuel, the heather for thatch, even the bog cotton for cushions. Such a lifestyle, however, was soon to be ended. The number of people was increasing, but the rents paid to the landlord were not. At a time when Highland landlords were increasingly looking to the south for their values, a healthy bank balance was more important than a large fighting tail. The Highland estates would have to become economical, whatever the cost to the indigenous people; if the 18th century was the age of reason, the 19th was the age of progress.

In some places, progress came brutally. Between 1812 and 1819, with the approval of the landowner, James Loch arranged that the people were cleared from the inland homes in the Sutherland glens where their families had lived for generations. Loch's account said that the enforced move benefited the people by allowing them access to the seacoast. He said that the men, once so lethargic, became as 'expert boatmen as any in the world.' Others had different views on this movement. Reverent Sage, the Achness minister spoke of a 'dark hour of trial' when 'man, woman and child' were evicted and fire applied to their homes. Donald Macleod a stonemason, who himself suffered eviction, wrote with even more anger. In *Gloomy Memories*, he wrote of 'people struggling to remove the sick and the helpless' before they were burned along with their homes. He wrote of the 'cries of the women and children' as two hundred and fifty houses were burned in a 'conflagration' that lasted six days.

These people were referring to the Sutherland Clearances, one of the worst episodes in a dark time that saw landowners sweeping away the past and the people in an attempt to make their estates more profitable. In place of the people that had inhabited the glens for centuries, these landowners placed sheep. Of all the Improvers, the Duchess of Sutherland, the employer of James Loch, has been most infamously remembered.

Her name was Elizabeth, and when her father, the last of the Earls of Sutherland died in 1766, she became heir to a vast Highland estate. In 1771, when Elizabeth was six years old, the family lawyers had already secured her right to be Countess in the peerage and *Ban mhorar Cataibh*, the Great Lady of Sutherland to the people. Few thought it ironical that she lived in Edinburgh, hundreds of miles south of her ancestral home. As was usual with absentee landlords, factors ran her estate, raising rent from tenants who were amongst the most materially poor in Britain, and evicting those who could not pay.

At only five foot high, Countess Elizabeth was not a tall woman, but she had the reputation of a beauty, and in her maturity she was fashionably buxom. A painter of country scenes and with a Romantic taste in literature, Countess Elizabeth was a cultured, urbane woman who would grace any drawing room. With chestnut hair and eyes, a shapely nose and round chin, Elizabeth does not fit the popular image of an ogre, yet her treatment of her Highland tenants retains the power to chill the heart. Together with her husband, George Granville Leveson-Gower, the Marquis of Stafford, Elizabeth cleared her Sutherland estates of five thousand souls; women, children and men. Unlike most landowners, she had no need of increased rent rolls, for her English properties made her unbelievably wealthy; she replaced people with sheep in the name of fashionable Improvement.

At the end of the 18th century, the prestige of a Highland chief increased if he could contribute a regiment of his clansmen to Britain's wars with France. The Age of Reason was also an age of incessant conflict with one war following another in a bloody sequence that culminated in the horror that came upon France in 1789. While the French Revolution shocked the ancient regimes of Europe, the execution of the aristocracy exposed the vulnerability of the British upper classes, which commenced the destruction of the French Republicans with genuine alarm. Unfortunately the Republicans proved terrifyingly capable, so that more and more of Britain's gold and men were poured into the molten pit of war.

Countrymen and city men were hounded into the army, but most of all, the recruiters looked to the Scottish Highlands, where lived, as Chatham remarked, 'a hardy and intrepid race of men.' Their recent past of rebellion made them ideal recruits, for they could purge their sins in battle for a Hanoverian king, and only their wives and mothers would mourn if they were killed. Highland chiefs, anxious to prove their loyalty to the Hanoverian monarchs, called up clan regiments. There was a regiment of Frasers, a regiment of Camerons, a regiment of Seaforth Mackenzies and Jane Maxwell, the personable young wife of the 4th Duke of Gordon, raised the Gordon Highlanders by placing the king's shilling between her lips and offering a silver kiss for each recruit. Some say she enticed the men with six pipers and a guinea, others that her beauty was enough, but her Gordon Highlanders became one of the finest infantry regiments in the world.

In 1799 Countess Elizabeth used more cold-blooded methods to raise the 93rd Foot, the Sutherland Highlanders, when she noted that General Wemyss was making heavy weather of raising a regiment among her tenants. Many men preferred to remain with their families rather than enlist for a war of which they knew little. Others had joined a rival regiment, which could not be allowed. Possibly for the first time, Elizabeth revealed the poison that lurked beneath her beauty. Those men who did not come forward, she stated, 'are really unworthy of attention, and need no longer be considered as a credit to Sutherland or any advantage over sheep or any other useful animal.'

The Countess was ruthless with those men who enlisted in other regiments. Writing of them as 'tenants…who thought proper in the course of the recruitment to show a preference of other regiments to the two which the Marquis and Marchioness recommended,' Countess Elizabeth ensured that their families were evicted as soon as possible. To show such vindictiveness to people who were helpless to respond reveals an ugly, petty nature. Taken beside the wholesale clearances of the early 19th century, the actions of Countess Elizabeth place her squarely among the most cold-hearted women in Scottish history. It is possible that, in her pride she did not even realise the suffering that her actions caused.

Making a census of her tenants, the Countess counted the eligible youths, set aside five hundred names and informed them that they would join her regiment. Such was the power of a Highland chieftain that the men obeyed. Such was their bravery that they fought with distinction. While they were doing so, the Countess began the eviction of the old men, women and children that remained. After Waterloo there was less need for regiments of fighting Highlanders and landowners could pursue their hobby of improving their land. The Clearances increased in ferocity. When George IV paid his state visit to Edinburgh in 1822, half a hundred Sutherland men, fully clad in tartan represented Countess Elizabeth, their shining claymores were ironic icons of their own impotence in the face of a class system that their kin had helped defend.

While one woman was a prime mover in the Clearances, many women suffered their effects. There is something mediaeval in the thought of a company of police and soldiers raiding a glen where people had lived for centuries, driving the inhabitants out of their homes and forcing them to either emigrate or move to the alien coast and adopt a whole new existence. Accounts of the clearances are harrowing, telling of women howling and tearing at the ground in their grief, of children running naked from burning houses, of a woman who drowned after she jumped into a river to escape. The Strathnaver clearances were perhaps the worst, with one girl, Betsy MacKay remembering her house set alight at both ends, and dogs set on the laggards. Donald Macleod, who wrote of the events as an eyewitness, told of the cottage of the 100 year old Margaret Mackay burned down, so she had to be dragged out with her blankets in flames. Five days later, Margaret Mackay died. Macleod may be a biased reporter, for forced evictions ruined his wife's health, but any exaggeration is only in the detail. The bitter, heartless facts remain.

Each clearance had its quota of horror, until the reader is sickened of cruelty and sorrow. There was the pregnant wife of John Mackay, who attempted to save her burning house by climbing onto the roof. She fell through the thatch and gave birth after agonising labour. There was the case of Henney Munro, the widow of a soldier who had fought for Scotland against Bonaparte. Henney Munro, like many women, had accompanied her man, and when he died in Spain she had returned to the glen of her youth. There was no red coated soldier to defend her from Improvement and Clearance. Her house, her possessions and furniture were burned as she struggled to save them. Only her memories remained.

In many cases the sheriff officers and burners struck when the young men of the glens were away at the shielings so there could be no resistance. Police backed the sheriff officer and his burners, often with a minister present to ensure that there was no recourse to spiritual help. No wonder the Highlands moved en-masse to the Free Kirk, where the landlords did not select the ministers. Sometimes Irish soldiers were used, men whose kin had been defeated in rebellion by regiments from the Highlands and who were keen to take sordid revenge. Many of those evicted were sent to the new seaports on the Sutherland coast, still under the authority of the same Countess Elizabeth. Macleod gives a description of the building of these neat little towns, where 'even female labour' was used. The master masons were Lowlanders, and supervised their Highland workforce that included sick and pregnant women, husbands, wives and children.

It was often the women, those descendants of Celtic warriors and Norse chiefs, who led any resistance to the evictors. In 1813 a body of men and women threatened a Northumbrian named Reid, who intended to evict the population of the Strath of Kildonan and replace them with sheep. An angry crowd chased away Reid, who reported the matter to the authorities at Dunrobin Castle. When exaggerated reports circulated, claiming that the people had risen in revolt, the 21st foot arrived to help the civil power.

Some of the men who waited for the Sheriff Officers in Strath Oykel in 1820 were veterans of the French wars, and they drove the evictors from their glen. The authorities responded with police batons, the clubbed muskets of the Easter Ross Militia and a bevy of mounted gentry wielding riding whips. Women carried stones in their aprons as they gathered to face the evictors, and there were casualties on both sides. One woman died after being shot, but the militia withdrew in haste as the Strath Oykel people chased them to Ardgay. Always able to win a battle, the Highlanders often lacked the skill of exploitation and leadership, so once their fight was over they returned to their homes. Their relaxation allowed the authorities to regroup, and with the aid of a persuasive minister of the Kirk, the tenants were cleared from their glen.

The example of resistance may have been infectious, for only a year later a mob of women and men from Gruids fell on a brace of sheriff officers, destroyed their eviction notices, stripped them naked and whipped them out of the area. Once again, however, the tenants lacked staying power and submitted to the military might of the army. They moved eastwards to become fishermen on the dangerous coast of Sutherland. The evictions continued for year after heartbreaking year, but as the older generation, reared on duty to the chief, died, the new generation was less pliable. They withheld their loyalty to a social class that had betrayed them, and in 1841, at Keneabin near

Durness, they retaliated with more spirit than Sutherland had seen for some time.

A sheriff officer rode in to evict people for rent arrears; to be hurled back with his writs burned. The police came twice, and each time furious women repelled them. As so often, the police had come when most men were absent at the herring fishing, ploughing cold seas. After two failures, the authorities tried again, the superintendent of police, Philip Mackay, the Procurator Fiscal and scores of sheriff officers and police marching to evict a handful of poor families from their homes.

The *Inverness Courier* thought that the women of Keneabin were 'in a highly excited state' as they met authority with volleys of stones, while the men matched the batons of the police with sticks. The police and Procurator Fiscal sought refuge at the Inn, but a crowd burst down the door with railings and threw out the police. Capturing the sheriff and the procurator fiscal, the Keneabin people debated what to do next. Some suggested following the traditional pattern of stripping these figures of authority of their clothes, and therefore their dignity, but the majority decided for the more lenient option of just making them walk back from where they came. As so often before, persuasion and threats changed victory to defeat and soon sheep replaced the people.

The middle years of the 19th century were turbulent for the north, where blight destroyed the potatoes and famine added its agonies to a tortured land. While some of the people reacted with apathy, others rioted against an authority that permitted ships full of grain to depart within sight of suffering people. Women joined their men in rioting in the ports of the northeast, so that the army fought with musket and bayonets, women threw volleys of stones and men boarded the grain ships in Wick harbour. Women fought against the convoys of wagons that carried grain from the starving land, so that Invergordon and Thurso saw what Highland women could do when they had lost respect for authority and their children were starving.

After the famine of the late 1840s, the evictions continued, with women still standing beside, or in place of, their men. Sheriff-officers reported that near Brelangwell, a mob of women had attacked them, burned their writs, torn the clothes from their backs and chased them away. A body of sheriff officers marching to serve eviction notices at Gledfield, Strathcarron was met by between sixty and seventy women and a dozen men. The women waited quietly, with shawls covering their heads, and when the sheriff officers ordered the police forward there was mayhem. A score of women and two men were badly hurt. Three police officers kicked their boots into head, face and breasts of fifty-year-old Christy Ross. Other women were similarly assaulted, with police batons causing horrific injuries.

There is no definite start or end date for the Highland Clearances, but the deliberate policy of forcibly removing people from the glens peaked during the 1840s and 50s, when the potato blight created famine in the Highlands. Perhaps 100,000 Highland people were paupers in 1846, and some of the landlords who had not resorted to mass evictions bankrupted themselves trying to feed their tenants. There is little doubt that the famine encouraged emigration, both forced and voluntary. Lord Macdonald cleared the district of Strath at this time, a scene witnessed by Sir Archibald Geikie, the geologist.

He heard the wailing of three generations of dispossessed before he saw the 'long and motley procession' of departing Skye people. Men whose fathers had fought the French, whose great grandfathers had clutched their claymores for their chief, whose ancestors had faced MacLeods, English and Vikings, now walked shamefaced to the white sailed ships. The 'minister with his wife and daughters had come out to meet the people and bid them all farewell.' There were similar scenes in North Uist in 1849, except for the resistance. Women waited for the sheriff officers who hoped to serve eviction notices on the people of Sollas. Again there were women throwing stones and fighting with the police. And again, after desperate rioting, the people agreed to the emigration, so Lord Macdonald could replace them with sheep.

The catalogue of shame and horror is long, but there were one or two gleams of humanity. At the end of the 18th century Alexander, the 23rd Chisholm chief, perhaps persuaded by his wife and daughter Mary resisted every attempt to evict any of his tenants in Strathglass.

After his death in 1793, his widow and daughter continued to protect the people. On one occasion a lawyer tried to force his ageing widow to sign an eviction notice, but Mary threw him out with threats and high words. As a counterpoint to the Duchess of Sutherland, Mary Chisholm should be better remembered, as should the brave women who faced the muskets and truncheons of authority with stones and their own bodies.

It is somehow reassuring to learn that woman also took a major part in the riots of the 1880s when the Highland crofters gained security of tenure and the evictions finally eased. Women were in the majority during the so-called Battle of Braes in Skye in 1882, as the men were at the fishing, and women took part in the riots at Aignish in Lewis in 1888. It is more difficult to admit that the Clearances might not be the only reason for the empty glens. When people heard about better conditions in the towns and abroad, many left the glens voluntarily. And while poverty remained in the Highlands, prosperity embraced thousands of the descendants of those who left. Freed of the tyranny of clan and chief, they worked for their own ends and their own families.

Chapter 10

Press Gangs and Powder Monkeys

> The boys and women who carried the powder...behaved as well as the men
> John Nicol

The sea wars against the French occupy many pages in any British history book. It was a desperate time, when mighty armies were encamped along the coastlines of Europe, waiting for a chance to invade and bring death and destruction to Britain. Only the Royal Navy kept them out, with heroes such as Admiral Duncan of Dundee, Cochrane, who Admiral Keith regarded as 'wrong-headed, violent and proud' and Admiral Nelson. However, not everybody in Britain regarded the Navy with admiration. For many thousands of seamen the Royal Navy was a prison, with bad treatment, bad food, low pay and no set time for release.

Whenever there was a war at sea, there was also a war around the coastal towns and villages, where seamen strove to avoid being forced into the Navy. In the days before conscription, the armed services depended on volunteers, quota men and pressed men. Volunteers were always preferred, but there were never enough idealists to man the great warships that defended Britain, while quota men were often regarded as a poor option. The Quota Acts of March 1795 compelled each county and port to provide a number of men for the Navy. While seamen who volunteered at the beginning of the war in 1793 received a £5 bounty, a grateful government gave the Quota men £70. Even so, port towns could never find enough quality recruits, and often took the opportunity to rid themselves of undesirables. Among the thieves, rubbish and riff-raff swept up by the Quota Act were the main perpetrators of the 1797 Naval mutinies.

At other times, the Royal Navy, in common with most navies of the world, resorted to the Impress Service. The term comes from the 'prest' money that was given to a man to enable him to reach a naval recruiting centre, often a tavern with a secure room, known as a 'press room' where the recruits were held until they could be sent to a ship. Throughout the ages, England had many laws that made it legal for the armed forces to forcibly impress men so that by the 1690s the majority of seamen serving in the Royal Navy had been pressed. James IV of Scotland had similar ideas, but Scotland seldom had a large navy, so Scottish mariners were reasonably safe from the press gang until after the 1707 Act of Union.

During the 17th century, the English Royal Navy made a few attempts to snatch Scottish seamen, but after 1707 it became much more persistent. From Shetland to Eyemouth, Orkney to Annan, Scottish seamen could rarely spend a peaceful night in bed in case the ogres of the press gang came searching for prey. Fear of the navy had an unusual side effect in Shetland, where in the late 18th century the minister of the parish of Walls and Sandend was closely monitoring the situation. 'One reason why few young men remain unmarried,' he wrote, 'is because, if not married, they are sure to be fixed upon... for the service of the navy, when a draft for that service is required from the country.' The minister continued, 'rather than be forced from their native soil, and the society of their friends, they will submit to many inconveniences.' It seems that the inconvenience of marriage was preferred to the danger, disease and discomfort of the Royal Navy.

Scotswomen, of course, were more than just a convenient excuse for men to hide behind. On more than one occasion they massed together to encounter and repel seamen from the most powerful navy in the world. It was in 1813 that a strange sail appeared off the Mull of Galloway and seemed to head straight for Portpatrick. By that year, the French wars had dragged on for twenty years and Scottish seamen had fought against most nations of Europe. A new war had started with the United States of America, as the leaders of that young republic eyed the vast lands of Canada. An unknown sail off Scotland could well be hostile. The Dumfries Militia marched to Portpatrick, Brown Bess muskets balanced on their shoulders and bayonets bouncing from their hips as the local Customs Collector mounted his horse and galloped northward all the way to Greenock to summon a warship. Until help came, the manhood of Portpatrick would have to fight alone, but they were a hardy bunch and collected whatever weapons came to hand as they crowded toward the harbour to see off this impudent American, or Frenchman or whoever the enemy happened to be.

As the vessel drew closer a little hesitation appeared in the waiting defenders, then sudden panic. Rather than the French tricolour or the Stars and Stripes, it was the interlocking crosses of Union that flew from this ship. Terrified of the press gang, the men ran for whatever shelter they could find, leaving the women and the Dumfries Militia alone on the shore. Folklore claims that it was the women who repelled the naval landing party, but there are no details of the encounter. However, similar stories exist from every coast in Scotland. Arbroath has the tale of Tibbie Hall. In 1803, when the press gang snatched her sweetheart, Tibbie led a mob of women who were determined to regain their men. Unfortunately the Impress Service was more deeply entrenched in Arbroath and the women were repelled, with Tibbie Hall becoming instead the first occupant of the town's fine new jail. In Cellardyke in Fife it was the fisherwomen who fought against the press gangs. Gathering stones in their aprons, they hurled them against the bluejackets who had landed to capture the fishermen.

Orkney has a whole host of stories; many of them collected by W. R. Mackintosh at the close of the 19th century. The Orkney women seem to have been a particularly redoubtable bunch, full of wit and guile as well as courage. One of the quietest was the wife of William Rich, who worked as a constable for the Impress Service. It was part of his job to select and capture strong young men for the navy, but he was not very successful. He was unaware that his wife operated a counter press gang service, and every time that Rich left the house on a secret raid, she would send warning to the intended victims.

There was also the case of Mrs Firth of Finstown. Her son George was returning from the whaling season at the Davis Strait and had disembarked at Stromness with the others of the Orkney contingent. His mother knew that the pressgang was on the hunt, so hurried all the way across the island to warn George. Sometimes she walked and often she ran and always she hoped to meet him before the press did. At last she saw him sauntering along the road in his seafaring rig, burned by the sun and carrying all his worldly goods over his shoulder.

'George, George!' Mrs Firth said urgently, 'quickly, put on these clothes!' She explained her plan even as she heard the hunting shouts of the press from over a fold of ground. Within seconds, George Firth was swathed in women's clothing, so that when the press appeared, all they saw were two women walking peacefully along the road.

While some women were defending their men against the Press, others signed articles with the Navy. When Thomas Watson was pressed from Cellardyke, his wife, Mary Buek joined him at sea. They remained together for years, with Mary giving birth to her daughter Margaret during the cannonade of Copenhagen and surviving the battle of Trafalgar. She also played a notable part in the aftermath of victory, for it was Mary who prepared Nelson's body for embalming. For many years the Navy termed rum as Nelson's blood, and swore that after his death the great Admiral's body was pickled in the precious fluid. There are also tales of men dipping into the embalming fluid for a quiet drink, or 'tapping the admiral' as they called it. Mary however, probably used a more efficient preservative.

There were a surprising number of women aboard warships in the 18th and early 19th century, and their presence seems to have been accepted as natural by most officers and all the men. The majority of these women seem to have been the wives of warrant officers, and they played their part in action as well as in normal seafaring life. John Nicol, a Scotsman who helped man a gun on *Goliath* at the Battle of the Nile in 1798 spoke of 'the boys and women who carried the powder. They behaved as well as the men and got a present for their bravery.' The women and boys who carried powder were known as 'powder monkeys' and their job was as dangerous as any other in the ship. They would run from the cannon to the powder store and back, carrying cartridges for the guns. They would be constantly on the move, dodging the rearing, bucking cannon, trying to ignore the sights and sounds of men who were torn to pieces by roundshot or mutilated by flying wooden splinters, while keeping alert from danger themselves.

Nicol continues 'I was much indebted to the gunner's wife, who gave her husband and me a drink of wine every now and then, which lessened our fatigue much.' Nicol does not say what part gunner's wife played in the action. Presumably she was also acting as a powder monkey, or else she helped her husband weigh the powder into the silk cartridge bags. The fact that the gunner's wife was able to carry wine indicates a measure of trust that would not be extended to many of the men. Drink and the British seamen were often poor companions, with the majority of naval crimes committed due to an excess of alcohol.

Nicol's final words concerning women were more sombre. 'There were some of the women wounded, and one woman belonging to Leith died of her wounds and was buried in a small island in the bay.'[1] The casual choice of the word 'some' indicates that Nicol saw nothing unusual in there being a fair number of women on board. Finally Nicol

---

1. There were a number of graves from this action discovered in April 2005. Perhaps one was that of the aforementioned woman from Leith.

said that one 'woman bore a son in the heat of the action; she belongs to Edinburgh.'

It is hardly surprising that the trauma of battle should bring on childbirth, and a fair proportion of children were born at sea. The Royal Navy, practical as ever, had a tradition in such matters and reserved an area of the gun deck for women in labour. If the child was male, he was known as the 'son of a gun' and was often bred up in the ship, to become a powder monkey and then a Royal Naval seaman in turn. The Navy could term such a man as 'begotten in the galley and born under a gun. Every hair a rope yarn, every tooth a marline spike, every finger a fishhook and his blood right good Stockholm tar.' There seem to be no folk memory of females born on board, but the law of averages suggests that many were. No doubt they were equally at home on board.

Some women also served as sailors aboard the wooden walls of Nelson's Navy. The historian Suzanne Stark in her *Female Tars, Women aboard ship in the age of Sail* wrote about at least twenty known female sailors in the 18th and 19th centuries. One of these was William Brown. Despite having her place of origin entered as Edinburgh in the muster book, Brown's nationality is questionable, not least because she was black. She became captain of the foretop of the battleship *Queen Charlotte* and served as a sailor for twelve years. As with many sailors, Brown ran away to sea to escape a bad marriage, enjoyed her grog and vanished from history. She was one of an unknown number of sea-women in the Royal Navy, but whatever the frown of officialdom, the tars that served before the mast winked at their presence. It was not until the 1980s that women were officially allowed to serve on board a Royal warship.

Women were also officially banned from serving on merchant vessels, although from time to time the odd woman emerged from her male disguise into the limelight of a press article. Occasionally there were female stowaways, such as the woman who disguised herself as a man, adopted the name of John Ibister and attempted to stow away on *Prince of Wales*, outward bound from Stromness in 1811. She was discovered, but others were more successful. The 'Indian Daily News' of 20 January 1868 reported that the troopship *Flying Foam* had recently berthed at Calcutta. On board were two female stowaways, one aged sixteen, and the other seventeen. The paper believed that both young women had been married to soldiers before they left Britain, and that the soldiers had helped their young wives stow away. The India bound soldiers appear to have cared for the two very young women on *Flying Foam* and the newspaper reported that they 'found berths in the veranda of the barracks,' but in this instance, the voyage was little more than a prelude to their real hardships. Other women demonstrated their adventurous spirit

In January 1873 a Whitby vessel sailed into Aberdeen, carrying a cargo of esparto grass, which was used in the making of paper. The newspapers made much of the discovery of a female sailor on board the ship. According to the newspaper accounts, the sailor was disguised as a 'smart looking young man' when he signed articles at Whitby and sailed with coal for Malaga. The voyage was rough, but the new sailor 'behaved himself like a man' and demonstrated 'great pluck for going aloft.' Indeed the Whitby sailor seemed very spirited, so that even the old hands were impressed. Nobody suspected that 'he' was in fact a 'she' until the vessel arrived at Malaga, when her gender was discovered. Dressed in woman's clothes, she worked her passage to Aberdeen as a stewardess. The newspapers described her as a 'stoutly built female and as her hair is not very long' she had a 'thorough masculine appearance.' While her erstwhile shipmates enjoyed 'many a hearty laugh' at her antics, the newspapers said that 'the female' gave 'no reason for her foolish freak.'

The anonymous woman of Whitby was only one of many women who posed as men for their own reasons. One of the most poignant tales concerned Isabell Gunn, who became a labourer with the Hudson Bay Company, in the guise of John Fubbister. In the eighteenth and nineteenth centuries, Orkney provided much of the manpower for the Company, so that Orkney boatmen worked under the vast Northern skies and the accents of Kirkwall and Stromness added colour to the Canadian forests. It was not uncommon for the Orkney men to marry the native women, bringing home wives from the Plains or the quiet creeks that shuddered under the terrible isolation of the Arctic. Isabell Gunn joined these men, working as part of a boat's crew on the hardly explored rivers that penetrated the wilderness west of Hudson Bay.

It was on the 29th December 1807, at Pembina Post on the Red River in what had not yet become North Dakota that the fur trader Alexander Henry opened the door to a visitor. At first he thought that the stranger was a young, sick lad from Orkney, and he invited the fellow Scot in. The youngster was clearly unwell, and lay on the hearth in front of the fire. As Alexander Henry recorded in his journal, the boy 'stretched out his hands toward me' and begged 'me to be kind to a poor, helpless abandoned wretch who was not of the sex I supposed.' Isabell Gunn was actually in labour, and with Henry acting as midwife, gave birth to a healthy son. Both mother and child returned to Orkney in September 1809, no doubt with enough tales to keep the grandchildren interested for years.

Some women had no desire to return home at all. For them, the sea and the company of rough living men was an escape from a life of abuse at home. In most cases, these women have remained anonymous, their identities never revealed, their stories never told. Others, normally through discovery, have left some memories of their life. However, these accounts are always frustratingly incomplete.

One such anonymous woman appears to have enjoyed a happy childhood in Aberdeen, until her mother died and her father married again. Perhaps jealous of the affection her new husband showed to his daughter, the stepmother treated the child cruelly. In an age where child abuse was nearly acceptable, the girl had no defence against the mental, emotional and physical abuse that the stepmother heaped on her. At last, when she was fourteen years old, she ran away to sea. Disguising herself as a boy, and calling herself Thomas Brown, the girl preferred the rough treatment by seamen to the cruelty of her stepmother. She found that she enjoyed a seaman's life, and learned many aspects of her trade. Not content with her position as an Ordinary Seaman, she learned how to work aloft and could stand her trick at the wheel. Perhaps because she had a woman's delicate touch, she became an expert in knotwork and the more intricate details of a sailor's profession.

For five years Thomas Brown played the part of a man, until she signed on a vessel apparently named *Flying Venus* at Liverpool. She worked assiduously throughout the voyage down the length of the Atlantic and across the Indian Ocean. Only as the ship neared Bombay did Thomas Brown give herself away. The full details will probably never be known, but it seems that one of the crew found out first, and then the master, Mr Little, came to hear of it.

Whatever his personal feelings for one of the more efficient members of his crew, Mr Little could not allow her to remain as a sea woman. With her disguise ruined, Thomas Brown may have been in danger; certainly she would be a distraction for the other members of the crew. In December 1867, Mr Little escorted her to the acting Chief Magistrate to seek advice. His Worship handed the sea woman over to Mr Bickers, the missionary for Bombay, who offered to look after her. Mr Bickers suggested that he either arrange passage home for the erstwhile Thomas Brown or 'some employment suited to her sex.'

After working with her for so long, Mr Little was reluctant to say goodbye to his prize. He did all he could to smooth her passage into a land woman by giving her 'an excellent character,' saying that she 'was of a quiet, retiring disposition' as well as 'one of the smartest hands on the ship.' Little more is known about Thomas Brown, who gave away very little about her earlier life. The captain raised some money for her, and arranged for a 'moderate wardrobe' of clothes, but when he left her in Bombay, the nameless sea woman disappeared from history. Hopefully she obtained a berth on another vessel and continued her career, but it is unlikely that her full story will ever be known.

Although there may be a gloss of romance about life on a sailing ship, there is nothing remotely romantic about working in the engine room of a merchant ship crossing the Atlantic during the Second World War. Nonetheless, that is exactly where a Scotswoman worked.

Even in peacetime life in an engine room meant long hours, hard dirty work and conditions that could range from primitive to atrocious. Wartime added the constant threat of death and mutilation. But engineering was Victoria Drummond's job, so she persevered. Named after her Godmother, the Queen-Empress, Victoria was born in Perth in October 1894, daughter of Captain Drummond, who was a Royal Advisor. Yet it was her grandmother whom Victoria seemed most to take after. Granny was a member of the Worshipful Company of Turners, working with a lathe and much skill to create marvellous article of wood and ivory. Perhaps Victoria learned by observation, perhaps she had a natural bent for practical matters, but either way she chose to be a marine engineer.

Although Perth is an inland town, the River Tay connects it to the sea, and Victoria would have been familiar with ships and shipping. Dundee itself, the centre of the British whaling industry and home to some fine shipbuilding companies, was only twenty miles away. Even so it was highly unusual for a young woman of eminent birth to choose an occupation known for its harshness. Victoria Drummond must have possessed an extraordinary personality to decide on such a career, and great determination to pursue it. The route to an engineer's berth was not easy. Victoria learned the ropes at a garage in Errol; about ten miles east of Perth in the Carse of Gowrie, where shipping can be seen creeping up the Tay. The manager possibly thought that this well-bred young woman was following a whim, and waited for her to tire. He allowed her to brush out the shop, to wash filthy machinery in paraffin and other menial tasks, but when it became obvious that Victoria was prepared to dirty her hands, he offered her an apprenticeship. Perhaps it was indicative of the future that her supervisor had been chief engineer on a Scottish ship.

Used to working with the hardy men of the Clyde, the supervisor treated Victoria in the only way he knew how. Engineering was a dangerous business and when a piece of molten solder dripped painfully onto Victoria's hand, the supervisor cut it out with his clasp knife and washed out the gaping hole with raw paraffin. It was a far cry from the Court of the queen, but Victoria revelled in the process.

Victoria moved from Errol to a Dundee shipbuilding company and then to Dundee Technical College. What is most remarkable is the lack of fuss that seems to have been made about her. This was just after the time of the suffragettes, when women barricaded themselves to railings and blew up pillar-boxes to gain the right to vote. Women such as Jex-Blake, who eased herself into medicine, have become famous, while Victoria Drummond is virtually unknown. Yet it is likely that she was the world's only female engineering apprentice at the time. It says a lot for the workforce of Dundee, and the instructors at Dundee Technical College, that they accepted Victoria. Perhaps people had more important things to worry about, with the Great War tearing the world apart and much of the manhood of Scotland enduring the mud of Flanders.

By 1922, when Victoria was 28 years old, she finally found a berth on a ship. Her first voyage was on SS *Anchises* on the short hop from the Mersey to the Clyde. Whatever the initial reaction in the engine room, and even then there would be many men that would welcome female company in their place of work, Victoria proved herself a competent enough engineer to be signed on for a second voyage. Rather than a short crossing of the Irish Sea, Victoria was destined for the long passage from Glasgow to Australia.

There was nothing glamorous about such a voyage. As Assistant Engineer on *Anchises,* Victoria would not have any opportunity to sunbathe on deck. Rather she was enduring the insufferable heat of the engine room, crawling on hands and knees to inspect the bilges among the dark and stench, or scaling the slithering coal in the bunkers. Shifting coal was one of the most under-rated dangers of sea-travel, with possibly hundreds of ships capsizing after badly stowed coal roared from one side of the vessel to the other. However, Victoria survived all the tedious, necessary tasks to arrive safely in Australia.

Perhaps it is significant that while the male passengers asked Victoria about her job, it was the women who sneered at her oil-stained hands and made comments about white linen in the engine room. It may be interesting to speculate just how much the opinion of supposedly superior women held back the cause of female employment equality, but it is unlikely that their attitudes concerned Engineer Drummond. The goddaughter of a queen and a native of Perth, she was surely aware that she was equal to any mere passenger. Drummond knew what real men were, for the firemen and trimmers who worked beside her in the bowels of the ship were, quite simply, some of the hardest men at sea. Most came from the dockside slums of Glasgow or Liverpool, Leith or London or Dundee; small men, undernourished from a harsh childhood, they had muscles wiry as a steel hawser and coal dust permanently engrained in their maltreated bodies. Nobody argued with the Black Gang, so if Victoria Drummond could work in their company, the words of a smoothly spoiled little flibberty-gibbet from the passenger deck were unlikely to touch her.

Victoria was not trying to prove a point. She was not attempting to press forward a theory of female equality. Instead she was pursuing her career, and her ambition was to become chief engineer. She remained as Assistant Engineer in *Anchises* for another two voyages, when she travelled the oceans and no doubt learned much about her trade and about the world in general. From *Anchises* she shipped on TS *Mulbera*, where the Chief Engineer praised her highly. But life at sea was changing; the twenties slid into the thirties and old fears were realised. People realised that the War to End all Wars had not quite worked as old monsters of superiority re-emerged from the European continent. It was then that Victoria Drummond gained her ambition of becoming a Chief Engineer.

It was a bad time to be a merchant mariner. Unarmed, slow, and utterly essential, the cargo vessels that were Britain's lifeline were targets of the venomous U-boat. Ships by the hundred were murdered as the sea-lanes became punctured with death in the most terrible of forms. If life at sea was dirty, dangerous and basic, death by torpedo was vile. Seamen died by choking on fuel oil, or by being blown to pieces; by burning alive in petroleum or by slow exposure. It was worse in the engine-room, where the Black Gang had the furthest distance to travel if their ship was hit. Death there was by scalding by fractured steam pumps, while the unlucky survivors, with their skin literally peeling from their flayed body, swam through oil thick, salt seas in the hope of rescue. To those who had the power of choice, a wartime engine room was regarded as no place for a woman.

And so an experienced, highly competent chief engineer remained frustrated on shore while her country, and the cause of democracy, fought with bloody fingernails for survival. The choice was simple: endure, suffer and possibly survive, or surrender to a regime that had more in common with a horror story than with humanity.

However, although British mariners fought to preserve their women, some foreign ships were less fastidious. On board SS *Harzion*, Victoria found herself mixing with a crew that could have come from the Foreign Legion. Almost inevitably, there was trouble, but rather than handle it bucko-mate style, Victoria resorted to a quiet voice. Perhaps the presence of a woman sobered even the hard-case mariners, perhaps Victoria possessed some natural authority, but she ended the fight. She spoke softly to her men, as she spoke softly to her engines, which, she claimed, could be coaxed or led but never driven.

The war continued. A dark, terrible war of secret submarines sending torpedoes into the bowels of civilian ships, of dogged, bloody-minded mariners continuing to do their job regardless of Hitler and associated horrors. In 1941, when the sea war was approaching a climax, German aircraft attacked Victoria's ship. Merchant mariners were not trained to fight; they were civilian volunteers, and Victoria was no exception. By remaining at her position in the engine room while the Luftwaffe bombed and machine-gunned her vessel, she set an example to her companions. Recognising her courage, the government awarded her an MBE, which was later augmented by the Lloyds War Medal for Bravery at Sea.

Unlike so many courageous mariners, Victoria Drummond survived the war. She also achieved her ambition of being a chief engineer. A woman of undoubted courage and resource, she is sadly neglected and her name is hardly known now.

Chapter 11

Only Weavers Wore Hats: Industrial Women

> All work, even cotton-spinning, is noble
> Thomas Carlyle

In the early 18th century, many parts of Scotland were dependent on linen. As early as 1725, Highland women made their own webs and bleached their own cloth, while Aberdeen, Glasgow, Forfar and Perth were fast becoming centres of linen manufacture. It was a small-scale process, however, with most people working at home amidst familiar surroundings. Women worked long hours while remaining matriarchs of a family unit that retained their man and children within shouting distance.

A century later the Industrial Revolution was in full swing, the character of Scotland was changing and women and children were sucked into the mills and factories that thrust up like parasitical growths along riverbanks and in towns and cities. In the early days, conditions were horrific. Used to working alongside their men at the handloom weaving or in the farms, women found it hard to adjust to the discipline of the machine and the clock. The heat and noise of mill and factory sapped the strength of the novice, overseers used brutality as casual coercion and the mingling of sexes could lead to a promiscuity that shocked the respectable. Sometimes the overseer or owner would be the worst example of immorality, for he could sexually abuse any female employee by using the threat of dismissal as a lever.

As large mills spread throughout Scotland, women spinners voiced their anger against this threat to their livelihood. At the beginning of the 19th century, feeling among the women spinners of Angus was so high that they spoke openly of burning down these mills that took their jobs and lowered their standard of living. Until driven there by starving necessity, they ordered their daughters not to work in the mills, for girls exposed to so much vice would not find a husband. However, the massive growth in the textile industry created thousands of jobs for the unskilled, so country people who had been cleared from the Highland glens or forced from Lowland farms by enclosures and increased mechanisation, could find employment, however unsavoury. In time, women predominated amongst the textile workforce, as their smaller hands and greater dexterity gave them an advantage over men. They were also seen as being more amenable to discipline than the men, who were usually made redundant on their 18th birthday. The only males to be retained were engineers, a handful of overseers and some with particular skills.

While Glasgow was a city of heavy engineering, Edinburgh was a centre of finance and Aberdeen acted as a market for farming and fisheries, Dundee was primarily a textile town. Women dominated the work force, both in the linen mills of the early nineteenth century and the jute mills of the latter quarter of the century; in 1851, 83% of Dundee's working women were employed in textile mills. While only 3% of married Aberdonian women worked, one quarter of Dundee's married women earned money, in a period when society expected women to look after the home and family. Dundee's employers preferred married women to their reputedly more flighty, less responsible single compatriots.

There were no regulations in the early days of industry, so men, women and children worked long hours in appalling conditions. The 19th century saw a gradual tightening of government influence, and a consequent lessening of hours spent in the mill. Althorp's Act of 1833 forbade children under nine from millwork and eased the hours of those aged between nine and thirteen. Unfortunately it was impossible to prove the age of a child until the registration of births began in 1855. Factories, as opposed to mills, continued to employ children until the Factory Act of 1863 forbade them. Often the Acts only added to the sufferings of terribly poor people who depended on even the pittance earned by a child. Many of the Factory Acts also diminished the role of women in factories, partly for the sake of their health, but also to help create a decent family wage for the husband, who was regarded as the main breadwinner.

The reality of factory life often contrasted with this patriarchal theory. Married women and daughters were frequently the providers for a family where the man could not find regular work, and men were relegated to a subsidiary position. In many accounts, these unemployed men were known as 'kettle boilers' and wives spoke with some pride of the husbands that kept their homes pin-clean and had their tea ready when they returned from the mill. In other families, the man's status and pride were so reduced that even his working daughters openly abused him, and the public house was his only refuge.

One of the most heavily industrialised areas of Dundee was Lochee, which the expanding city absorbed in 1859. By the 1840s there were three large and various small mills in Lochee, with adults and children, men and women, working long hours. In 1850 the Cox family founded their Camperdown Linen Works, which in time would employ five thousand people, the majority of whom were women. As none of the Lochee mills supplied houses the workers had to rent privately or find a boarding house. Not surprisingly, housing was rudimentary, with two story cottages and the ubiquitous Scottish tenement. However, the situation was better than in other parts of the city.

Sanitation was sparse, for not until 1868 did the Dundee Water Company insert three miles of pipes. One area, known as Tipperary on account of the influx of Irish women looking for work, continued to rely on the Lochee Burn for sewage disposal. In 1881 there were 12370 people living in Lochee, in 2493 houses, giving an average of 4.96 people per house. Many of the women shared one-roomed flats in what were all-female households where two or more wages ensured a relatively comfortable lifestyle. In other homes, married women lived with their husbands, so if there were no children, or the children were older, there were at least two wages. Families with young children often faced financial hardship as they struggled with a single wage and multiple mouths to feed.

Women's wages varied; the average weekly wage was between 8/- and 9/- (40 – 45p) a week, but textile workers wages fluctuated according to the market. Weavers' wages rose 20% between 1886 mad 1890 and in 1905 spinners earned around 12/- (60p) a week, weavers perhaps 3/- (15p) more. However, wages in Dundee remained among the lowest in Scotland, with unfortunate women from the worst quarters of town earning a mere 6/- (30p) a week for hand sewing jute sacking. Following the trend with Scotswomen and their money, many of the mill workers saved from their wages, however small. James Cox, owner of the massive factory, offered to give financial advice to 'any of the girls' that wanted to 'lay out their little savings to the best advantage' and added that some 'have such sums that…you would be astonished.'

Perhaps Lochee was different from the rest of Dundee, but there seems very little unemployment in 1881, with early morning trams carrying men to work at Dundee docks and in the quarry and building trades, while the women worked locally in the mills. The 1881 census reveals that in the Tipperary area, there were 261 adults, of whom 151 women and 52 males were employed in mills or factories, with only one woman employed elsewhere. Fifty-five men had jobs outside the mill. Although there was a regular omnibus service to Dundee, the women in Lochee had a selection of shops that included a specialist store for Lady's Furnishings, butchers bakers and even a tearoom.

It is possible that Lochee enjoyed better living conditions than other parts of Dundee for while the 1905 Dundee Social Union Report calls the centre of Dundee 'particularly congested' and the Overgate area too 'thickly populated', Lochee was seen as 'unrepresentative.' Possibly the superior housing with 'two storey buildings' helped explain Lochee's lower infant mortality rate, despite having the highest percentage of married working women. In comparison, the St Mary's district had the next highest number of working women and the highest mortality rate.

In 1905 Lochee's 430 married working women with children had to share a single crèche, which the municipal health visitor criticised for 'overcrowded and unsanitary conditions.' However, the charge of between 1/6 and 2/- a week was cheaper than those imposed by child minding neighbours. Perhaps the Reverent Connel of Lochee, and Miss A, B. Cox, both members of the Social Union, influenced Edward Cox's decision to provide another nursery in 1909. The remainder of Dundee shared three crèches, so that only the fortunate had access to such formal facilities.

Mothers and children suffered together. Women, exhausted after a twelve-hour day, had neither time nor energy to spend on her offspring, who were often brought up devoid of affection or education. It was Engels who coined the phrase 'wild weeds' to describe the lives of such neglected unfortunates, who were taught nothing by the often drunken child minders and often made poor mothers and wives when their time came. Children grew up ignorant and neglected by their exhausted parents. Forced into mills at too early an age, many were deformed by unnatural working positions, white faced with lack of fresh air, emotionally, mentally and physically crippled. They knew nothing of the world save the necessity to work. Factory and millwork perhaps made money for the few and put Britain in the forefront of the world, but the Scottish people, man woman and child, paid a high price.

The municipal list of female voters for Lochee in 1884-1885 has 44 names. At that date, women were not able to vote in parliamentary elections, so presumably these women voted in council elections. While most of the women were registered as 'householder', there were two grocers and one flesher, or butcher. One, Mrs Betsy Smith, owned a house, shop and bleaching green, while two others, Ann Steel and Mrs Soote, had two addresses. No doubt these women rented out their second houses.

By the 1870s there were 70 mills in Dundee, with 30,000 women amongst the 40,000 jute mill workers. Contemporary reports are fairly uniform in their descriptions of the bold eyed, overdressed mill lassies that swaggered through the streets. Outsiders thought them coarse and were repelled by their use of snuff to expel the jute dust from their nostrils. Even worse was the sight of drunken mill women being carried to the police cells in hand carts. Yet despite the alarmist reports, debauched women were a minority in a city where hard work was the norm. For most working women of the latter part of the 19th century, 'perambulating' around the shops, gossiping loudly and whistling to reveal their freedom from the restraints of the mill were the few pleasures in life.

There is evidence of some culture among the women of the mills, with the power loom weaver Ellen Johnson writing poetry about the hardship of the poor. Interestingly, she also wrote with some affection for the factories in which she worked. There would be few employees today who would write anything so sentimental as her 'Dear Chapelshade Factory,' but ideas and opinions alter with each generation.

Women adapted to working long, hard hours and created a sign language and accent that penetrated the remorseless clatter of the mill machinery. They also had their own unique caste system. Weavers were seen as responsible, mature women and dressed accordingly in hats and gloves; they often disdained to talk to the lower paid spinners, who they regarded as irresponsible. Weavers believed that they made better wives, and often left the mill when they married artisans or engineers who brought in decent money. Despite the relatively reasonable conditions of Lochee, Dundee had a terrible reputation for bad housing and low pay, so that many of the inhabitants were small, slight and unhealthy.

Life for married women was not a continuous honeymoon. Men who had spent long hours in physical labour found no pleasure in returning to a tiny flat noisy with a brood of children. He would often retire to the public house, leaving the unfortunate woman virtually trapped with the children twenty-four hours a day, every day. With no mechanical aids to make housework easier, the married mother had a life of constant toil and little pleasure. Drink, disease and slum housing occupied the attention of many social reformers of the 19th century, and they had ample scope for their efforts in Dundee. One of the best remembered was Mary Lily Walker.

Dundee born and bred, Mary Lily Walker was the daughter of a lawyer who died while she was young. One of the very first female graduates of the University College, Dundee, where she studied Latin, Chemistry, Maths and Biology, she left university to nurse her dying mother for some years, then studied for her BSc at St Andrews. Although Dundee remembers her social activities, Walker was also an accomplished scientist, writing some notable papers.

In May 1888 Walker was a prime mover in the foundation of the Dundee Social Union, whose purpose was 'to improve the condition of the dwellings of the poor, to provide opportunities and cultivate a taste for healthy enjoyment and to promote the well-being of the inhabitants of the town.' There were to be no limits on 'class, religion or condition.' Walker spent some time in London, working under Octavia Hill, the great English social reformer, at the Women's University in Southwark. Obviously interested in helping the poor, she worked for a further year in Blackheath with an Anglican sisterhood known as the Grey Ladies. Walker must have been genuinely impressed by the work of these Grey Ladies, for she adopted their grey nuns habit, and wore it even after she left London to return to Dundee.

Distressed by the living condition of the workers of Dundee, Walker also began a movement to have restaurants for nursing mothers, many of who were also working. Concentrating on the most vulnerable, Walker pushed forward Scotland's first hospital exclusively for children and Scotland's first school for disabled children. The Industrial Revolution and its associated poverty created many young disabled people, victims of rickets, mill accidents, long hours in cramped positions or children born with defects due to their mother's unhealthy working life. In 1891, working with Emily Thomson and Alice Moorhead, Dundee's first women doctors, Walker founded a woman's clinic and chemist's dispensary in the Hilltown.

Walker was particularly concerned with the poor housing of the Dundee people. Although the Dundee Improvement Act of 1870 had created some fine streets around the Whitehall area, huge numbers of people continued to live in shocking conditions. When the Social Union purchased ten properties in some of the worst areas, with the idea of letting them out to deserving tenants, Walker supervised the scheme. She managed the houses and arranged for the rents to be collected, but also ensured that the children were properly looked after when their parents were at work. As well as helping a number of families, this work enabled Walker to scientifically study Dundee's social problems.

It had been Walker's intention to persuade the Scottish Episcopal Church to establish a branch of the Grey Ladies in Dundee, but this did not happen. Instead she bought a house in Wellington Street, near the poor area of the Hilltown. Naming her house Grey Lodge, she used it as her headquarters to help the local community while furthering the developing science of Social Work. Indeed, it could be said that Mary Lily Walker was the first professional social worker in Dundee, if not in Scotland. Joining Dundee Parish Council, Walker was in a better position to further her aims of improving the conditions of factory women and children. She was busily employed when the Boer War started in 1899. As the army needed more and more men, it became apparent that industrial society was creating a race of undersized, under strength Britons who were not fit to fight. The government began to take measures to improve the health of the people.

In the meantime Walker and her team of four female sanitary inspectors studied many of Dundee's homes. Working with the Londoner Mona Wilson, Walker wrote Dundee Social Union's Report on *Housing and Industrial Conditions and Medical Inspection of School Children*. This 150-page book revealed the social horrors of 6000 Dundee houses. The facts were starkly portrayed with none of the colourful rhetoric of earlier reports, but the result still has the power to shock. Dundee in Edwardian times seemed every bit as bad as it had in the early years of Queen Victoria. Poor sanitation, overcrowded rooms, filth; the poor of Dundee lived in unimaginable squalor. Driving her point home, Walker published lists of statistics comparing working and middle class children. In each case, working class girls were smaller and lighter than their more affluent contemporaries were. When they were thirteen years old and on the threshold of maturity, Dundee girls weighed an average of nearly a stone lighter than girls from England.

After reading Walker's Report, the Government requested a more lengthy investigation. Walker responded with the 1905 Social Union Report, possibly the most comprehensive investigation into working class housing of its time. When the House of Commons read the report, there was an immediate outcry to improve conditions in the city. Mary Lily Walker, however, did not wait for the government to act. In 1906 she opened Scotland's first restaurant purely for working mothers, with a moderate charge for most customers and no charge for the poorest. In the Social Union Report, Walker had pointed out that when new mothers returned to work in the mills, the babies suffered from a lack of breast-feeding. The restaurant was staffed with women who gave free health advice to mothers with young babies, encouraged breast-feeding and visited mothers in their own homes.

In 1912, Walker's Infant's Clinic had a staff of women doctors, and she had also established a milk depot for young children. Still not content to rest on her considerable laurels, Walker was involved in research for the State Insurance Act. Together with Captain Scott, Mary Lily Walker founded a holiday camp for the deprived and orphaned boys of *Mars*, the training ship that was anchored in the Tay.

Walker died in 1913, but even in death tried to help the working women of Dundee by leaving her house as a social work centre. She is well remembered in Dundee, with the Grey Lodge Centre continuing her work and the 1905 Social Union Report still used for research.

Naturally, many women in other Scottish cities also had to endure shocking living conditions. With the gentry fleeing Edinburgh's Auld Toon for the New Town, by the 1840s the historic closes and wynds were scenes of Third World squalor. Dogs, horses and chickens shared rooms with humans; the closes were deep with human excrement and men, women and children slept on beds comprising heaps of dusty straw. Alexander Smith, visiting the Cowgate, where once Earls and Duchesses had strolled, spoke of 'shoals of hideous faces… sodden countenances of brutal men, women with loud voices and frantic gesticulations, children who had never known innocence.'

George Bell wrote of Blackfriars Wynd, where 1000 people were squeezed into 142 houses and where a woman shared a 6-foot square room with rats, mice and rubbish. Thomas Guthrie, the Minister for the Cowgate in 1837 spoke of 'crowds of half naked creatures, men, women and children shivering with cold and hunger.' He visited houses 'where there were starving mothers and starving children with neither bread, bed nor bible.' The underbelly of Edinburgh was a sink of debauchery and horror, with dismissed servant girls selling themselves to survive and desperate men from Ireland and the Highlands crouched cold and cramped in doorways. This was the Edinburgh of Burke and Hare, where lone women could be killed for profit and soldiers from the castle poured kill-me-deadly whisky down their throat for a few minutes relief from misery.

Glasgow was no better. A reporter in Glasgow in 1839 found lodging houses with up to twenty people of both sexes, some naked, sleeping on the floor. The night-time Glasgow streets were a riot of drunken fights and even the police avoided the airless backcourts. The 19th century may have been a constant war for of progress, but the casualties were many.

Every city and town where there were factories and mills needed a workforce, and in very many cases women filled the ranks. Women were the backbone of Britain's Industrial Revolution, their sweat, toil and tears created much of the wealth that poured into the nation's coffers. In return, these same women received very little. Only a few dedicated people such as Mary Lily Walker, were concerned enough to try and raise their quality of living above that of desperation. Even so, it was not until 1918 that the Government decided to build decent homes for the working people, and even now many thousands of Scottish women struggle to bring up their family in conditions that are less than ideal.

Rural conditions too, could be grim. The mythological country cottage with roses around the door and a smiling, clean housewife who spent her days making healthy food and feeding the hens never existed. Indeed, rural housing was often worse than in any city tenement, with dampness, overcrowding, a home tied to the job and no facilities or shops close by. The growth of mechanisation in the 19th and 20th centuries hit the rural poor hardest of all. As the number of jobs decreased, rural workers moved to the cities, and those who were left faced long hours at low wages. The farmer's wife, herself as hard working as anybody in the country, often proved a tyrant to her tenants, while crofters in both the east and west of the country struggled desperately on often marginal land. Crofting was always subsistence farming, but when faced with cheap imported food, the crofters could only reply by relying on the unpaid labour of wives, sons and daughters. Often the women would farm the land while the men took to the sea. The return home after each herring season was an anxious time, with the women hoping that the fish had been plentiful and storms few.

Young people regarded agricultural work as mere drudgery and many women were glad to escape to the relatively better paid, cleaner and more feminine tasks of the domestic servant. Others remained where they were. Rural counties also seemed to have a higher percentage of illegitimate births, particularly where large-scale farming took place and the farm labourers were mainly young men who lived in communal bothies. Each of these large farms would have a maidservant who helped the farmer's wife with housework and food preparation, and contemporary ballads are full of references to illicit, if highly enjoyable meetings between maid and horseman in barn or byre. Often the couple would marry after the event; sometimes there was no need. Sex to countrywomen was a natural progression to womanhood, something to be enjoyed as a break from the routine of work and labour.

Other women had more inhibitions. Middle class Victorian women were often unsure what to do with a man even after she had one. Some grown women had so little understanding of life that they were unsure from what part of their body a baby might exit, provided that one could be placed inside in the first place. Perhaps some married men used this ignorance as an excuse to visit the prostitutes that could be found in most towns. There was no excuse for middle class married men to seek the sexual favours of their own maids. The bars across their bedroom windows that ensured that these maids could not slip out to find a lover of their own class were little protection from a prowler within the house.

Until well into the 20th century, there were gangs of women labourers that travelled around the farms. Bondagers worked long hours at menial tasks such as hoeing or picking potatoes, 'tattie howking.' Often the daughter of horsemen, ploughmen or other rural employers, the women worked in all weathers, often with a male gang master. Many seemed to have enjoyed the experience, despite the hard work; there were compensations such as female companionship, sometimes the freedom of working alone and certainly fresher air and more variety than working in the mills. Overall, women's work was hard, repetitive and poorly paid, whether they were in the countryside or the city.

Chapter 12

All at Sea

> I will go back to the great sweet mother
> Mother and lover of men, the sea
> Swinburne

For centuries, Scotland was a nation divided by culture. In the East and South were the Lowlanders, who traded with Europe, while in the Far North were the people of Orkney and Shetland who knew the sea like a friend. In the West were the Highlanders and Hebrideans, who used the sea as a highway to the islands.

Folklore and remaining Gaelic documents provide only sparse clues to what was certainly a rich and diverse culture, and one in which women played their full part. For instance, there is the tale of the nuns from the Monach Island who often took out a birlinn to cruise the Hebridean seas. On one occasion, a sudden storm capsized the boat and all the nuns were drowned. But many Hebridean women sailed these western seas. On another occasion MacDonald of the Isles was crossing the stormy Minch to see his son in law, MacLeod of Harris, and his new grandchild. Half way across the water a thick sea fog crept in. MacDonald's birlinn ran into another vessel and quickly sank. The commander of the other vessel was MacDonald's daughter, mother of his grandchild, and seeing that her father was drowned, she continued her voyage to Skye to take possession of Dunvegan Castle for her husband – or so the story goes.

Even if these tales are apocryphal, they contain no surprise that a Hebridean woman could sail or even command a boat. The Hebrides bred tough women.

Shetland is another of these places where the sea has always been as important as the land. It was once said that an Orkney man was a crofter with a boat but a Shetlander was a seaman with a croft. Until the advent of aircraft, Shetlanders used boats as other people used coaches; they were essential for transport. Although it was the men of Shetland who sailed the deep seas or who manned the famous sixereens at the fishing, Shetland women could sometimes be seen in inshore waters. In the 18th century many of the coastal farms would place their animals on small islets for pasturage, and the daughters of the house were as likely to care for the stock as were the sons. It was around 1708 that two young girls from the island of Uyea off Unst rowed out to the islet of Haaf Gruney to milk the family's cattle. The name Haaf Gruney means the 'green island', and this little islet is indeed a fertile place for pasturing cattle. The girls would have a small yoal, double prowed, clinker built and so light that she moved as gracefully as the waves themselves. It was a routine journey that they had made a hundred times before, but as they returned a storm blew up.

The girls rowed for home, but their combined strength counted for little before the power of the Atlantic gale that blew them eastward across the sea. After days in the yoal, they were driven ashore on a rocky coast, and strange people crowded around them. At first there was consternation, for the girls and the strangers could not understand one another. Then one of the girls made the sign of the Cross and the strangers relaxed. One young man in particular smiled to the prettiest of the girls and from being wary strangers the people became fellow islanders.

The girls had drifted across to the Norwegian island of Karmoy. They remained in Norway, married local men and were accepted as part of the community. Such incidents were probably more common than is generally realised at a time when island communities were cut off and there were no radios or newspapers to bring peoples closer together. However, by 1886 communication was far more advanced, so that stories from one end of Scotland became widely known in the other. Such was the case in the voyage of Betty Mouat.

Betty had been born in 1826 and had been lame all her life. Like many Shetland women, she supplemented the produce of her croft at Scatness in Dunrossness by knitting and selling shawls. In early 1886 she experienced a stroke and decided it would be best if she visited the doctor at Lerwick. It was 14 years since she had last travelled so far, and she struggled down to Grutness to catch the weekly boat to the island's capital.

At that period the boat was *Columbine,* a 50 feet cutter rigged vessel with a crew of three, and Betty boarded with a bundle of forty shawls to sell, for her neighbours had asked her to take theirs as well. She also carried a bottle of milk and a couple of biscuits to sustain her on the journey. *Columbine* was not well equipped for passengers, but Betty limped down the companionway to the small cabin while the crew worked on deck. After *Columbine* cleared the bay and was off Voe a sudden squall blew up. Alone in the cabin, Betty held a loud tearing, then the strained voice of the skipper, 'the main sheet's broken!' She would listen, possibly nervously, as there were more voices sounding, and a sudden order to get the boat away. By the time Betty realised what had happened, she was alone in *Columbine.*

After the main sheet broke, the skipper had been washed overboard. The remaining members of the crew launched the small boat to save him, but, underestimating the strength of the waves, they found that the sea forced their boat back to the land, while *Columbine* drifted, stern first out to sea. Left alone in the cabin, the semi-lame Betty struggled to keep herself from being thrown to the deck as the sea tossed *Columbine* around. The cabin hatch was open, so cold water poured in as the wind screamed frantically through the rigging and the sail flapped uncontrollably against the mast. It was Friday 30th January that *Columbine* left Grutness, and not until Wednesday that Betty saw the snow-whitened hills of an unknown land. Agonisingly, the sea drove her away again, steering *Columbine* up a rocky coast of skerries and islands. On the Sunday, after threading through a series of fanged reefs that would have torn the hull from any vessel, *Columbine* was tossed onto the only beach on the island of Lepsoe. Like the sisters from Uyea, Betty Mouat had been driven from Shetland four hundred stormy miles across the sea to Norway.

Betty Mouat's voyage made her into something of a celebrity. She travelled by ship to Hull and from there by train to Edinburgh. It was her first trip on a train, and the crowds that waited for her were nearly as alarming as the storms at sea. Some asked her about her experiences, others merely stared while the bold demanded a hair from her head. However, Betty eventually returned to her croft, which she never again left. She lived for another thirty years, a notable survivor of the North Sea.

Earlier in the same century, a remarkable woman from Saltcoats had lived most of her life at sea. Betsy Miller was born in 1792, just as Britain was about to enter yet another long war with France and at a time when shipping thronged the seas of the world. It is difficult to imagine now just how many ships there were, and how important maritime trade was, but in an age when everything travelled by sea, when roads were deplorable, ships were small and labour intensive, sea trading was more than important to Britain: it was irreplaceable. Saltcoats shared in this shipping bonanza, with vessels leaving the port for both domestic and transatlantic destinations. At times it could be a rough place, with so many strange seamen reeling from the taverns, and in 1793 a group of men formed the 'Protection Society of Saltcoats.' For a fee of one shilling, these men guarded women and the unwary through the dark closes. Sometimes seamen stalked the shore, their swinging lanterns casting alternate light and shadow as they shouted out the state of the tide to those mariners whom were waiting to sail into the Firth of Clyde. Saltcoats also had three shipbuilding yards, all of which were busy producing more tall sailing ships. One such was *Clytus*, a brig that was built, phoenix like, from the remaining timbers of a wrecked Dutch warship. *Clytus* was just one of the vessels owned by William Miller who was a combination of shipowner and timber merchant.

William Miller fathered four children; a son named Hugh and three daughters, of whom Betsy was the oldest. As was usual in those days, the financial future of the family was expected to rest in the hands of the son and heir. What was not so usual, Betsy joined Hugh in the seafaring life. Disregarding the superstition that a female on a ship brings bad luck, William Miller employed the fifteen-year-old Betsy as ship's clerk. Within the year, and under the watchful eye of an experienced Sailing Master named Simons, Betsy was acting as navigator between Saltcoats and Dublin. This was not a romantic life for a young woman, for *Clytus* was a coaster, a maid of all work that operated mainly between the Clyde and the Irish ports of Dublin, Cork and Belfast. Betsy navigated the stormy North Channel and the Irish Sea, always aware of the possibility of meeting a privateer, for the French war continued. Betsy seems to have taken this in her long skirted stride, as she did the conditions on board.

It was a common belief that the most efficient British seamen were those brought up in Scottish coasters or the Geordie collier brigs, but the life was hard. During the frequent squalls, the seamen would take turns in the main chains, tied to the weather main rigging with a canvas waistband. Here they would take soundings, tossing the lead line and slowly chanting their findings. Tacking in foul weather was worse with the crew continually at the sheets and braces, hauling with hands cracked and raw under the salt water. As a clerk, Betsy would have avoided the worst of this type of work, but the evidence suggests that she became an expert mariner and no crew would have much respect for a captain who had never performed elementary seamanship.

So Betsy Miller, skirts clinging to her legs and hair plastered to her face, might well have hauled and cursed and bled with the best of them. Sometimes carrying timber, often loaded with two hundred tons of coal, *Clytus* would not be a clean ship. One description compares life on board a collier as 'sleeping in a travelling mine, sometimes in a bunk, sometimes in a hammock, but always aware of being in a world of coal.' Working in a collier was not for the delicate, for while the crew shovelled and sweated and worked, the master had to take risks to bring his cargo to its destination. Betty would live her life with coal dust everywhere, covering everything, gritty between the teeth, stinging the eyes, itchy on the scalp.

Perhaps surprisingly, Betty thrived. Carrying coal to Ireland and limestone back to Scotland, she rose from apprentice to command and made *Clytus* her own. Seafaring was a tough, masculine world and no doubt there were many sardonic comments among the fourteen-man crew when Betsy first took station on the poop, but the sea was in her blood and her natural resilience soon earned their respect. Ultimately the perverse streak that frequently surfaces in the Scottish character would make the crew proud to serve under Britain's only female sea captain. In time Betsy Miller was termed '... a hardy yin: a reg'lar brick' and even '... a sonsy woman, weel favor't, neither wee nor tall, an' wi' as much sense o' humour as made life aboard gang pleasantly.'

Quiet understatements these, at a time when life at sea could be a continuous nightmare ruled by the rope's end and the boot, when it was not unknown for a ship's boy to be sent naked to the masthead and apprentices to disappear without trace. To inspire loyalty in hard-bitten seamen, Betsy Miller must have been quite a character. She had to be. Things were not going well for her father. When Hugh died at sea off Ardrossan, it marked a violent downswing in Miller's luck that led to his destitution. His death in 1847 meant that Betsy was the family breadwinner, with a £700 mortgage on the ship to pay and two dependant sisters. Knowing only the sea, Betsy continued to trade and it is possible that she blossomed under the challenge. *Clytus* was only a coasting brig, a small, two -masted vessel with a square mainsail and probably a fore and aft mizzen, but she was conspicuous in having a deckhouse on her poop. As the only female on board, Betsy needed some basic privacy so, rather than share with the crew in the crowded forecastle; she created her own queendom in the deckhouse. Here she could be both captain and lady, keeping apart from the rough –living mariners before the mast while being close enough to supervise and command.

Captain of a coal boat or not, Betsy retained her femininity, and her frilly white caps became a byword in the trade. She was known to peer out of her deckhouse to watch her crew, white mutch bobbing as she asked 'Hoo's she daein noo, lads?' A realist as well as a fine seafarer, Betsy always carried a shroud in case *Clytus* should be wrecked and her body recovered. Not for her the pauper's grave paid for by a gold earring. Perhaps it is true that during particularly severe weather when *Clytus* was in danger, Betsy donned the shroud to be prepared. On one occasion however, *Clytus* was storm bound in Irvine Bay and the short, high waves for which the Clyde is notorious were pounding her but Betsy did not resort to the shroud. Rather she dressed up for the event.

'Lads' she said, 'I'll gang below and put on a clean sark for I would like to be flung up on the sands kind of decent – Irvine folk are nasty, noticin' buddies.'

Clytus survived that storm and the crew put down their escape to their captain's change of clothing. Possibly her seamanship also helped. With debts to repay and sisters to be fed, Betsy Miller could not afford to stop working merely because of bad weather. As the *Times* of 13th March 1852 reported 'she weathered the storms of the deep when many commanders of the other sex have been driven to pieces on the rocks.' Betsy commanded *Clytus* for a full twenty-two years, so that the Earl of Eglinton mentioned her while debating the Merchant Shipping Act in 1834. There will probably never be a challenge to her position as the only registered captain and owner of a British merchant sailing ship. Once, however, her 'romantic and adventurous spirit' – or sheer necessity – forced Betsy to continue in weather that even Clytus could not master, and the brig was forced onto the sands at Saltcoats.

Both vessel and crew were saved, but the captain was concerned about her cat and canary. 'Thank God there's nae lives lost' Betsy said when told they were fine. Her crew, of course, knew this very human side to her character and could often persuade her to break out the grog to hearten them during a rough patch. So Betsy Miller knew men and how to get the best out of them. She seems to have used a mixture of rough kindness, bribery and genuine, seafaring skill.

This skill was evident, as she used no pilot to guide her into the tricky little ports on the Clyde and Irish coasts, and the reputation was carried from Belfast to Boston and possibly beyond. In 1915 the 'Ardrossan and Saltcoats Herald' spoke of her trading across the Atlantic and south to the Caribbean and even to the East Indies. 'She was known all over the world' the report noted 'and bore an honourable reputation as a capable and upright trader and shipowner.' In the best tradition of Scotswomen, Betsy was careful with money, keeping a ledger with details of all her financial transactions. Capable of hiring and firing her crew as well as coping with the day-to-day business of cargo management, she was an all round sea merchant and equal to any of the bitter tongued male captains of her time.

Betsy's thrift and hard work first reduced, and then cleared her father's debts and she probably enjoyed life a little. The money she earned kept her sisters well above the poverty line until Betsy bought the solid 'Clytus House' in Quay Street, Saltcoats. Eventually, however, hard living at sea took its toll and in 1862, aged 69; Betsy Miller made her final voyage before settling in Clytus House, no doubt walking purposefully down to the harbour to watch critically and enquire after *Clytus*. 'Hoo's she daein noo, lads?'

Chapter 13

The Fisherwomen

Them that guide the purse rule the house
Walter Scott

Fishing was a way of life around all the coasts of Scotland in the nineteenth century. In all seasons, in most weathers, the fishing boats would creep from the small harbours; the open beaches and often even from cracks in the rocks. They would be under sail if the wind was in the right quarter, under oars if it was calm. The smaller boats would work inshore, depositing creels for crabs or lobsters or working the long lines for haddock. The larger boats could work thirty, fifty, two hundred miles from shore, or sail as far as Shetland or Great Yarmouth as they hunted the shoals of herring.

It was a tough life, with injury or death a constant possibility and it was an anxious life for the women that they left behind. Not that the women had much time to worry, for they worked every bit as hard as their men did. When their men were line fishing, women often gathered the bait from the beach, getting up in the black small hours to pad along the sand or shingle. Either that or they would buy the mussels from a merchant, haggling heartily to obtain the best price.

While gathering the bait was tough, it was only part of the process. Next the mussels had to be 'sheeled' which was often a community task. Two or three women would gather together with basins and 'sheeling knives', which were often just cut-down kitchen knives. They would prise open the shells and collect the contents in a jar, then, when they had enough, would bait the hooks on the long lines. That was a heartbreaking, tedious job, for a line held 1500 hooks or more, and the smaller the mussel, the more the fisherwoman needed to thrust onto the hook. It was no wonder that women preferred to buy the larger Dutch mussels rather than the small variety from Montrose Basin, the Tay or the Eden. By the 20th century some fishermen switched from long-lining to seine-net fishing, mainly because they wanted to save their wives the tedious labour of baiting. Unmarried men had to employ a woman to do the work, while others willingly paid their wives for their efforts.

When the men returned from sea, exhausted, sodden and emotionally drained from the constant possibility of death by drowning, the women still had work to do. While the men were at sea the women would have baited one line, now they would help to clean, or redd another. This redding was another tiresome, tricky job, with nimble fingers removing any rotted, uneaten bait or any pieces of seaweed or other debris from the wickedly sharp hooks. On other days the women marketed the fish. They carried their great baskets of fish to the city or market towns or around the isolated cottages of the country. These baskets were called creels in some parts of the country, ripps in other, but were always capable of holding 150 pounds of fish. Quick of wit as of tongue, the fisherwomen would bargain with her customer and often had the last word. Well aware of their value, fisherwomen were never awed by social standing.

When the Newhaven fisherwomen attended the London Fisheries Exhibition of 1883, Margaret Flucker met Princess Beatrice and the Prince of Wales. 'Hoo's yer mother, my lamb?' asked Mrs Flucker of the princess.

The Fisherwomen

The Prince of Wales smiled, 'you will not know who I am?' he said, quietly.

Mrs Flucker told him exactly who he was, 'wha doesnae ken you! You're the Queen's auldest son!'

When they were still in their early teens, many of the fisher girls began to follow the herring. They travelled to the herring ports around the coasts of Britain. Aberdeen, Stornoway, Arbroath, Great Yarmouth, Scarborough; all knew the chatter and constant work of the Scottish fishwife. The women usually travelled by train, although special chartered vessels carried them to the great gutting centres of Shetland. While the men worked at sea to catch the fish, the women worked on land, curing the fish. They worked in teams of three, two gutting the herring, the third packing the fish in careful layers before adding enough salt to ensure that the fish remained edible. Scottish fisherwomen were the best gutters and packers in the world and worked at an incredible speed, from the first landing of fish until there was nothing left to pack. Sometimes they would work from six in the morning until midnight, wielding their terrible knives by the light of oil lanterns. In some of the larger ports the women might be under cover but in most they were out on the quay or by the harbour, braving the bitter North Sea winds or the blast from the Atlantic.

Wearing an oilskin apron or an oiled, pleated skirt with a bib that stretched from breasts to thighs, knee length boots and a headsquare, the herring gutter was ready for work. When the first boat came in, the catch was weighed and emptied in a silver cascade of fish into the farlans, the rectangular wooden boxes around which the women worked. With the fish were sprinkled with salt for ease of handling, and with thumb and two fingers tightly bandaged against cuts that would sting with the salt or fester terribly, the gutter raced to fill the barrels. A skilled gutter could dispose of a herring in just over a second. The packers would be as busy, with the girls often having to lean well into barrels nearly as tall as themselves to layer the herring onto the coarse grained salt.

Despite their sheer exhaustion, the women often sang. Mary Bella Finlay, a fisherwoman from Whitehills said 'I sometimes think we sang to stop ourselves crying,' but others enjoyed the camaraderie and the freedom. In a good season a skilled woman could earn as much as a man, and many of the youngsters enjoyed this first taste of freedom from parental supervision. It was also an opportunity to hunt for a handsome young fisherman who needed a wife to share his burden of life.

Once married, the woman would take care of the family finances. The woman controlled the money; few fishermen would dispute their right, or their capability, just as no fisherwomen would think of boarding a boat. In the few breaks in their labour, the women might relieve their high spirits by throwing herring heads or fish guts at rival teams, or by exchanging mock-friendly insults.

> 'The lasses o' the Ferry
> They busk braw.
> The lasses o' the Elie,
> They ding a';
> The lasses o' St Monans
> They curse and ban;
> The lasses o' Pittenweem
> They do the same
> The lasses o' Anster
> They drink strong ale
> There's green grass in Cellardyke
> And crabs in tae Crail.'

While the women of Fife chanted, those from the Western Isles squabbled happily in Gaelic and the Blue Mogganers from prosperous Peterhead abused the girls from Boddam:

> 'The *Annie* it sailed round the coast
> And a' the hands on it were lost

Except the monkey that climbed the mast
And the Boddamers hanged the monkey o!'

The rhyme, like the legend it was based on, is slanderous. In 1674 the Court of Session proclaimed that if a vessel was driven ashore by foul weather and there was no life left aboard, that vessel was deemed a wreck. However, if life remained, the vessel was not deemed a wreck and the locals could not claim the flotsam and jetsam. Legend claims that in 1772, a vessel named *Annie* was wrecked at Boddam, hard by Buchan Ness in the great granite fist of northeast Scotland. The same legend said that wreckers had lured the ship ashore with a signal fire, hoping to loot the wreckage. All on board were dead except for one monkey, presumably a pet or mascot, and the Boddamers hanged this unfortunate creature so it could not claim the cargo. Once the monkey was dead, the Boddamers gave it a Christian burial, presumably to make amends. To settle any debate, there is no documentary evidence for this tale.

Life for the fisherwomen was not all hard work and capers; there was also a fair share of grief and tragedy, with the occasional flashes of heroism. The fishing communities were often noted for sincere religious beliefs. During the Jacobite persecutions in the 18th century, Episcopalian priests were imprisoned in Stonehaven tolbooth. Many of fishwives from Skateraw hid their babies inside their creel before walking along the rugged coast to present it at the barred cell for the pastor to perform the baptismal ceremony.

In the 19th century, and probably before that, women often used to carry their men out to the fishing boats. It would be a cold task, with the woman having their long skirts kilted to the waist as they waded through the surf to the boats. There was nothing deferential in this carrying, for in the days before waterproof clothing, a man with cold wet feet would be unable to concentrate on his work and would quite possibly be a liability.

It was not until after the great storm of November 1848, when 100 Scottish fishermen lost their lives, that people seriously considered their safety. Until that date most Scottish fishing harbours were small, with narrow entrances that were hazardous even in good weather and evilly dangerous in bad. Many fishing villages had no harbour at all, and boats were launched from the open beach. Women helped in both the launching and beaching of boats, often with waves breaking over their heads as the women grappled with the heavy boats.

Returning to their home creek was often the most dangerous part of any fishing voyage, and there are countless incidents where fisherwomen watched helplessly as their men drowned just offshore. Sometimes the women were not content to merely watch. In the 19th century Cellardyke in Fife was home to some of the most daring of Scottish fishermen. They were known as 'Dykers' and fishermen from other harbours spoke with awe of their ability to smell out the fish. One such man was William Watson, but one stormy autumn morning his boat capsized while just outside the harbour.

The watching crowd witnessed terrible scenes as their husbands, sons and fathers struggled in the savage seas. Most fishermen wore heavy clothing against the cold, and thigh length leather boots with iron segs that gave them a grip on boats that were slippery with fish. Unfortunately these same boots weighed them down so it was nearly impossible to swim. William Watson, however, was not inclined to tamely drown and he struggled toward the shore.

In an age where modesty equated with respectability, Mrs Watson threw off her heavy woollen skirt and waded deep into the sea. She kept one eye on her man, the other on the bursting waves, and threw herself forward. Most of the crowd thought that she was gone, but Mrs Watson was a strong woman. She pushed herself forward and reached for her man, whose strength was now beginning to fail. Grabbing him in arms strengthened by years of carrying creels, she dragged him ashore. From that day onward Mrs Watson's man was known as 'Water Willie.'

Death and tragedy were commonplace for the Scottish fisherwomen. Most of the boats were family owned and crewed, so when a boat went down, it was possible for a woman to lose her husband

and sons at the same time. The acceptance of such suffering can be seen etched on the faces of those fisherwomen who stare levelly from Victorian photographs. There is sometimes humour in the eyes, but more often tragedy and hardship have ground away all emotion, leaving only the bare granite of women who accepted hardship as a way of life.

One such woman was Agnes Birrell. She was from a seafaring family, with her father from Kinghorn and her mother from Anstruther. Marrying James Davidson, a fisherman and the son of a fisherman, Agnes settled down, baiting and redding lines, repairing nets, attending to the family finances. In the 1820s, the boats from Cellardyke made a trip to the Eden every autumn to gather mussels for the long lines, and that September James Davidson was on his father's boat. The voyage along the coast went well, and soon the boats were filled with the mussels and lay in the river ready for the return. A westerly wind was rising, so the more experienced men advised that the boats remain where they were. James and the other young men disagreed. A hatful of wind was not enough to keep them from their wives and sweethearts.

Shaking their heads at their own folly, the men hauled up the great dun sails and put out to sea. The Cellardyke fleet crossed St Andrews's Bay, tacked around the Carr and headed across the Hurst, but conditions worsened. As a sudden cross-sea struck the Davidson's boat, a massive wave exploded on top of her, filling her so she lay exposed to the next swell that crashed over the low gunwale. Like so many of the open Scottish boats, the Davidson's boat capsized and, with his father holding him in his arms, James Davidson sank to his death.

Sitting alone in Cellardyke, listening to the waves thundering against the sleek black rocks, the widow Davidson nursed her newborn son and felt the grief burn inside her. However she was still young and time eased the pain. She met another fisherman; a handsome local man named Thomas Reid. They married and Agnes mothered more children, carrying them with her when she sold her fish or painted and tarred her husband's boat. Perhaps it was Agnes who pointed out that his boat was older than most in Cellardyke, but she would certainly be present when he bought a new boat and launched it into the small harbour.

That would have been a proud day when *Nancy* set out, newly painted and ready to provide for the family. Agnes was no longer a young woman; she had been married to Thomas for many years, although every time she looked at her eldest son she would be reminded of James Davidson. It was on St George's Day, 23 April 1846 that a terrible gale battered the Firth of Forth. Agnes would listen to the wind howling around the gables of her house and the breakers crashing against the harbour wall and think of her man out there on the sea.

Perhaps the minister brought the news, or perhaps another fisherman. There would be the dreaded knock on the door and when Agnes answered the messenger would be standing there, wet, cold, with his eyes looking everywhere except at her. 'It's the husband,' he would say, and Agnes would know the black despair and terrible loneliness of grief. *Nancy* had sunk about fifteen miles from the Isle of May.

Seven men had drowned, leaving six widows including Agnes, and fifteen orphans. Agnes was not alone in her suffering, but that was little consolation. The sea had not yet finished with Agnes. It claimed her brother Thomas next, then three of her brothers-in-law. On the 8th December 1859 her brother William and eldest son both drowned. Six years later another son, Thomas, and two of her sons-in-law died when their boat sunk deep in the North Sea.

In a life tainted by tragedy, Agnes Birrell or Reid lost two husbands, two of her sons, two sons in law, two brothers and three brothers-in-law and an unknown number of nephews and friends to what she termed the 'weary sea'. Overall she lost over twenty of her close relatives, but she never gave up and never left the sea. In a hard working village, she was renowned for her labour, gathering limpets, mending nets, keeping her family and her independence so that she was 'never to be obleeged' to anybody. After a lifetime spent in the shadow of the sea, Agnes died on the 25 February 1873, aged 69. Like so many people of that age, she accepted her life as God's will, and on her death bed she was content to be joining her family who were 'not lost but gone before.'

Women such as Agnes Birrell or Reid epitomised the dogged endurance of the Scottish fisherwomen. Although life at sea is not as hazardous as it was, fishwives still watch their men sail without the certain knowledge that they will return. And many also continue to hold the purse strings.

Chapter 14

High Adventure

> I travel not to go anywhere, but to go
> R. L. Stevenson

For many, the image of women in the past may have been of meekness and humility, generations of females who were content to live in the shadow of their men, accepting their lot with gratitude as they seldom strayed more than a few miles from their domestic comfort. As well as being a gross insult to those women, this view is also an affront to their men. What self-respecting man would want such a milk-and-water creature as a partner for life? Luckily, this view of women is false. While many women, like many men, had no choice but to work within close proximity to their homes, others indulged in much travelling and high adventure.

On some occasions, the adventure took turns that were unforeseen. Helen Gloag could never have foreseen that her proposed emigration to America, an adventure enough in itself, would have seen her settling in quite a different country. She was born near Muthill in Perthshire in January 1750. At that time the Episcopal religion, with all its Jacobite associations, was banned in Scotland, so the Episcopal Gloag family had Helen secretly baptised in St James Church, Muthill on 14 February 1750.

Andrew Gloag was a blacksmith and moved his family to the Mill of Steps. He must have been proud of his green-eyed daughter with her red hair, pale face and high cheekbones, but after Helen's mother died he married again and his new wife had less time for her stepdaughter. While still in her teens, Helen became attached to John Byrne, a local farmer who was eleven years her senior, but the new Mrs Gloag attempted to end the friendship. Perhaps it was the deteriorating relationship with her stepmother that convinced Helen to immigrate to South Carolina. In May 1769, along with a party of her female friends, she boarded a ship at Greenock and headed west across the Atlantic. She was just nineteen years old.

At that time pirates from the Barbary Coast of North Africa still infested the Atlantic, and a pack of xebecs attacked Helen's ship. A xebec was a three masted vessel with 20 cannon and 200 men. The pirates captured the unarmed merchant ship and Helen was now a prisoner of the Sultan of Morocco.

The pirates separated the genders, with the seamen and male passengers chained to the benches and used as galley slaves, while the women were thrust down below, to listen to the creaking of the ship and worry about their future. The arrival of the xebec to Salle was not encouraging, as the walls of the town were decorated with grinning skulls and decomposing human heads. Helen would hear terrible tales of torture, of the previous sultan's harem of 2000 women, of his thousand children and of his habit of strangling his own female children at birth.

The stories may have been exaggerated, but there was no disguising the hatred of the people of the port, who spat and jeered as the captives were led in chains from the ship to the slave market. Those women who were deemed unsellable were handed over to amuse the guards, while the best looking, including Helen, were displayed on the slave block. There can be few experiences worse than being sold as a slave, and Helen must have suffered agonies as she was pawed and examined by the buyers, until a merchant eventually bought her.

Helen the slave was handed as a gift to the Grand Vizier, Ibn Abdullah; the Sultan of Morocco. Since Ibn Abdullah ascended the throne in 1757 he had proved less of a despot than his predecessors. However, he was shrewd enough to realise that much of his income came from piracy, while slavery was seen as part of life. He also had enough sense to see the quality of his new Scottish slave and, in time he promoted her from concubine to wife number four. As such, Helen also bore the title of Empress, and it seems that she used her new position to perform good deeds.

In 1769 a party of Barbary pirates captured Mrs Crisp, an English traveller in Minorca. Passed into the Sultan's harem, Mrs Crisp expected the inevitable to happen, but instead she was freed, unmolested and unharmed. In the subsequent book that she wrote, Mrs Crisp wondered if it had been the Sultan's 'Irish' wife who had caused her freedom. Helen may also have been influential in bringing an English doctor, William Lempriere, into Morocco in 1789. When Doctor Lempriere examined the women of the harem, he met only three of the Royal wives, but mentioned that the fourth, which he believed to be English, was in Fez. By that date, Helen would have been in her late thirties, and it was customary for the Sultan to send any wife over thirty into exile, together with her children.

It seems that Helen had great influence over the Sultan. Perhaps due to her prompting, he banned the shipping of Negro slaves from Morocco and released any Briton that was captured. Eventually the practice of slavery faded from the country. More importantly for British seamen, the Sallee pirates no longer cruised for prey, so that seamen had one less anxiety. It may also have been due to Helen that the Sultan entered into trade agreements with Britain. These agreements were extremely important, for in the early 1780s, Britain was fighting a difficult war against much of Europe and the rebellious American colonies. When the Spaniards laid siege to Gibraltar in 1782, the Sultan of Morocco helped the British defence. Sultan Mohammed, with his eyes wide open to the changing world, also invested in trading towns, with his new port of Mogador on the Atlantic coast. In an amazing piece of benevolence, the Sultan also graciously permitted Christian monasteries to exist in his strongly Islamic country.

Throughout all the changes in Morocco, Helen continued to be a wife and mother. She had two sons by the Sultan and corresponded frequently with her family in Scotland. However, everything altered in 1790, when the Sultan died. With Helen's sons too young to occupy the throne a civil war erupted. Helen sent her two sons to one of the new Christian monasteries in Teuton. While a British flotilla readied itself to intervene, a British officer crossed to Morocco to find out the truth. Unfortunately, both of Helen's sons were murdered before the British arrived.

Around 1792 Helen disappears from history. Perhaps she also died in the turmoil of civil war, or perhaps she was treated as an Empress and spent a long life in honourable retirement. Either way, her remarkable life deserves to be remembered, for not many Scotswomen became Empress of Morocco.

Other women also had adventure thrust upon them and coped as well as they could. One such was Eliza Fraser, the wife of Captain Fraser of *Stirling Castle*. Originally from Stromness in Orkney, Elizabeth Fraser had grown up with the sea, so it was natural for her to marry a seafaring man. In 1836, *Stirling Castle* sailed from the Thames with a cargo of ale, but was damaged when a brig ran foul of her. Collisions at sea were fairly common at a time when lighting regulations were not strictly enforced, but the more superstitious of the seamen spoke of bad omens at the start of a voyage. More important for the master, the collision necessitated repairs that delayed their departure. However, they left the Thames at last, and with a crew of 18 mainly young seamen, arrived safely at Sydney.

In these days Sydney docks had an unenviable reputation as one of the roughest areas of the world, so Eliza must have been glad to see her crew safely on board as *Stirling Castle* slipped out on her northward voyage. She would be doubly glad for she was heavily pregnant and probably hoped to reach somewhere more civilised to give birth to her child. Unfortunately, a week later, the ship ran aground on a section of the Barrier Reef a few miles to the north and east of Rockhampton. Geographers have since named that particular place Eliza's Reef, for the experiences that the woman from Orkney was about to survive would resound throughout the world.

The Great Barrier Reef is one of the natural wonders of the world, a 2000 mile long coral barricade that stretches along much of the Eastern coast of Australia. When it became apparent that there was no chance of saving her, Captain Fraser gave the order to abandon *Stirling Castle*. There were eleven people on board the longboat and seven on the smaller pinnace when they slipped into the warm, violent sea. Mrs Fraser was with her husband in the longboat, but either it had been damaged in the grounding, or it was overloaded, for it soon filled with water.

Captain Fraser gave orders for the pinnace to take the longboat in tow and they steered toward the nearest settlement, the penal colony of Moreton Bay. As they navigated through the maze of tiny islets and coral reefs, Captain Fraser ordered that the crew collect shellfish and whatever water they could find. All the time, the longboat was sinking deeper into the sea. Mrs Fraser reached her nadir when the pains of childbirth came onto her, and with no privacy or medical care, she gave birth while sitting waist deep in warm seawater in a sinking boat, under the unforgiving Pacific sun. It may have been merciful that the child died after only a few minutes, but that would be no consolation to the mother.

After a succession of tiny coral islets, the sight of the large, green island must have been like heaven. Now known as Fraser Island, it is 75 miles long, the largest sand island in the world, and when the survivors of *Stirling Castle* hauled up their boats, proved to be plentifully supplied with fresh water. Believing that they had reached mainland Australia, Captain Fraser ordered that they walk to Moreton Bay, and they headed inland. Weak, sunburned, exhausted and with the Frasers suffering from the trauma of losing a child, they would be extremely vulnerable when the local aborigine tribesmen appeared. The Kabi Kabi tribe seemed friendly at first, but as they realised the weakness of the shipwrecked group, their behaviour altered. After bartering kangaroo meat for whatever possessions the newcomers had left, the Kabi Kabi attacked.

There was no contest. The spear carrying tribesmen stripped the survivors, leaving Eliza with a single garment. After weeks with ten men in an open boat, and the birth of a child, it is unlikely that Eliza was concerned about her modesty, but clothing was essential as protection against the sun. The Kabi Kabi divided the seafarers between them, using the seamen as slaves and torturing or killing them when they could no longer work. The next six weeks must have intensified the nightmare for Mrs Fraser. She witnessed the murder of her husband, saw the mate burned alive and became a chattel of a vicious Stone Age tribe. Alive with fleas and lice from the Kabi Kabi, Eliza, with her skin coloured like one of the tribe, had to clamber up trees infested with insects and biting ants to bring down honeycombs.

Then, weeks after her capture, the aborigines held a grand celebration, with laughter and dancing, feasting and drink. As Eliza watched, there was a hiss from the undergrowth and a white man slithered across to her. His name was Graham, and he was a convict. Eliza followed him, to learn that the ship's cook had escaped and made his way to Moreton Bay from where a search party had been organised.

It is heartening to learn that Graham received his freedom as a reward for rescuing Eliza, but the remainder of her story is not so pleasant. The story of the shipwreck and the ordeal of the survivors soon spread, and Eliza was treated as a heroine wherever she travelled. It was common in the Victorian age for the public to collect money for the relief of survivors of shipwreck and the widows of those less fortunate. Eliza accepted all that came her way and, even after she married the master of the ship that carried her home, continued to apply for relief grants. This behaviour lost her the respect of the public, and it seems that her marriage did not last, for she became a sideshow at a travelling circus, with a charge of 6d to see the white aborigine.

Australia seemed to be a popular destination for adventurous Scotswomen, and most made a better final impression than Eliza Fraser. One of the most unusual was Big Aggie. Born in Govan and brought up in Ayrshire, as a teenager Agnes immigrated to Australia. She soon met a man named Hugh Buntine, originally from Kilwinning. He was eighteen years her senior but after a brief courtship they married.

The discovery of gold in 1851 changed Australia from a quiet backwater to a dynamic destination. Footloose wanderers from half the world descended upon the near empty colony of Victoria, scraping for the yellow metal and quarrelling with the authorities and each other. Men left their jobs in offices and factories to join the mad search for gold; they abandoned secure careers to lift a shovel and dream of riches. Ships swung uselessly at anchor in Hobson's Bay as their crews deserted in mass to swap the muscle tearing labour of a seaman for the prospect of a life of wealth. Victoria became a wild place of gun toting diggers, with loose morals, dirt and the occasional wild celebration as strikes were made.

Agnes and Hugh realised that there was money to be made in the diggings, but without staking a claim or panning the now crowded rivers. Instead they launched a haulage company that supplied the diggers with the necessities of life. With horses at a premium, the Buntines bought in some bullocks, which were better suited to haul heavy wagons over the rough tracks of the Bush. While Hugh opened a store a Forrest Creek, Agnes climbed into the driver's seat and became one of Australia's few female bullockies.

On her first trip, Agnes, or Big Aggie as she was known, carried a ton of cheese and half a ton of butter from Melbourne to the goldfields of Bendigo, ignoring the dangers of bushrangers and the irritations of flies. The bush was no place for glamour, so Agnes wore her long skirt over man's breeches that were tucked into heavy boots as a protection against dust and snakes. With a huge cabbage tree hat and a long overcoat, she looked vastly overdressed in the heat, but nobody cared to argue with Agnes. Perhaps it was her size that made even the hardiest of diggers walk wide of Aggie, or perhaps it was the pair of pistols that were handily thrust through her belt. More likely it was the reputation of her quick Scottish temper and readiness to dispense instant justice.

On one occasion, at the outback town of Bald Hills, one of the many drunken diggers watched a young girl walking past. In her crinolined skirt and demure poke bonnet, the girl was causing no offence at all, but the drunk followed her with his tongue and hands busy. Unfortunately for him, Big Aggie was jolting past on her wagon. Without hesitation, she dismounted and swung her long stock whip, slashing until the drunk was on the ground, begging for mercy.

'You may be as hard as you like,' said Aggie, 'but even here in the bush a man should be civil'

Such actions earned Aggie her alternative name as the White Mother of Gippsland. However, she had to work for her reputation. The Buntines followed the diggers from one gold field to another, opening stores and transporting food and goods. Floods and fires were a constant danger, but always Agnes struggled through. Bush fires in Australia move at frightening speed as the dry vegetation and especially the eucalyptus trees explode with the heat. A flare-up in early 1863 was remembered as Black Monday for its intensity. For a while the fire seemed to have Agnes surrounded as she lumbered through smoke and sparks with her eyes narrowed and her hat thrust low over her brow. Whipping up her bullocks, she raced to find a sandy patch of ground where there was little to burn. Keeping the fire-and-smoke-maddened bullocks as calm as she could, Agnes sat out the leaping flames, thankful for the heavy clothing that repelled the worst of the sparks. Singed but stubborn, Agnes finished her journey.

Even when Hugh died, Agnes continued with her wagons, a formidable Scotswoman working through some of the worst terrain and with some of the wildest men in Australia. She was well into her fifties when she ceased being a bullocky and remarried; she had earned her quiet retirement at Flynn's Creek.

Isabella Bishop, or Bird, was a different type of adventurer. Edinburgh born, she travelled to write and created an extensive, fascinating journal, ironically entitled *Englishwoman in America*. She first left Scotland in 1854, when she was 23 years old, and visited a great chunk of the remote quarters of the world. As well as Canada and the Eastern United States, she travelled west to the Rocky Mountains, home of Mountain Men and untamed native tribes. Still not satisfied, she kept moving, to Persia and Kurdistan at a time when white women were virtually unknown. Each journey seemed to bring her to wilder parts of the world, to the Sandwich Islands, Yezo, Korea and, almost unbelievably, Tibet. In 1881 she married Dr John Bishop, who, not surprisingly, was also footloose. Eleven years later, the Royal Geographical Society recognised her, electing her as the first ever woman Fellow of the Society.

Many of the Scotswomen who travelled abroad in the 19th century hoped to find a husband. A letter from Catherine Dickson, a domestic servant in Australia told her female Scottish friends to come over, for 'they will all get married if they come out here. Crippled ones, deaf and dumb females, all get married over here.'

Some women, such as Elizabeth Macquarrie, were already married when they sailed south. Wife of the Governor of New South Wales, Elizabeth not only helped her husband but also tried to mitigate the terrible hardships of the orphans, Aborigines and female convicts. Other women were solitary travellers. The Falconer Museum in Forres has a fascinating collection of paintings. They show the appearance and costumes of tradesmen from India in the 1870s, and were painted by a Scottish woman traveller. Constance Frederika Gordon Cummings came from Altyre, but wandered around the backwaters of Asia for twelve years, painting the ordinary people. At a time when the Indian Mutiny was a recent memory and the North West Frontier seethed with unrest, Constance must have been a woman of some character.

Other women moved abroad for personal reasons. Anne Drysdale from Fife never married, worked her own farm and ordered her own life. When it became obvious that Scotland's damp climate damaged her health, she upped sticks and sailed to Australia. Landing at Melbourne, she moved to Geelong, where she squatted on 10,000 acres of prime farmland. Obviously a pragmatic woman, Drysdale would not be known except for her diary, which tells of sheep farming and dingoes, the Australian weather and the price of wool.

The 1880 census of Idaho contains the names of many Scotswomen, all of whom are recorded as 'keeping house' or 'helping mother.' These two phrases disguise a world of work and hardship. Nellie Allen, a young woman from Keith, spent her pioneering life scrubbing floors while tending the livestock and children of the Regan family. For all its hardships, Nellie preferred life in America to domestic service in Scotland where servility was expected. Instead Mrs Regan recognised her worth, and one day approached her with a strange request. 'If I should die out here,' she said, 'would you marry my husband?' There can be no greater tribute from a wife.

Another Scottish adventurer, but from a different social level, was Ishbel Marjoribanks, the wife of the diplomat Lord Aberdeen. While in Scotland Lady Aberdeen had founded the Haddo House Association to educate her Scottish tenants. In time this association became the Onwards and Upward Association that helped rural Scotswomen. She continued her charitable associations while travelling with her husband to Ireland, then to Canada, where he was governor-general, and back to Ireland. As she journeyed throughout Canada and the Western United States, Lady Aberdeen founded the Canadian Nursing Organisation and an organisation to provide books for isolated settlers in Canada. She also led the Canadian National Council of Women and was president of the International Council of Women. Nominated for the Nobel Peace Prize, she died in 1939, another of Scotland's influential women.

Many of the Scotswomen who travelled abroad remain anonymous. Few kept a diary, or wrote of their exploits, or left a memorial. However, every pioneering family who left Scotland for a new start in life would include at least one woman. Sometimes her man would die or, disheartened by bad weather or crop failure, would simply pack up and leave. Then it was up to the woman to keep her family together by sheer determination and hard work. Sometimes they failed. Often they succeeded, but their exploits are unknown. However, there are occasional gleams of knowledge that highlight the pluck of pioneer Scotswomen.

Donald Sutherland was one of the foremost explorers of New Zealand, and he settled with his wife deep in the heart of the rugged South Island. When he died the snow and ice of the New Zealand winter isolated the Sutherland's house. Stuck in the cabin with the corpse of her man, Elizabeth Sutherland revealed her pragmatic streak. Rather than try to bury her husband, she hauled back the floorboards and pushed his body onto the frozen ground beneath the house. Covering the hole with her bed, Elizabeth left him there until the spring thaw made travel possible. Only then did she call the doctor and have her man properly taken care of. Such a blend of pragmatism and verve surely marked many of those Scotswoman who lived their lives in high adventure.

Chapter 15

Scotswomen and Drink

> There are two things a Highlander likes naked, and one of them is malt whisky
> F. Marian McNeill

Mrs Elizabeth Garnett was horrified. It was 1875, and, when navigators blasting and hacking out the route for Scotland's new railways, one of the drunken, hard-swearing men had decided to sell his wife. He put her up for auction at the navigator's camp, asking for only one shilling, or a gallon of beer. Apparently there were no takers as any of the navvies that still possessed a shilling would keep it for drink.

Drinking has long been a part of Scotland's culture. From the middle ages, ships imported beer from Europe and claret from France, while ale was brewed and whisky distilled locally. Not until the Victorian age was heavy drinking viewed as a problem. Although men historically drank more, women have long been involved as brewers and distillers, ale sellers and consumers. Indeed keeping an alehouse was one of the occupations where women had complete equality with men.

Today whiskies come beautifully packaged, a throat warming liquid welcome encased in a bottle carrying a colourful label of a Highland glen, or a stag at bay beneath some famous brand name. The *Antiquary; Lochranza; The MacAllan,* or *Cream of the Barley*; the names are as evocative as the reek of peat on an autumn evening. It was Aristotle who remarked that seawater could be made drinkable once it was distilled, and perhaps some wandering Celt added the wisdom to the knowledge that she, or he, had gathered while journeying.

Settling in Scotland, the Celt experimented and drank the produce. The process required fire, water and cereal. Fire was easy to make, cereal could be grown and there was never a shortage of water in Scotland, so in time *Uisqe Beathe,* the water of Life developed. The name *Uisqe Beathe* soon became Scotticised to whisky, which is as easy on the Lowland tongue as the drink is on the palate. Whisky became so popular that in 1579 there was a shortage of barley for food. The Privy Council passed an Act saying that 'only Earls, Lords, Barons and Gentlemen for their own use, shall distil any.' This Act was a foretaste of a drive to make whisky an elitist drink. Naturally, it was also the beginning of resistance to any such foolish notion.

In the 18th century whisky was readily available for everybody. Elizabeth Grant, in her *Memoirs of a Highland Lady,* said that 'whisky drinking was and is the bane of that country.' Even 'decent gentlewoman' she said, 'began the day with a dram' and 'the very poorest cottages could offer whisky.' Whisky had entered the culture of the nation, and when the government began to tighten up regulations and imposed drinking taxes, whisky smuggling and illicit distilling became common. At one time there were more than two hundred illicit stills in Glenlivet alone, and Scotsmen and women preferred the milder smuggled distillation with its better flavour.

Whisky was also illegally distilled in the Lowlands. Mary and John Cairns lived at Carlops, in the shadow of the Pentland Hills. Together with a weaver from nearby Monkshaugh, they began to distil whisky in Harlaw Muir and sell the produce locally and to the passengers of the Edinburgh stage. An illicit still is easy to hide in the fold of a muir, but there is always a distinctive aroma, and when it became obvious that there was money in the Cairns' home, the gaugers came to call.

Legend says that a woman warned the Cairns of their uninvited guests, and they managed to move all their equipment, but the gaugers also searched the house.

Right in the open and beside the door, a barrel of whisky stood brazen and defiant with its bunghole open for all to inspect. The gaugers were in the house, sniffing away, but Mary was a woman of wit and resource. She had been pouring soor-dook – butter milk – through a filter and now placed the filler, smeared as it was with milk, into the open bunghole. Ignoring this innocuous barrel, the gaugers left, suspicious but empty-handed.

Women became expert distillers, possibly because they also operated many of the change houses and inns. Often distillers worked in remote glens, from where they could watch for any prowling exciseman, but whisky could also be distilled in towns and cities. Often the houses of poor women were used as a cover, such as the case in Glasgow in December 1821 when a woman on the Poor Roll was fined £5 for having an illicit still in her house. On another occasion in July 1822, a young smuggler was thrown into Glasgow jail until he could pay his fine. At a time when debtors could languish in prison for years, the jailer had no compulsion in allowing the smuggler's mother and sister to visit. They left some time later, but when the jailer checked on the prisoner later, he found a laughing woman. The smuggler had escaped in his sister's clothing, leaving her in his cell.

Not all women were so innocent. At the beginning of the 19th century, a woman named Kate Steen had such a reputation for witchcraft that even the hardiest exciseman hesitated to raid her Kirk Oswald home. She would sit there; spinning happily, while under her spinning wheel was a deep cellar, filled with smuggled brandy and whisky.

Even more formidable was the Stromness witch Betsy Miller. Betsy was a famous witch in Orkney who made a living selling favourable winds to whalers. When Captain Phillips of HMS *Widgeon* began a systematic hunt for the numerous Orkney smugglers, he faced strong resistance from Betsy Miller. On one occasion she threatened a naval sentry with blindness if he prevented her from entering the captain's cabin. When the sentry stood aside, Betsy slipped into the cabin. Her eyes dark in a face weathered by wind and years, she stood in her hand-woven gown and tartan shawl, staring at the captain. Not surprisingly, he ordered her to leave.

'George Phillips,' she replied, 'you come from a proud, wilful race, and most of your brood have met death by sword, bullet and violence. Beware how you deny Betsy Miller!'

Intrigued and probably unsure what to do with such a powerful woman, Captain Phillips waited to hear what she had to say. Betsy Miller recounted the history of his family over the past half-century and more, including some intimate personal details that he had not known himself. However, the captain was a brave man and when she ordered him to take his ship and return, he only laughed.

With her attack on Captain Phillips blunted, Miller acted against the crew. When the captain sent his men to watch the haunt of a known smuggler, Miller appeared on the headland, cursing the men until they mutinied, refusing to remain longer. Other men reported sick, believing that Miller had bewitched them. Even though Captain Phillips threatened to burn down her home unless she removed her curse, Miller continued the war, aiding the smugglers at every turn.

Muckle Kate Ferguson was another woman who seemed to know a lot about smugglers. In the 19th century she was reputed to be the fattest woman in Scotland. She was named Kate Stewart, when she was born at Landrick beside Loch Venachar, but marriage changed her name to Kate Ferguson. It was Kate who took over the licence of the Inn at Brig o' Turk in the Trossachs, and Kate who entertained the excise men who dropped in for a wee refreshment while on their way to hunt for whisky smugglers. It may be coincidence, but after visiting Muckle Kate's, the Excisemen were seldom successful. It has been suggested that Kate delayed them long enough for messengers to reach the smugglers.

Kate however was better known for her weight than her hospitality. Perhaps the food at Brig o' Turk was of excellent quality, but Kate put on weight until at 25 stone she dominated her Inn. After the railway reached Callander in 1858, Kate would often travel to Edinburgh or Glasgow, even though her size forced her to sit in the Guards Van rather than a conventional carriage. A popular hostess who could speak fluent English as well as her native Gaelic, Kate became something of a personality. People travelled miles just to see her, and to marvel at her eccentricities. While talking to her customers, Kate sat in a huge chair, with a large leather purse hung from her skirt. Her staff of local serving girls brought food and especially whisky to the customers, and took their money to Kate, who dropped it into her purse. She had a rule that no change was given, so customers either paid the exact amount, or lost their money. Nobody argued with Muckle Kate Ferguson and even Queen Victoria came to visit.

'We stopped at what is called Ferguson's Inn,' the Queen wrote, 'but is in fact the very poorest sort of Highland cottage. Here lives Mrs Ferguson, an immensely fat woman and a well known character, who is quite nice and well dressed.'

After meeting the Queen, Kate's fame increased further, so that her smiling face decorated postcards throughout Scotland.

The landlady of a coaching inn on the Edinburgh to Moffat road achieved a different type of fame. The inn welcomed travellers eager to relax from a lonely stretch of road, with bare Border hills on either side. There was no other habitation for miles. Knowing that she had a monopoly, the landlady would often place two or more people in a single bed. Sometimes she resorted to trickery to make just a little more money. It was not unknown for a man to be sleeping alone in one of the dark rooms when the landlady knocked timidly on the door and slid into the room. She held a single candle, allowing just enough light for the half-asleep visitor to see that she was attractive, and very scantily dressed.

'Pray, good sir' she would say, dropping a curtsey, 'but do you have room for a neighbour in your bed?'

'With all my heart!' The traveller would reply, throwing back the bedclothes to welcome this unexpected bounty.

'Thank you, sir,' said the landlady, and ushered in a carter, or other traveller, soaking wet from the road and reeking with whisky.

Scotswomen even travelled abroad to spread their famous Scottish hospitality. When the MacDonald family from Castle Douglas immigrated to New Zealand, they opened a small inn at Otaki. As well as providing hospitality for travellers, they sold drink to whoever popped in. Unlike other new countries, New Zealand did not have a colour bar, so the local Maoris were as welcome as anybody else. The Maoris seemed to appreciate the service, so when they had a local feud, Maori fought Maori around the walls of the inn while Agnes MacDonald and her husband continued to work, ignoring the occasional stray shot. Agnes became quite attached to her Maori customers. When she realised that many were dying of disease, she obtained a medicine chest for the colonial authorities and, only a few years after the Maori Wars that claimed hundreds of lives, worked amongst the tribes. Not many Scottish innkeepers had such experiences.

Sometimes an innkeeper is remembered because of her association with the famous. Isabella Shiel Richardson ran an Inn beside St Mary's Loch in Yarrow for many years until her death in 1878. Her clients included Sir Walter Scott, James Hogg and John Wilson, better remembered as Christopher North. With Isabella, or Tibbie Shiel, these literary giants let down their hair and relaxed. Born in 1783, Tibbie began her working life as a servant to Mrs Hogg, whose son later became the famous Ettrick Shepherd. In later life Tibbie mentioned her friendship with the teenaged James, saying he was 'an awfu' fine man. He should hae ta'en me, for he cam' courtin' for years, but he just ga'ed awa' an' took another.' Instead, Tibbie married an English mole catcher, until in 1823 they moved into a small cottage by St Mary's Loch. Next year her husband died and Tibbie began to take in paying guests. As the cottage was small and crowded with Tibbie's children, the guests had to 'just lie on the floor or on gate.' Always respectful of the Sabbath, Tibbie ensured that her guests attended family prayers.

Tibbie's hospitality became legendary, with fourteen varieties of soup and Green Groset St Mary, better known as Tibbie's Gooseberry wine. One of Tibbie's favourite stories concerned the Ettrick Shepherd, a genius with his pen that spent much of his working life as a shepherd. One day Hogg had been drinking heavily, so that he sat surrounded by a pile of empty bottles. When he demanded more, Tibbie told him that he had drunk enough; there was no more for him.

'Tibbie, Tibbie,' Hogg implored 'bring in the loch!'

No doubt Tibbie could have related far more and far worse about her clientele, but perhaps part of her success was because of her confidentiality. When she died, hundreds travelled from all parts of Scotland to mourn her. Like Muckle Kate, Tibbie Shiel was a legendary woman.

However, the Victorian period saw a decided swing against alcoholic drink. Influenced by the Church and a new cult of respectability, many thousands of people decided to stop drinking altogether. This temperance movement began when people began to drink spirits rather than beer or ale. There had been good reasons for the inhabitants of cities in particular to regard ale as a healthy drink, for many city wells were horribly polluted, contributing to major cholera epidemics. Following the 1868 outbreak, an analysis of Dundee's Lady well revealed it to be 'nothing but a very thoroughly purified sewage.' The whisky culture, however, was seen as a threat to family life, especially when many working men were paid inside public houses or even paid partly in whisky. When spirit duty decreased from 6/2d to just over 3d per gallon in 1832, the consumption of whisky soared. When news of the temperance idea spread from the United States, some Scots took notice.

It was the Misses Allan and Graham who started one of Scotland's first temperance societies in Glasgow's Maryhill in 1829, and the idea soon took hold. The women had plenty of local ammunition, for an estimate of 1840 said that 10% of all Glasgow houses sold drink. Temperance tracts dwelt on the harm that drink did to family life, comparing a husband who drunk away his wages so the family lived in fear and poverty, to a teetotal husband with a comfortable, happy home.

But many women also continued to enjoy a drink. The mill workers of Dundee had a perhaps-undeserved reputation for drunkenness on a Saturday, while the main streets of many other towns, from Leith to Glasgow, were filled with drunken men and women on a Saturday night. There were many that believed that Temperance was aimed at controlling the working classes, rather than curtailing drink. Spirit duty rose and society discouraged women from entering public houses, so by the 1870s, most Scottish pubs were male dominated establishments where decent women would hesitate to tread. Men spent their day at work and much of their evening in the pub while women remained at home. Many social reformers, however, believed that Scotland's addiction to alcohol was a social and not a gender issue. The answer, they thought, was better housing.

Women were vociferous in many Scottish temperance meetings and tens of thousands urged their husbands and sons to curtail their drinking. However in 1922 women got a real opportunity to fight against the massive male drinking culture. Edwin 'Neddy' Scrymgeour was the son of a Chartist, a staunch Christian, a Socialist champion of the poor and a member of the Prohibition Party. He had stood for election in Dundee in every election since 1908, and lost. Many people had disapproved of his anti-war stance between 1914 and 1918, but in 1922 he had a new chance for success. With all women over 30 now enfranchised, the number of Dundee voters increased by 77%, Scrymgeour's vote increased by nearly the same percentage.

The women had struck back against the evils of drink although the final victory rested with the government who raised the tax on spirits to an unprecedented level. Licensing hours decreased, and for much of the 20th century, Scottish pubs became sawdust and spit places of austerity and rugged drinking. Occasionally there was a lounge 'for the ladies', normally a dingy room with extremely limited access to the bar and perhaps a chair or carpet for comfort. By the end of the century the opening times had relaxed again, pubs were becoming more comfortable and, as more women were working, their spending power was recognised. The wheel seems to have gone full circle, with as many women as men now spending time in the public house or lounge bar, drunken women once again joining the men that stagger along the streets and drink related diseases affecting both men and women.

Chapter 16

Local Girl Done Good

There is no sunlight in the poetry of exile. There is only mist, wind, rain, the cry of whaups and the slow clouds above damp moorland
H. V. Morton

It is said that a prophet is without honour in her own country, and nowhere is that better illustrated than in the number of Scotswomen who have left their marks in other countries, while being almost unknown at home. These women have worked in an amazingly varied field of endeavour, often in appalling conditions, and have been remembered in various ways, if rarely in Scotland.

One of the bravest of all women was the missionary Mary Slessor. Born in Aberdeen in 1848, the second of eight children, her shoemaker father moved the family to Dundee when Mary was aged eleven, and she became a half-timer in the Baxter Brothers mill. She learned the ugly side of life early as her alcoholic father beat her and she experienced loss as her father and four of her siblings died. Like so many mill workers, Slessor was never tall, but her red hair warned of a quick temper. As soon as she was fourteen, she became a full timer, working a twelve-hour day and squeezing in evening classes as well. She spent fourteen years in the mill, and revealed a genuine Christianity that moved her to work as a Sunday School Teacher.

Slessor added to her busy life with voluntary work with destitute children in the sordid slum of the Cowgate. In 1874 Scotland was rocked by the death of David Livingston, but stories of his work were so powerful that in 1875 Slessor applied to work as a missionary with the United Presbyterian Church's Foreign Mission Board. Slessor's mother blessed her proposal: 'You are my child, given to me by God and I have given you back to him,'

After training in Edinburgh the 28-year-old Slessor sailed for Calabar in West Africa, one of the wildest places on Earth. A Scotsman, Dr Ferguson, had founded the Calabar mission in 1843, but after centuries of exploitation by slave traders the area was in turmoil, with human sacrifices commonplace, child sacrifice acceptable and the Ekpo secret society attacking slaves and women. Undaunted, Slessor set to work to spread Christianity, humanity and sheer common sense in the village of Old Town, fifty miles up the Calabar River in what is now Nigeria.

Many of the Africans lived in total savagery, while the Scottish missionaries were prim, correct and possessed of a proper Victorian standard of morality. Slessor, with her background of hard labour in the jute mills, had known poverty at first hand and was not afraid of work. It was unheard of for a Victorian female missionary to wear trousers, but Slessor thought them more practical in the forest than a long trailing skirt. It was also unusual for a female missionary to be forthright and assertive, but Slessor hacked through the worst of the African forest in her travels and spoke her mind to anyone. She carried loads alongside her African porters and climbed trees with an agility that women were not supposed to possess.

When Slessor arrived at Chief Okon's village, she was the first white woman that many of the natives had ever seen. They crowded around her, so astonished that some touched her skin to see if she was human or supernatural. On one occasion Slessor came across a sexual orgy, with powerful warriors abusing young women, so, yelling, she lifted her umbrella and attacked, routing the naked men. She relied on the force of her personality, faith and the superstition of the Africans to protect her. Operating in the area where Juju was created, she capitalised on the African belief that a powerful spirit protected her. Her spirit guardian was Jesus Christ. Warriors who were not yet out of the Iron Age became dedicated Christians. There were cannibals in the hinterland, disease and witchcraft everywhere and danger was so constant that Slessor accepted it as a fact of life.

After a while, Slessor adopted a loose dress that kept her cool, and despite snakes and insects, walked barefoot through the bush. Realising that someone special was among them, the Africans began to call her 'Ma.' Although she dedicated her life to Africa, Slessor also watched over her family in Dundee. In 1879 she returned, to move her mother and sisters from the unhealthy town centre to the outlying village of Downfield. Four years later she came again, this time shaking with malarial fever and accompanied by a little girl who she had rescued from sacrifice. Nonetheless, Africa called her back. When Slessor took over the running of Old Town she insisted on high standards of hygiene as well as Christian morality. When she heard of the deaths of her mother and sister in Scotland, she continued with her missionary work. In her forties now, she met a 25-year-old fellow missionary named Morrison who proposed marriage, but Slessor was planning to travel deeper into Africa. Morrison was not permitted to accompany her to the lands of the Okyong, where life was even more dangerous; he died in the United States as Slessor toiled with the horrors and rewards of missionary work.

Slessor travelled to Okyong in a royal canoe. Thirty-three loinclothed natives chanted deep-throated songs as they paddled to the thrum of a drum. It was a far cry from the factory hooter and the crowds in the Overgate. Opposed to the imposition of Western laws on people who had their own traditions, Slessor never stopped working, helping men, women and children, but even as she advised and taught, her hands were busy with knitting needles and wool. She was appointed an administrator, with power to judge the native people, but her first priority was always for the most vulnerable. One vice-consul who visited her saw a 'little frail old lady…crooning a black baby in her arms' and with a 'very strong accent.' When a 'hulking, overdressed native' intruded in her meeting place for women, 'she jumped up with an angry growl…seized him by the scruff of the neck, boxed his ears and hustled him out.'

It was the custom in many parts of Africa for the death of a chief to be marked by the ritual massacre of a number of people. When a local chief died, Slessor hastily bundled the threatened natives to a compound where she could watch over them and remained on guard for several days and nights until she deemed it safe. Totally committed to Africa, she married David Adeyemi Adeyemo, with whom she had two children. Known as the 'White Queen of Okoyong' she judged and cared for people within a 2000 square mile area, working despite the arthritis that crippled her. When she died in January 1915, crowds of people came to watch her funeral procession, the police stood to attention and government officials watched as her Union Flag draped coffin was lowered into the grave at Mission Hill, Calabar.

Mary Slessor must be remembered as one of the greatest of all Scotland's missionaries. The Church of Scotland Overseas Council gave perhaps the most telling comment. 'Her friends were from all walks of life, from Ma Erme, the sister of the chief who remained pagan to the end of her days, to Mary Kingsley.' A woman who could communicate with such diverse people must have been special indeed.

Fanny Wright was another local woman who became well known abroad. While Slessor worked in West Africa, Wright worked for human rights in the United States of America and is widely considered the mother of women's rights in that country. She was born in Dundee on the 6th September 1795. At that period Dundee was noted as a Radical town, so it is not surprising that her father, a skilled worker, was also radical. In common with many Scots, he sympathised with the aims of the early French Revolution and had Thomas Paines' *Age of*

Reason published in Dundee. Although he died shortly after her birth, Fanny seems to have inherited some of his beliefs, for her entire life was one of protest against oppression. More practically, she also inherited his entire estate, which made her a relatively wealthy young woman.

Brought up by relatives in England, Fanny proved her idealism at the age of eighteen when she wrote *A Few Days in Athens*, a philosophical romance that closed with a declaration of the brotherhood of man and was dedicated to Jeremy Bentham. Surprisingly for a work written by a young woman, the book received much critical acclaim. Returning to Scotland when she reached 21, Fanny lived with James Mylne, her great uncle, who was a lecturer at Glasgow University. It might have been the atmosphere of intellectual stimulation in Glasgow, or the ideas of Robert Owen the co-operative pioneer, but Fanny's radical ideas began to dominate her life. In 1818, at the age of 23, she sailed to the United States. Together with her sister, Fanny lived in New York, where she wrote a political play, *Altorf,* which was performed on Broadway.

On her return to Scotland, Fanny published another book, *Views of Society and Manners in America*, which again proved so successful that one reader, the Marquis de Lafayette, invited her to Paris, the revolutionary capital of Europe. When Lafayette, an admirer of the United States, emigrated in 1824 Fanny followed. In 1825 she published her *Plan for the Gradual Abolition of Slavery in the United States, Without Danger of Loss to the Citizens of the South.* Following the teachings of Robert Owen, she believed that slaves should be allowed to earn enough money to buy their freedom. Accordingly Fanny bought 2000 acres of land at Nashoba in Tennessee and started a plantation for helping the nine slaves that she bought. Her idea was to train and educate the slaves as well as keep them safe. Although she was of relatively gentle birth, Fanny worked beside the slaves in the forest and fields, but her physical strength did not match her will and she suffered a breakdown. Her idea for the slaves to work their way to freedom within five years also failed due to bad harvests, financial troubles and arguments between whites and blacks.

In the summer of 1826, Fanny moved to Robert Owen's Utopian community at New Harmony in Louisiana to recover her strength. Robert Dale Owen had recently arrived from New Lanark and described Fanny as 'tall, commanding figure, somewhat slender and graceful.' He thought her face was 'delicately chiselled' but 'masculine rather than feminine.' Inspired by her relationship with Robert Dale Owen, Fanny Wright altered the character of Nashoba from a haven for slaves to a Utopian settlement. It was in this period that she began to develop her own ideas about the place of women in society. Nashoba became notorious, perhaps unfairly, for free love and equality between the sexes. Fanny Wright had not succeeded in abolishing slavery; now she concentrated on ending the practice of traditional marriage, which she also believed to be wrong. 'The proper basis of the sexual intercourse to be the unconstrained and unrestrained choice of both parties,' Fanny Wright claimed. Perhaps her ideas would not be viewed as radical today, for she aimed for equality between men and woman, an end to the traditional woman's vow of obedience, an opportunity for women to retain their personal identity and possessions and easier divorce.

Unfortunately these ideas did not receive a favourable response and in 1828 Fanny embarked on a new career as a public speaker. Her first notable speech was in New Harmony on the 4th July 1828, where, according to tradition, she became the first woman to speak in public in the United States. She visited many American cities, giving lectures against slavery and in favour of universal suffrage. The American audiences did not always welcome her, partly because of the content of her speeches, but partly due to misogyny. In one notable speech in Baltimore, a bodyguard of women in full Quaker costume ensured that she would not be assaulted by some of the men in the audience.

Fanny also wrote extensively on sex and marriage, education and woman's rights. Women who were educated as equals, she argued, would enhance men's lives, not threaten them. Women, through education and association with men, would lose their frivolity and disorderliness, while men who associated with educated women would lose their rudeness and pedantry. Fanny wrote in the Socialist journal, *Free Inquirer*, which she lauded as the first United States periodical 'for the purpose of fearless and unbiased enquiry on all subjects.'

Despite her strictures on marriage, in 1838 Fanny married a Frenchman Guillaime D'Arusmont whom she had met at New Harmony. Perhaps predictably, their marriage failed and Fanny took her daughter with her to Cincinnati. She continued to lecture and write for the remainder of her life. Divorced in 1850, Fanny died three years later. Her legacy is immense; the first woman to speak in public in America, the first woman to campaign against slavery, a very early exponent of women's education and suffrage, Fanny Wright wakened the eyes of America to new thoughts from Britain and Europe. It is no wonder that the United States has several Fanny Wright societies, but although she is well remembered in the United States, she is barely known in Scotland, although there is a small plaque in her honour in the Nethergate, Dundee. If ever there was a case of a prophet without honour in her own country, Fanny Wright was that prophet.

It is doubtful whether more than a handful of Scots could name Catherine Spence, originally from Melrose in the Borders, but she is well remembered in her adopted Australia. In 1839 the legal practice of David Spence, her father, failed, and the family decided to immigrate to Australia. David Spence found a house on the outskirts of Adelaide in South Australia. While he found his way into local government, his teenage daughter Catherine became a governess and then a teacher. Catherine flourished, writing notable novels, working as a journalist and dabbling in politics. She is remembered for advocating Proportional Representation, and has been featured on Australian stamps.

Margaret Burns, born in Edinburgh was also interested in education for females. Educating to New Zealand, she rose to become the first Principal of Otago High School, the first New Zealand High School purely for girls. As with so many Scotswomen of the 19th century, Burns was intensely religious and gave freely to charity.

Another Scottish educationalist was Louisa Dalrymple, who left Scotland for New Zealand in 1853. After involvement in establishing the Girls High School in Otago, Louisa decided to push for Higher Education for women. For years, she argued that women should be given equal treatment. Perhaps it was her Scottish stubbornness that made her wear down the authorities, who eventually agreed. It is to the credit of New Zealand, and Louisa Dalrymple, that the University of New Zealand was the first in the British Empire to award a degree to a woman.

If Louisa Dalrymple is known in New Zealand and not Scotland, Williamina Fleming operated in a much vaster arena. Another Dundonian, she was born in 1857, became a pupil teacher at the age of 14 and six years later married James Fleming. Only a year later the Flemings immigrated to Boston in the United States, where Williamina was to spend the remainder of her life. Williamina was pregnant when her marriage failed, but Scotswomen, with a reputation for intelligence and high standards of cleanliness, were favoured as domestic staff and Professor Edward Pickering employed her. Pickering was Director of the Harvard College Observatory, and must have made a favourable impression on Williamina, for she named her son Edward Pickering Fleming. From a cleaner, Williamina rose to become a general clerk at the observatory and within a few years was in charge of the photographic library.

Although humanity had been studying the stars for some centuries, it was not until the late 19th century that astronomers began to use short focus lens photography to systematically map the heavens. By mapping and classifying the stars, Williamina became the most important female astronomer of the 19th century. Williamina lectured at the Chicago World Fair of 1893, choosing the bold subject 'A Field for Woman's Work in Astronomy.' After the undoubted success of her work, none could argue. Six years later, she became the first female Curator of Astronomical Photography at Harvard. Williamina recruited a team of twelve females to assist in her investigation of over 190,000 photographic plates. These women, and others who worked with her, recalled that she always demanded perfection.

The work was intense, calling for absolute accuracy as she catalogued and measured the position of thousands of stars. Working without the benefit of modern technology, the mathematical background must have been colossal. She also spent hundreds of hours preparing the Harvard Annals for the printer, impressing her colleagues and staff by her aptitude for rapid understanding of thousands of unrelated facts. The sheer volume of research is staggering. In 1890, Henry Draper's *Catalogue of Stellar Spectra* included Williamina's classification of 10351 stars, a collection that remains perhaps her most significant contribution to astronomy. Stars that were not part of her index were labelled as 'peculiar.' By 1911, Williamina had discovered ten of the 28 known novae, stars that display sudden bursts of radiation. She also located 222 variable stars and 52 nebulae, while her *Stars having Peculiar Spectra* was published in 1912.

Williamina's work however was not unrecognised. In 1906 the Royal Astronomical Society made her an honorary member, only the fifth woman and the first American to be so honoured. Williamina was a member of French and American Astronomical societies, while Wellesley College appointed her an Honorary Fellow, and the Astronomical Society of Mexico posthumously awarded her a medal for her work in discovering new stars. All the time that she was working, Williamina Fleming ensured that that her son Edward obtained a sound upbringing and education. When she died in 1911 she was a noted member of the international astronomical world, so the leading journals of her day were effusive with their tributes. In common with so many other Scotswomen who made their name overseas, Williamina Fleming is hardly remembered in her native Scotland.

Kate Sheppard also made a major impact in her adopted country while hardly raising a ripple in her home pond. Born in Islay in 1848, she immigrated to New Zealand and took a very active part in the cause of woman's suffrage. A journalist, Sheppard is remembered as the most outspoken supporter of female suffrage in New Zealand, and perhaps the most effective. When New Zealand became the first country in the British Empire to grant female suffrage in 1893, Sheppard opened and ran Women's Groups up and down the country, campaigning for women's rights and women's issues. When she died in her eighties, Kate was only a few months short of witnessing the first woman elected to the New Zealand parliament. Her face is familiar in New Zealand from the ten-dollar bill where she keeps a watchful eye on progress, but she is hardly known in Scotland.

Perhaps these women needed to travel outside Scotland to further their careers, and Scotland's loss was certainly another's gain, but it would be interesting to speculate what their lives would have been like had they remained at home.

Chapter 17

The Suffragettes

> Let men say whate'er they will
> Woman, woman, rules them still
> Isaac Bickerstaff

The Members of Parliament sat in solemn debate within the Gothic formality of Westminster. Grave and bearded, they spoke with sombre dignity, until the sound of a brass band blasted their words away. Dumfounded, they stared at each other, and rose to walk to the terrace beside the Thames. There, on the busy river, was a steam launch, with a brass band playing loudly and a small, extremely neat woman brandishing a bold banner.

'Women's Sunday' it read 'June 21. Cabinet Ministers Specially Invited.'

As the powerful men stroked their beards in wonder, a police launch steamed up and shepherded the intruder away, but she had done what she intended. It was June the 18th 1909 and Flora Drummond, the Suffragette from the Island of Arran, had struck another blow toward women's right to vote. It was not until 1906 that the *Daily Mail* christened members of the Women's Social and Political Union as suffragettes, but the name stuck, and has been transferred to any of the movements for women's votes. The history is long, always difficult and often honourable.

In 1832 the First Reform Act increased the number of people who were allowed to vote. Although many people hailed the Act as a great step forward, there were more who were greatly dissatisfied, for all the Act had achieved was to allow a certain number of middle class people to join the ranks of the privileged. The great mass of people was deprived of any say in the running of the country. A careful few noticed that, for the first time, the Act stipulated that only men were allowed to vote.

At the end of the decade, the Chartists demanded electoral reform, with some suggesting that women should also be enfranchised. The 1840s brought much social unrest, unemployment, repression and hunger, but an upturn of economic fortune in the 1850s saw the country settle down, although demand for electoral reform remained. In 1867 another Reform Act saw the number of voters rising, with Glasgow alone increasing its electorate from 18000 to 47000, all male.

1884 saw more reforms, so that all male house owners, men who had held their tenancy for at least one-year and selected lodgers, could vote. Women still were not permitted to choose a political candidate. However, not everybody agreed. As early as 1866 Emily Davis and Elizabeth Garrett Anderson petitioned parliament for women's suffrage. The following year, John Stuart Mill the philosopher and social reformer argued in parliament that women should have the vote. His suggestion was received with some derision, and outvoted by 194 votes to 73. Although the seed had been sown, Britain, when Queen Victoria was Queen-Empress of quarter of the world, when most women were undereducated and underpaid, was barren ground. Women were unlikely to gain suffrage.

However, there were signs that the absolute refusal to see women as responsible thinking beings was beginning to crack. In 1869 the Municipal Franchise Act allowed single female ratepayers the right to vote in local elections. Married women, as chattels of their husbands, were not allowed this privilege until 1894. Then followed a series of small advances, such as the right for women to vote for, and even participate in School Boards in 1870, or as Poor Law Guardians in 1889, and finally in Parish and District Councils in 1894.

Strangely, while men such as John Stuart Mill campaigned for votes for women, there were many women opposed to the idea. Octavia Hill, Florence Nightingale, Beatrice Webb and even the queen did not agree that women should have the vote. Many people believed that women simply did not have the intellect for politics, and certainly lacked the physique for the hassle of the hustings. William Cremer, MP openly admitted that if even a few females were enfranchised, eventually all would be, so that women would outnumber men. As 'creatures of impulse and emotion', women could not reason as men did, and therefore the country would decline.

Despite the rumblings of discontent, women's suffrage was not a central issue in politics. Social interests such as housing, education and health were seen as more important, as was concern over defending and building the Empire. There were also party concerns; with the Liberals believed that women would be more likely to vote Conservative. The Labour Party, on the other hand, shied away from directly addressing the question, concentrating instead on general adult suffrage.

While the politicians hedged the question or paid lip service to women's issues, some women decided that more direct action was needed. If men would not help them, then women would help themselves. When it was obvious that petitioning politicians was not effective, a number of groups formed to force the issue. In 1867, at the time of the second Electoral Reform Bill, a woman's suffrage society was founded in Edinburgh. This party was active in collecting signatures for the massive petition for woman's suffrage that parliament rejected, but this setback only strengthened the resolve of the women. Further branches were opened in Perth and Dundee. With the failure to achieve complete success, interest in the cause waned throughout the 1870s, so that by the mid 1880s only the Edinburgh branch remained alive.

In 1897 Mrs Emmaline Pankhurst forged a number of small women's groups into the National Union of Women's Suffrage Societies. Mrs Emmaline Pankhurst believed that women's suffrage was only the first step in obtaining many social reforms. In October 1903 she brought a number of women to her house and formed the Women's Social and Political Union, the WSPU, with more aggressive tactics. Rather than sending petitions and writing hopeful speeches, militant women interrupted political meetings, heckled politicians, organised rallies and even broke the law. Naturally, Scotswomen were at the forefront.

The Woman's Social and Political Union was different from previous women's movement. It was highly organised, and its members were instantly recognisable. Mrs Pankhurst instigated a uniform for her women. They wore clothes of three colours, each carefully selected to highlight an aspect of their belief. They wore white to symbolise the purity of their private and public life; nobody was ever to accuse the WSPU of economic or moral scandal. They chose purple to show the dignity and freedom of their members, and green as a symbol of hope the green of spring. Most of the WSPU members were from the upper or middle classes. Working women had neither the time, nor the energy to spend in campaigning for the vote. Most of them barely had time to spend with their family. Many were too exhausted after a week of hard shifts at the mill or factory even for that.

It became common to see determined women striding along the main streets in Glasgow, Dundee or Edinburgh, clad in a white golf jersey, a purple or green skirt and a hat decorated with green ribbons. Many of the boldest also wore a sash with the unambiguous words 'Votes for Women.' Some grooms may have felt vaguely uneasy as their bride turned up for the wedding ceremony in a long white frock with the purple sash across her right shoulder, but there seems no evidence that such a uniform ever stopped a wedding. Indeed, many husbands supported their women, for the suffragettes were not an anti-male organisation. Scottish members frequently sported a purple and green thistle as their symbol, proving their Scottishness as well as their commitment to woman's suffrage.

One of the most energetic leaders of the movement was Flora Drummond. A telegraphist; Drummond qualified as a Postmistress, but was turned down because at five foot one, she was one inch too short. Undaunted, she put her talents to use by being one of the first members of the WSPU. Still in her twenties, Drummond became the National Publicity Officer. Her exploits became legendary. In 1906, the Prime Minister had visited Scotland to attend a meeting in Glasgow. His speech had been interrupted by the diminutive, sturdy figure of Drummond heckling him with her demands for women's suffrage, and it had taken a pair of hefty stewards to remove her.

Two years later, Drummond was again to the fore when another Scotswoman, Mary Phillips, was due to be released from Holloway Prison. Mary Phillips was also a suffragette, who had been jailed three months earlier for taking part in what was termed an illegal demonstration. Drummond ensured that her release was marked by intense celebration. She waited at the gates of Holloway, and when Phillips stepped outside, a female guard of honour met her. They were distinctively suffragettes, with white dresses that reached to their ankles, tartan sashes and brooches and Scottish glengarries. Beside them was a horse drawn wagonette that itself was adorned with huge thistles and snatches of purple heather. To ensure that there was no doubting their identity, Drummond had a large WSPU banner, with the additional slogan 'you maunna tramp on the Scots thistle, laddie.'

The banner was a direct challenge to Drummond's old sparring partner, the Prime Minister. The minute that Philips stepped to freedom, Drummond gave orders for four female bagpipers to start to play *Macpherson's Farewell*. If there was no mistaking Drummond's commitment to the cause of suffrage, neither was there any ambiguity about her nationality.

The wagonette picked up Philips and re-united her with her parents as Drummond danced an impromptu Highland Fling to entertain the crowd that had gathered. Never one to miss an opportunity, Drummond also gave a speech about women's suffrage, stating that the WSPU was determined to 'get the Scottish thistle behind Asquith.' Flora seemed to enjoy pipe music, for she ensured that pipers led all her parades, both in Scotland and in England. She also made sure that she was instantly recognisable by adopting a characteristic uniform.

Disdaining any clothing company that catered to traditional female styles, Drummond chose the military tailor of Toye and Company to make her uniform. Riding her horse at the head of her processions, she wore a greatcoat with gold epaulettes and a gold sash with the words 'Votes for Women' and 'General' embroidered in purple and green silk. She also wore a peaked cap and black leather boots, making her a formidable and highly individual, figure.

Drummond gained her title of General during the great London demonstration of 1909, the same Women's Sunday to which she had invited Cabinet Ministers. Seven processions marched across London, all converging at Hyde Park, where eighty speakers at twenty separate platforms addressed the converted, the doubtful, the interested and the plain sceptical. Newspapers reported that half a million women attended the marches and meetings, many from abroad. Unfortunately, such meetings often attracted the wrong sort of people, and the initial arguing turned to violence. Mounted police rode in to stop what could have been a nasty situation.

While Women's Sunday was noted for the attendance figures and violence, the Edinburgh demonstration later that year, organised by Flora Drummond, was more of an entertainment, albeit with a serious purpose. Uniformed and mounted, Drummond led the procession along Princes Street as female pipers sweetened the air, but the thousands of spectators gaped and pointed at the decorated floats that depicted the achievements of Scotswomen. The suffragettes had researched diligently to reproduce historical personalities such as Flora MacDonald, Queen Margaret, and Lady Grisell Baillie.

Hundreds of women also paraded in the clothing of their employment. As well as students from Glasgow School of Art wearing clothes that they had designed and made themselves, there were fishwives and nurses, factory operatives and clerks. A notice above each group proclaimed their occupation, driving home the message that Scotland's women worked hard for the nation and deserved the vote. All ages marched, from the white haired fishwives who had seen three generations of their men sail to danger on the North Sea to the nine-year-old piper, Bessie Watson. Yet despite the numbers, there was no trouble.

Perhaps eight thousand women crammed into Waverley Market, to hear speeches by the leaders of the suffragette movement. Drummond gave her usual rousing performance and scores of women hastened to join the cause. Entrepreneurs jumped on the rolling bandwagon, creating clothing and souvenirs for the more affluent of the suffragettes. As well as the run-of-the-mill material such as tablecloths and scarves, there was a game called Panko, named after Mrs Pankhurst.

With the success of the Edinburgh meeting fresh in their minds, the Scottish suffragettes planned more meetings, more marches, and more demonstrations. There was a procession in Dundee, and a violent demonstration when a body of suffragettes charged into Kinnaird Hall to disrupt a speech by Winston Churchill. As the police and stewards dealt with this bold frontal attack, more suffragettes led by Adelia Pankhurst, daughter of Emmaline, sneaked into a building that overlooked the hall and began to hurl missiles at the skylight. With the possibility of serious injury from broken glass and stones, the political meeting was severely interrupted. Police had to locate the stone-throwers, arrest them and then quieten down the mob that had formed to watch the fun. Five suffragettes were arrested, and offered the choice of a £5 fine or ten days in jail. They chose the latter and promptly declared a hunger strike.

Unhappy at the publicity that the suffragettes were receiving, and unwilling to allow any high-profile prisoner to die in custody, the Scottish Office ordered that the prisoners should be force-fed. If the suffragette still refused to eat, a doctor would examine her and she were deemed fit wardresses would force her onto a chair, thrust her head back and open her mouth, into which milk was poured. The woman would struggle, spitting out the liquid as she choked. At that point the doctor would take tubes from the trolley and push them up her nostrils and down into her throat.

Naturally the woman would struggle, so often this procedure also failed. If so, the wardresses would hold her in a half sitting position while the doctor opened her mouth and placed a cork gag between her teeth. With her mouth thus wedged open, the doctor took long tube from the trolley and manoeuvred it down her throat.

On this occasion, however, the prison doctor refused to force feed them, and after four days without food, the suffragettes were released. When they walked free of jail, Flora Drummond was waiting, with a statement already prepared for the press. Drummond claimed that the release was a triumph for Scottish justice, for force-feeding, already common in England, would not happen in Scotland.

Heckling politicians was a favourite tactic of the suffragettes. Lila Clunas of Dundee had argued with Asquith, then Chancellor of the Exchequer, when he spoke at Newport in Fife in 1907. She also chained herself to the railings outside number 10 Downing Street, while the Asquith children and their nanny watched from an upstairs window. Back in Dundee, Clunas had interrupted Churchill's election meetings so often that the stewards threw her from her seat, tearing her clothes in the process.

After the excitement of 1909 the suffragettes called for an amnesty, hoping that they had persuaded parliament to grant them the vote. Instead the politicians hedged the issue, while the women's anger grew. The 1911 census gave the suffragettes a splendid opportunity to demonstrate their ingenuity and power. Why, they argued, should we be included in the count, when we are not recognised as equal citizens? By the terms of the census, a count had to be made of everybody who was in every house in Britain on a certain day. Accordingly, when the day of the census came, the women travelled away from their homes and crammed into offices, halls and coffee shops in Edinburgh, Dundee, Aberdeen and Glasgow. Other women just refused to pay taxes, and when the authorities sold their possessions, they hoped that sympathetic suffragettes would bid for those they treasured most.

Non-violent action, however, seemed to achieve nothing. While the papers were full of accounts of the clever tricks of the suffragettes, the more extreme started a guerrilla campaign. They set fire to buildings or pillar-boxes, smashed windows and generally cried havoc. In May 1911, the suffragettes bombed Edinburgh's Royal Observatory. The explosion awakened Professor and Mrs Simpson but did not do a great deal of damage. The message beside the bomb, however, was clear, 'How beggarly appears argument before defiant deeds. Votes for Women.' There were spots of blood to prove that at least one of the bombers had been injured, and a second note that read: 'From the beginning of the world every stage of human progress has been from scaffold to scaffold and stake to stake.'

In East Lothian, suffragettes burned the historic church at Whitekirk. In Perthshire the suffragettes set light to a trio of mansions around Comrie, a bright torch to illuminate their hopes, but arson was a step too far. After playing softly with the women, the Scottish authorities hardened their attitude. Forced feeding was introduced in Scotland. The first suffragette to suffer was Ethel Moorhead, a Dundee suffragette who accused of the Comrie arson attacks. Undaunted, or perhaps infuriated, the women fought back. They tried to set fire to Burns' Cottage and vandalised paintings in art galleries. Even the Royals were not safe as a suffragette took an axe to a portrait of the King and others harassed the world's leading family whenever they came to Scotland.

Among the most vocal of the protestors was Lila Clunas. When the King and Queen visited Dundee in 1914, she waited for them, yelling 'Stop forcible feeding!' as the Royal carriage rolled past. On other occasions Clunas organised her suffragettes, from the less militant Women's Freedom League, to chant 'Votes for Women!' in unison during political meetings. Violence became accepted wherever the suffragettes appeared. When Mrs Pankhurst was due to speak at St Andrews Hall in Glasgow, both the police and the WSPU knew that there would be trouble. As the police waited to arrest the leader of what was rapidly becoming a female terrorist group, the suffragettes made defensive plans. They strung barbed wire amidst the bright garlands of flowers that decorated the front of the speaker's platform. They also arranged for a bodyguard for Mrs Pankhurst, tough women who were ready to fight the police fist to fist.

At six in the evening, two hours before the meeting was due to start, a number of police descended into the basement of St Andrews Hall, where they waited for Mrs Pankhurst. More police formed a barrier around the building where crowds were already gathering. Plain-clothes detectives scrutinised the women who entered, and by half past seven the hall was filled with suffragettes. It was after eight o' clock that Mrs Pankhurst stepped onto the platform, and while the crowd cheered, the police filed in to make their arrest. Simultaneously, one of the bodyguards stood up, produced a pistol, aimed at the leading policeman and fired. As the report of the shot echoed round the hall and the policeman flinched and turned aside, his colleagues, believing that he had been hit, drew their truncheons and charged. They were brave men, to face a pistol-wielding suffragette while armed only with sticks, but in the event, the bodyguard had only fired blanks.

There were a few minutes of mayhem in the hall as club-wielding women of the bodyguard, aided by many of the audience, attacked the police. Tables and chairs crashed to the floor, women screamed and swore, but the police arrested Mrs Pankhurst and carted her off to jail, where her treatment was possibly slightly better than that accorded to most of her rank and file followers.

Although the suffragettes claimed to be political prisoners, they were treated no better than other vandals, fire-raisers and disturbers of the king's peace. Stripped of their finery and made to wear rough prison clothing, the women, often from the middle and upper classes, spent their sentence in menial labour. They ate ordinary prison food and were sometimes kept in solitary confinement. Although most endured these privations, others, deprived of support and perhaps expecting glamour often became disorientated and confused. At least one woman was released after enduring a nervous breakdown. When the British public voiced their disquiet with such treatment of women, the Home Secretary conceded that suffragettes were to be treated as first class prisoners, with better conditions and privileges.

The women continued to campaign. There were long walks for publicity, such as in the autumn of 1912 when seven women marched from Edinburgh to London. There was continued refusal to pay taxes as some women adopted the slogan of the American Revolutionaries 'No Taxation without Representation.' One of the most prominent tax evaders was Lady Steel, whose late husband had been the Lord Provost of Edinburgh. Her possessions were publicly auctioned at the Mercat Cross.

By 1911 Flora Drummond was so well known that the authorities banned her from appearing at a by-election meeting. She arrived nonetheless, to be promptly grabbed and thrust into an upstairs room, with the door firmly locked behind her. While the crowd outside jeered at her discomfiture, Drummond realised that her room contained the food for the after-meeting buffet. More importantly, it also contained the drink. Knowing her countrymen, Flora lifted one of the dozen bottles of whisky and flourished it to the crowd. 'If someone finds a ladder and sets it against the window, I'll give them a bottle of whisky!'

A ladder was appropriated and Drummond passed over the whisky, and then climbed to freedom. With the crowd now on her side, she treated them to a grand speech on women's right to vote, concluding with a rousing 'votes for women!' that raised a cheer.

The suffragettes seemed to have some success in 1913 when Asquith's Liberal government proposed giving the vote to female householders and wives of householders. Asquith had not been persuaded by the actions of Flora Drummond and her compatriots; rather some of his colleagues believed that many fundraisers from the suffragette ranks were supporting the Labour party. Unfortunately, the timing was wrong, for the Conservatives and Irish Nationalists combined to defeat the bill. The Irish Nationalists were afraid that an influx of women would cut their representation in Westminster. Asquith did not repeat the experiment.

It is arguable exactly how effective the suffragette campaign was achieving female suffrage. When the First World War broke out in August 1914, the leaders of the suffragettes agreed to suspend their activities until victory had been achieved. During the next four years, women worked in factories throughout Britain and took over the jobs of men who were fighting at the front. In January 1918, most women over the age of 30 gained the vote. Ten years later, all women over 21 could vote. That particular battle had been won, but there were many more to fight.

Chapter 18

Political Women

Stop the world, Scotland wants to get on
Winnie Ewing

The entry of women into politics was drawn out, tortuous and, ultimately effective. Women were first recorded as having become involved in industrial disputes as early as 1768, but at that time their arguments were purely local. It was the Great Reform Act of 1832 that specifically stated that only men should enjoy the vote, although before this date there had been no female politicians. When the Chartist movement began a few years later, the emphasis was on advancing the working class through self-help and improvement.

In 1840 the National Association of the Chartists provided reasons for admitting women to their ranks. The Association stated that women were not exempt from legal punishment 'any more than men' so they should share 'in the enactment of laws to which they are amenable.' The Chartists also pointed out that female householders were expected to pay direct taxes, while all women also paid indirect taxes, and 'there should be no taxation without representation.' Married women, said the Chartists, exercised influence over their husband, while 'far more important, women are the chief instructors of our children.' Finally, the Chartists said that 'much of men's happiness depends upon the minds and dispositions of women' so men should 'promote the education and contend for the social and political rights of women.'

There were women among the Chartist agitators who marched and rioted in the 1830s, with women from factories in Aberdeen notably vocal. The Chartists, however, were too advanced for their time. Despite marches and political disturbance, petitions and protests, their hopes gradually faded as minor government reforms eroded their numbers.

Women were generally paid less than men were, even if they performed the same work. On marriage, the husband controlled his wife's possessions, and if there were children, the husband controlled them too. If a woman was unfortunate in her choice of man divorce was difficult, although much less so in Scotland than in England. The 19th century, however, saw some small advances that acted as a portent of the future. In 1839 women gained the right to have custody of their children under the age of seven, while wives had to give their consent before their husband disposed of her freehold land. How often this consent was sought, and how often it was coerced, is another matter. For the majority of women, however, owning land was not even a dream, yet alone a remote possibility. Dependent on a man for financial security, women also found that by mid century, 'respectable' women did not work. Convention thus relegated the millions of hard grafting women into a sub-stratum of society.

During the second half of the 19th century, the pace of improvement quickened. The Conjugal Rights Act (Scotland) of 1861 eased life for married women, as did the 1877 Married Women's Property (Scotland) Act. As the century progressed, fewer married women participated in paid, formal work, although many worked as childminders, in family businesses or in home-based sweated labour. Nevertheless, the army of women who operated the machines in mill and factory were disinclined to meekly accept male authority. Before the 19th century women had never gathered together in such numbers and had never had the opportunity to speak, women to woman, about women's concerns. Rather than the hoped-for compliant workforce, mill workers had a history of defiance and political agitation. In the 1870s there were 46 strikes among Dundee's female mill workers, some perhaps encouraged by Mary Macarthur's Woman's Trade Union League that burst into the political arena in 1874.

While the Reverend Henry Williamson formed the Dundee and District Mill and Factory Operatives Union in 1885, in an effort to solve disputes by conciliation and debate, women often preferred more direct action. Two years later the Scottish Woman's Trade Council was formed, then a whole host of organisations, including the Women's Protective and Provident League.

Margaret Irwin was prominent within the Women's Protective and Provident League, and later was elected as secretary of the Scottish Trade Union Congress. Other women to work within the STUC Parliamentary and General Councils included Isabella Blacklock, Kate Maclean, Agnes Gilroy and Isobell Barrie.

The mill girls did not win all their early struggles. In 1888 a group of six mill workers realised that they were paid a halfpenny a week less than their male counterparts. That sum does not sound a great deal today, and perhaps it did not in 1888, but the principle of equality was at stake and when the manager refused a pay rise, the girls went on strike. The management retaliated by arresting the strikers and parading them through the streets of Dundee. It would be many years before the mill women obtained equal pay.

Dundee mill girls became renowned for the lightning strikes that saw them take to the streets in chanting, gesticulating crowds that congregated in the Cowgate, mocking their employers. Impoverished and overworked, they responded with defiant songs that reflected what they would like to do, rather than the reality of their position.

'The shifters they're all dancin'
The spinners singing tae

The gaffer's standing watching
But there's nothing he can dae.'

Mary Macarthur, together with the Social Union, helped found the Jute and Flax Workers Union, which combined the raw energy of the mill women with the bargaining skills of John Sime. Members of the JFWU were involved in suffrage campaigning in 1907.

In 1911, perhaps 80% of the female spinners of Cox's Works were members of a union and participated in a strike against new working practices that would see a 50% increase in work load. Although the names of the ringleaders are not recorded, contemporary accounts tell of a 'girl with a green felt hat.' After three weeks the strike ended, with no clear winner. It may be significant that one clause in the settlement guaranteed that a woman named Bridget King would be allowed back to work, under a different foreman. Perhaps Bridget King was the wearer of the green felt hat?

Voting rights for women advanced slowly throughout the 19th century. The 1867 Reform Act granted women the right of voting in Poor Law Boards and town councils. Four years later married women and women property owners were able to vote in local elections, with other women following a decade later. By the end of the 1880s women could stand for election in county and parish councils, and in 1907 in town councils. Dollar in Clackmannanshire had the honour of the first female councillor, with Laing Malcolm being elected that same year. Six years later she won a notable victory by becoming Provost of the town. In the meantime, working women continued to fight for more modest gains. Not only the mill girls were militant. In one famous encounter, Dundee's domestic servants warred with their mistresses over dress, hours and holidays.

In 1918 women over the age of 30 finally gained the right to enter mainstream politics. Within a very few years, female politicians were proving their worth. One of the earliest was Katherine Marjory, the Duchess of Atholl.

Katherine Marjory had been born in Perthshire, the daughter of the historian Sir James Ramsay. Used to privilege, she was educated at Wimbledon High School in England, and then at the Royal College of Music. At the age of 23 she married the future Eighth Duke of Atholl, and very soon after proved her social conscience by working with the sick and wounded of the Boer War. She also used her musical talents to organise concerts for the troops, who must have appreciated the thought as they sweated and suffered on the African veldt.

Ironically, at this stage of her life, Katherine Marjory opposed woman's suffrage. When the First World War broke out in 1914, she again helped in hospital and morale boosting work, and in 1917 became the Duchess of Atholl. When the war ended, Marjory stood for parliament, becoming the Conservative MP for Kinross and Perthshire in 1923. Thereafter her rise was steady. Between 1924 and 1929 Marjory was the first female Conservative minister when she was appointed Parliamentary Secretary to the Board of Education. As such, Marjory was successful in defeating government policies that would have weakened the education of the poor. Marjory was not only interested in British affairs. For a decade from 1929 she fought to improve the condition of women and children within the British Empire, but her interests extended far beyond what many might see as traditional women's concerns. Marjory was one of the first politicians to be openly disturbed by the growing influence of Hitler. Obtaining an uncut version of *Mein Kampf*, she had it translated and encouraged government ministers to read of Hitler's philosophy and intentions.

War and the threat of war dominated the 1930s, so while Marjory opposed the European policy of non-intervention in the Spanish Civil War, she also refused to support British help for the Republicans. Her book *Women and Politics* is still worth reading, while her *Searchlight on Spain* became a best seller soon after its release in 1938. A woman of great principles, she lost her seat in parliament when she opposed Chamberlain's Munich Agreement, with the press calling her the Red Duchess because of her hostility to Hitler. Although Marjory was out of politics, she did not retire from life. For the next two decades, she

Political Women

helped the many millions of displaced people in Europe. The Red Duchess was the first prominent Scottish women politician and she left a fine legacy for others to follow.

During the First World War collective political action by Scotswomen saw its finest hour. The war machine was hungry for men, so that Scotland was drained of male labour, which poured over to France and Flanders, Gallipoli and Palestine like a kilted khaki tide. While these men were enduring the nightmare of trench warfare, women occupied their work places. Women worked on trams, in munitions factories, in welders' yards and shipyards, and while they worked they worried about their men at the front. They knew, by the mournful casualty lists published in the newspapers, by the shocked faces of their bereaved colleagues and by the broken men who returned home, just how bad the war was. They also worried how they could feed their families on the rations allowed to them. Then the Glasgow factors imposed a massive increase on their rents.

It was a situation that mirrored the Clearances of the previous century. Once again the factors had chosen to strike when the men were absent. Once again there were threats of eviction, and once again the women of Scotland faced the forces of authority head on. The women refused to pay their rent, saying that they would not let a single soldier's wife be evicted.

The rent strike began in Govan and Partick, with women banding together. Baillie Mary Barbour was the guiding light of this urban revolution. She knew that the law stated nobody could be evicted between sunset and sunrise, so arranged for women to gather at those houses threatened by eviction before dawn, and remain until dusk. Soon women from other areas of Glasgow became involved, barricading the mouths of their closes and fighting the forces of authority. 'Our husbands are fighting Prussianism in France,' one placard read, 'and we are fighting the Prussians of Partick.' Perhaps 20,000 women were involved, most of them ordinary housewives, but some, such as the suffragette Helen Crawford, were more politically aware.

Men too, supported their women, with the Clyde shipyards and engineering works threatening strike action. When Britain faced siege by submarine, when shipping carried the lifeblood of the nation, its army, food and supplies, the Clyde shipyards were beyond value. Faced with massed wife power and the possibility of disruption to ship repair, the government capitulated. The Rent Restriction Act ensuring that there would be no evictions and no more rent increases until the war was won.

Even more important, the women's action persuaded Lloyd George to concentrate on house building after the war, creating the 'Homes Fit for Heroes' slogan that gave the fighting men hope for a better future. The 1919 Addison and 1924 Housing Acts began a programme of council house building that, whatever its faults, rehoused tens of thousands of Scots in homes that were far superior to the crowded unsanitary tenements that disfigured Scotland's towns and cities.

Another highly successful female MP was Florence Horsburgh, an Edinburgh woman whose family originated in Fife. Horsburgh gained the MBE for creating a network of food vans and canteens during the First World War. After the war she worked with Countess Haig to help disabled soldiers.

Horsburgh had not intended a political career, but was asked to raise support for a Unionist politician. Impressed by her oratory powers the Scottish Unionist whip, Colonel Blair, recruited her for his staff. Although she was on the campaigning trail during the 1920 election, it was not until 1930 that the party adopted her as the prospective parliamentary candidate for Dundee. At that time there was a double vote system, and in 1931 Horsburgh became an MP with the Liberal Dingle Foot. She had the double distinction of being Dundee's first woman Member of Parliament, as well as Dundee's first Unionist MP.

Interestingly, the woman mill workers of Dundee appear to have voted en-masse for Horsburgh when she replaced Edwin Scrymgeour, the Temperance candidate. Two years after her election, Horsburgh was selected to become one Britain's four delegates to the League of Nations, a position she held until 1936. She was re-elected in Dundee in

1935. The following year she became the first ever woman to move the Address in reply to the Queen's Speech on the opening of Parliament as well as the first politician to appear on television.

In 1937 Parliament passed Horsburgh's Methylated Spirits (Scotland) Bill. This Bill was intended to curb the use of Red Biddy, a potentially lethal concoction of cheap wine and Methylated spirits. Two years later she became the first woman to move two Acts of Parliament when she toughened the adoption laws so that children could not be sent abroad to unknown parents. Horsburgh's awesome list of achievements continued; in 1939 she was awarded the CBE and became Parliamentary Secretary to the Minister of Health, then Parliamentary Secretary to the Ministry of Food. In 1945 Horsburgh became the first Scottish female Privy Councillor but lost her seat as Labour swept to power. She had better luck at Manchester Moss Side in 1950 and the following year was appointed as Minister for Education. From 1953 to 1954 Horsburgh became the first Conservative woman to have a cabinet position.

Florence Horsburgh was also the first ever woman to be awarded an Honorary Diploma of the Royal College of Surgeons, and also helped establish the United Nations. From 1959, one year after the House of Lords admitted women; she became a life peer as Baroness Horsburgh, as well as a member of the Council of Europe. There can be few people whose life has included so many firsts, and who was responsible for breaking so many barriers. Florence Horsburgh deserves a mention in any list of significant Scotswomen.

Today there is nothing unusual about a woman politician, and Scotland has had many that will be remembered. Other parties as well as the Conservatives have made their political mark. For Labour there was Clarice McNab, Wendy Alexander and Margaret Herbison and for the SNP Winnie Ewing, Wendy Wood and Margo MacDonald. The Scottish Socialists and Liberal Democrats have also had a quota of vibrant personalities.

Since the late 19th century, women have been involved in Trades Unions, either for occupations that involve only women, or for those that have a mixed gender membership. Given the history of Dundee, it is perhaps not surprising that the first woman to be the General Secretary of a Trade Union should be a Dundonian. Born in 1920, Margaret Fenwick first fought the management when, as a 15-year-old apprentice weaver, she argued for equal pay with older weavers who were doing the same work. She won her argument, and that same year joined the Jute, Flax and Kindred Textile Operators Union.

Fenwick became the Assistant Secretary of the Union at the age of 28, but first came to public attention in 1961 when mill managers announced a 5% pay raise for men, but only 4% for women. The announcement rekindles decades-old discontent about pay inequality, but only when Fenwick called for a strike was the matter addressed. With both women and men out on strike, the managers conceded to Fenwick's demands and both genders received an equal award. Men were still paid more but Fenwick's negotiations gradually won small concessions until the pay equalised in 1975.

By that time Fenwick had become the first female General Secretary of the Union. To concentrate on her Union activities, Fenwick gave up her weaving work. She proved a successful campaigner, becoming a member of the Jute Joint Council and always working for better pay, conditions and holidays. In 1973 she was awarded an MBE for her services to the jute industry.

Scotswomen continue to involve themselves in politics, on either side of the political fence and at every level from Union members to top-flight politicians. At one time there was hope for Wendy Alexander to be nominated as First Minister for Scotland, and perhaps in the not too distant future Scotland might well have a woman First Minister. The old time suffragettes would raise a sturdy cheer; then, being Scotswomen would probably criticise her policies and plan a vigorous protest.

Chapter 19

Women and War

> Women adore a martial man
> William Wycherley

Ever since the Dark Ages, war has been a business for men. While knights and soldiers marched boldly off to war, their ladies and wives remained behind to care for the children and manage the house. However, through the ages there have been a surprising number of women involved in military affairs, some on the sidelines, and others right in the forefront of battle.

One of the most controversial was Christian Davies, also known as Mother Ross. Dressed like a man, with her tricorne hat, long red coat and heavy riding boots, Davies carried the carbine and sword of the Scots Dragoons, the regiment with whom she rode and fought in the 1690s. The Historical Records of the regiment presume that she was brave, but also point out that she was a 'very coarse woman.' Perhaps nothing else could be expected in that period of brutal discipline and even more brutal battles.

Many women would know army life as the mother, sister or wife of a soldier. Their experience of war was of waiting for news and of constant dread that their man would not return from the field. When tragic news arrived, there would be deep mourning. A verse from the traditional song of the Jacobite wars puts their feelings succinctly:

'Ochone, ochone, O Donald O
Ochone, ochone ochrie
Nae woman in this whole warld wide
Sae wretched now as me.'

In the 17th century there was a distinctive mercenary tradition in Scotland. Thousands of men poured into Europe to fight in the great religious wars. Many of the officers brought their wives with them. Although most were anonymous, occasional references in letters and diaries bring others to life. When Colonel William Forbes was wounded in the groin at Nurnberg, he seemed to spend his convalescence writing letters. In one he related how the surgeon removed 'more than 130 pieces of bone' from his wound, and then mentioned a Captain Wardlaw, 'whose wife is a Forbes,' and who had not been paid. The tie of clan was powerful as he demanded help for Isabella Forbes, whose husband was killed in action and who was struggling to care for what sounds like an adopted family. The children's father was Captain Pringle, while their un-named mother had been killed by a cannon ball at Brieg. Scotswomen appeared to haunt the danger areas of Europe.

Throughout the 18th and 19th centuries, many Scottish regiments discouraged officers from marrying until they reached a certain rank. Young subalterns simply could not afford to keep up with mess bills and tailor's bills as well as the financial demands of a wife. When they did marry, officer's wives found themselves part of a new family, with a definite social system. The Colonel's wife was as much in charge of the women as the Colonel was of the regiment; her word was law. On the other hand, a Scottish regiment was a family; the Colonel's wife was the matriarch who gave advice and ensured that everything ran smoothly and properly. If the regiment were posted abroad, a good Colonel's wife would hire the best servants for her women, and check their work for efficiency.

Wives abroad also shared the discomforts of their men. When Lady Errol accompanied her husband to the Crimean War in 1854, she lived in his tent very near to the Russian lines. With equipment at a minimum, there was only one camp bed between them, and when, many years later, a grandchild asked if the bed had been hard, Lady Errol shook her head.

'I don't know my dear,' she replied, 'His Lordship had the bed and I slept on the ground." Military chivalry, it seemed, had ended.

Compassion, however, had not. Mary Seacole was the daughter of a Scottish father and a black mother. She grew up as a slave in Jamaica, and when the Crimean War broke out she used her own money to reach the front. While Flora Nightingale has been rightly remembered as the Lady with the Lamp, Mary Seacole worked just as hard to nurse the sick and wounded soldiers. Using herbal remedies that she possibly learned from her mother, Mary became immensely popular with the soldiers, and when she came to Britain, Queen Victoria met her.

During the 19th century and for much of the 20th, every regiment could expect at least one posting to India. There were many reasons for ordinary soldiers to dread the prospect. As well as the distance, dust and disease, the only relief from barrack room boredom was the possibility of active service. During the reign of Queen Victoria, military expeditions were frequent, but in 1857 the Mutiny shattered the Honourable East India Company and altered the relationship between Indian and Briton. Indian sepoys had been discontented for a number of years, but matters came to a head when a rumour spread that the British were trying to destroy their caste by smearing cartridges with animal fat. The resulting explosion of violence saw army wives, including Scotswomen, murdered in Cawnpore and besieged in many places, most notably Lucknow. The near contemporary *History of the Revolt in India* numbers the people who were trapped within the Residency at Lucknow. It mentions 'Ladies: 69. Ladies, children of: 68. Other women: 171. Other women, children of: 196.'

The Englishwoman Julia Ingles, wrote about the experiences that she shared with a number of Scotswomen, and her account could serve as a microcosm of a Victorian officer's wife. Only 23-years-old, she was on her way to church with her 43-year-old husband, Colonel Inglis of the 32nd, when the mutiny reached Lucknow. Packed away to safety, she promptly caught smallpox, but when the mutineers began to ravage the city she rose from her bed. 'It was fearful to see how near the wretches were to us,' Ingles reported, as her husband made preparations to defend the city.

Food was rationed, with women receiving three quarters of the men's allowance. 'Our ladies were…put to sore straits as the siege continued,' Ingles wrote, 'they had no servants and had to cook their own food and wash their own clothes.' As always in such situations, most women accepted the challenge. They tended the sick and wounded, checked supplies and ammunition and loaded the muskets for the men. Even as mutineer's bullet's killed their husbands, and smallpox, scurvy, cholera and dysentery ravaged their ranks, women continued to work.

Ingles was present as kilted Highlanders cut their way through the Mutineer lines, but the newcomers were themselves besieged. Colin Campbell led the final relief expedition, and his address to the 93rd Highlanders, some of whose great grandfathers had enlisted for the Countess of Sutherland, was memorable.

'We have to rescue helpless women and children from a fate worse than death…keep well together, and use the bayonet.'

The 93rd did as they were ordered, despite heavy casualties. It was a Scotswoman, known to history as Highland Jessie, who first heard the pipes of the relief column whispering across the stifling heat of India. Fittingly, they played *The Campbells are Coming* and the women and children, including Julia Inglis were rescued. Her adventures, however, were not over, for she was again fired upon at Cawnpore, but came safely through to Calcutta and shipped home, only for the ship to be wrecked off Ceylon. Julia survived that too, and lived until 1904.

In 1891, most of the military tension in India concentrated on the North-West Frontier, where Russian troops were annually expected to invade. However the North-East frontier could also be troublesome. Manipur was one of the small states of that frontier, a land of hills and heat, forests and insects with no road link to India. It was nominally independent, with a small garrison of Ghurkhas, a political officer named Frank St Clair Grimmond and Ethel, his wife. When a civil war erupted, the British sent 400 Ghurkhas to restore order, but their initial attempt failed. The Manipur army captured and murdered a peace deputation of senior British officers. Frank St Clair Grimmond was among the dead. When none of the junior officers stepped forward Ethel St Clair took command.

There were many miles of jungle between Manipur and the nearest British garrison, and Ethel did not know how the Manipur army would react, but she marched at the head of her small army. After a hot, steep climb, Ethel brought them 3000 feet up a jungly hill, when she met a detachment of Ghurkhas under their British officer. Only then did she break down at the loss of her husband. The *Illustrated London News* termed Ethel as the 'Heroine of Manipur' while the government awarded her the Royal Red Cross and a life pension. Today she is largely forgotten.

Despite such escapades, warfare was a relatively rare hazard for army wives in the heyday of Empire. Loneliness, heat and disease were much worse, so the highways, byways and forgotten garrisons of Empire were the last post for many women and children. Today grass grows rank over graves that once were tended with care and sorrow, while tombstones crumble in the tropic heat. The original messages were often poignant. 'The Lord giveth and the Lord taketh away, blessed be the name of the Lord,' was a favourite for children in the middle of the 19th century. Others were bolder, such as the Malta grave for four and a half year old Missie, 'I'm gone to Jesus, will you come?' The Empire may have been glorious on the map, but the women who gave the best years of their lives to its creation, and who cried over the graves of their men and children, must have cursed that so much of the world should be tinted pink.

Throughout history, some women have looked fondly on men in uniform. In return, soldiers have responded with smiles, promises and often a sexual experience. Sometimes women fall for soldiers of another nationality, such as the young woman from Penicuik who befriended a French prisoner of war in 1814. When the girl became pregnant, her friends advised her not to say who the father was, for the French were still the enemy. Advised to blame a local boy, the woman shook her head fiercely. 'That won't work,' she said, 'what would I say when the bairn begins to speak?' That story may be apocryphal, but it does illustrate that sexual attraction could far outweigh national considerations.

It was more common for a Scotswoman to marry, or at least favour, a Scottish soldier. The army, however, often frowned on such liaisons. In 1795 army regulations ordered officers to prevent the men from marrying. In 1848 the standing orders of the 90th regiment, the Perthshire Light Infantry, stipulated that no women were to be allowed to live in the barracks unless they were 'useful in cooking, &c.' Furthermore, men were 'on no account to marry' without the permission of the commanding officer. The Orders pointed out the 'inconveniences' and 'evils' that befall a regiment 'encumbered with Women: poverty and misery are the inevitable consequences.' The officers were ordered to deter the men from marrying, while the men, apparently, would in time 'be much obliged to them for having done so.' In 1867 there was a Royal Commission on recruiting, during which a Colonel Collingwood Dickson reported that Scotswomen were apt to marry a soldier 'at once without reflecting,' while young women in England were more careful.

P

Perhaps there was good reason for the officers not to wish their men to marry. Life for a soldier's wife in the 19th century was brutal, sordid and often tragic. There were no designated married quarters in the barracks, so only a thin blanket screened the marriage bed from a roomful of men. Privacy was an unheard of luxury, there was no consideration for children and poverty was expected. Wives were expected to pay for their room and keep by doing the washing, cooking and general small tasks for the men of their regiment.

To most of the ordinary soldiers that garrisoned India in the early 20th century, women were something that existed in a different life. Still only permitted to marry if the colonel permitted, soldiers watched the married quarters roll with despairing eyes. Officers above the rank of Captain, warrant officers and sergeants could marry but only one in ten of the privates were allowed a wife. It was no wonder that men visited the red light districts such as the Nadge in Poona. Some regiments had unofficial brothels, others held periodical medical inspections, but homosexuality and masturbation were not unknown. Perhaps the officers, fresh from their male-only public schools, believed that single-sex institutions were normal, but the men often longed for a more natural lifestyle.

There was an old saying in the army. 'Officers had ladies, sergeants had wives and the rankers had women'. If life could be tough for officer's ladies, it was hell on earth for the women.

Whatever the army thought about women, sometimes Scotswomen showed their disapproval of the army. During the American War of Independence, an Irish regiment was stationed at Perth. There were no barracks for the men, so together with their wives; they were billeted with the townsfolk. Under stoppages for some misdemeanour, the men were paid even less than their normal starvation wage, so it was hardly surprising that many scoured the countryside for food. The army disapproved of such private enterprise and awarded up to 500 lashes for those caught. At length the washerwomen were disgusted at the sight and sound of men being publicly flogged, and attacked the officers responsible. According to the *Traditions of Perth*, the women caught the adjutant, stripped him of his trousers and treated him to a 'handsome flogging on the bare posteriors.'

When war came, or the regiment was sent overseas on a tour of duty, only a certain number of wives were permitted to accompany their men. At the beginning of the 19th century, British army regulations stipulated 60 women for every 1000 men. Each regiment selected those travelling by lot, and the remainder was left behind to cope as best they could. Some took in washing, some worked in the sweated labour trade, and a number joined the desperate army of prostitutes that swarmed around every port and barrack city in Britain. They were not disloyal to their men; merely starving in a country that their husband was helping defend. At a time when overseas postings could last a decade or more and disease killed tens of thousands, the wife knew that she might never see her man again.

Army wives, however, were tough. During the long French wars of the early 19th century, many marched with the army. They helped carry the packs and muskets and nursed the many sick. After each bloody battle, the wives searched through piles of dead and horrendously wounded men for their husbands. Sometimes they had to fight off the terrible creatures who stripped the wounded of possessions and clothes and often slit their throat. A painting showing such a scene hangs in the Deutsches Historisches Museum in Berlin, possibly by William Heath or the Scottish artist John Heaviside Clark. Among the women and children searching for their menfolk, a Scotswoman holds the head of a dead Highland soldier while her two children look on. It is a picture of anguish and agony that shows some of the true sordid horror of war. There is also a French print of 1815 that shows a Highland soldier and his wife and children. The wife appears suspiciously well dressed in a long dress of plaid, under a light coloured cape. She has a fashionable hat on her head and carries a basket. Although the picture will be idealised, it does show the army wife as a real human person, not the victim or demonised myth often portrayed in British sources.

When the army advanced across Spain or Holland, the wives marched in the rear, with only the lucky hitching a lift on an ammunition cart or baggage wagon. When the army retreated, the women, often encumbered with children, followed. Many trailed behind or fell victim to cold, exposure or rape by the pursuing French or local villagers. The widows suffered most, for a woman without a husband had no helpmate on campaign. For that reason there was little mourning period, a wife could become a widow on Monday and a bride by Friday. The first marriage might have been for love, but the second was sheer necessity.

The wars of the 20th century made many changes to the relationship between Scotswomen and the army. The start of the First World War saw men rushing to the colours. Some men, such as those in agriculture and the merchant navy, were exempt from military service even after conscription, but many still volunteered. It was not unknown for women, particularly those from middle class backgrounds, to hand out white feathers as a mark of cowardice to men they considered were shirking their duty.

During the First World War, Elsie Inglis, a Scottish female surgeon, sent all-woman ambulance units to the front in France and Serbia. She also established military hospitals in Serbia in 1916. The Austrians captured her, but sent her home, whereupon Inglis formed a voluntary hospital corps and travelled to the Russia, where she remained until the Revolution. Although male surgeons and doctors were often hostile toward women such as Inglis, the sick and wounded soldiers welcomed their presence.

At home, the need for men at the various fighting fronts caused a labour shortage. At first managers filled their vacancies with men taken from retail work, retirement or unemployment, but women were soon recruited, quickly trained and expected to work alongside the men. By 1918 women were working in finance and commerce, in local and national government, in transport and in the service sector. The most remembered image, however, is of women who worked in the munitions and chemical factories. Many had been transferred from domestic service; others had recently left school.

Work in the munitions factories was hard, unpleasant and often dangerous. Most of the women accepted that their work was temporary, and all realised that women had been working in factories for well over a century. However, by emphasising the part that women played to win the war, government propaganda highlighted their importance. It is possible that after the Suffragette campaigns, the government used their wartime efforts as an excuse to award women the vote. By 1922, post war depression ensured that few of the 'duration only' women were working.

Only two decades after the War to End Wars, the armed services were again at full stretch to defend an ungrateful world from tyranny. Once again women were called into unfamiliar roles, and once again they responded with skill and dedication. Between 1939 and 1945, the number of women workers increased dramatically in every sphere from engineering to transport and the building trade. Some worked in the factories that made strips of foil that were dropped to fool German radar during the invasion of Normandy. Women worked as blacksmiths and welders; outdoors in shipbuilding yards, operated cranes and drove ambulances. One of these women workers was Bella Keyzer, who worked as a welder in the Caledon shipyard in Dundee during the Second World War. Unusually, she returned to work in the mid 1970s, when the Equal Opportunities Act began to bite. Although she was the only woman manual worker amongst hundreds of men, she did not experience any ill feeling. Indeed, she said, the only problem was when the hooter sounded to mark the end of the day, when the flood of departing men nearly rushed her off her feet. Some women worked as lumberjacks in the Women's Forestry Service. Although their wages were slightly over half what men earned, many remained in the labour market after the war. They had tasted economic freedom and liked the flavour.

Many countrywomen took in evacuees from the cities, while all over Scotland women took in refugees from countries overrun by the Germans.

Not all women were patriotic. Jessie Jordan was born in Glasgow in December 1887. After a harsh childhood, Jesse became a talented dressmaker, exhibiting in the 1901 Glasgow Exhibition. Unfortunately, there were few careers in dressmaking, so at the age of 16 Jesse became a maid in various parts of the country. In Dundee she met Frederick Jordan, a German waiter.

In 1907, at the age of 18, Jesse and Frederick moved to Germany, where they married. After the birth of a daughter, Frederick was called up for service during the First World War, but he died of pneumonia. When Jesse sorted out his belongings she is said to have found a letter from another woman. Deeply hurt at losing what was to prove the love of her life, Jordan learned hairdressing and started a salon in Hamburg, but by 1919 the war had ended and there was prejudice and bitterness against the British. She returned to live with her mother in Perth, but by now she was an outsider. In 1920 Jordan returned to Germany where she married a relative of her husband. At first everything moved smoothly. Jordan, who seemed to have a great deal of talent, opened a small chain of hairdressing shops, but in 1936 her second marriage failed and again assumed the name of her first husband. As she was about to return to Scotland, a friend asked her to 'verify certain information that was already in the hands of the Germans.' With no reason to feel loyalty to Britain, bored and deeply unhappy with life, she agreed.

Back in Scotland, Jesse obtained £150 from a German aunt and opened her own hairdressing business in Dundee. Her business seemed to prosper, so she could afford to hire a cleaner, leaving her time to style hair and attend her other occupations. However, the cleaner, Mary Curran realised that Jesse spent a great deal of effort in making maps. When Curran found a plan of the Tay Bridge, with the word 'Zeppelin' emblazoned across the front, she knew that Jesse was something other than a hairdresser. Further investigations unearthed a map of Scotland and a leaflet of code words, plus a number of letters from the United States, at least one of which was to be forwarded to Germany. With Europe buzzing with suspicion, German armies marching into various countries and talk of war on many lips, the cleaner advised her husband of her discoveries and together they told the police.

The Dundee police took Curran's discoveries seriously and, together with MI5, mounted a full-scale surveillance operation against this hairdresser who had so recently come from Germany. After fifteen weeks, they had collected enough information to act. In addition to maps showing Britain's coastal defences and military installations, the police discovered that Jesse was collecting letters from German spies in the United States. On March 2nd 1938 the police arrested her at her shop.

Jesse was tried at Edinburgh Sheriff Court. She agreed that she had photographed Southampton Docks and that she had acted as a post office for mail between the United States and Germany, but pleaded not guilty to spying. She had also mapped the Fife and Dundee coastal defences and drawn government buildings, but although she was found guilty, the judge was lenient. Sentenced to four years in prison, Jesse was interned during the war and afterward deported back to a shattered Germany, where she died nine years later. Perhaps it would be easier to see Jesse Jordan as another victim, but she was also a traitor to her country.

During this war, many women also donned uniform. As well as joining the Land Army that grew food for a nation that was again under siege, where the most common complaint concerned the cut of the uniform. Others joined the WRENS or the WRAAF or worked as nurses dealing with horrific wounds at bases themselves under threat of shellfire or bombardment.

With the return of peace, many women were reluctant to return to the poor housing and poor wages of the pre-war days. Thousands preferred to work in retail or light engineering firms rather than in the old mills with their long hours and low wages. Some had learned new skills and gained new confidence, while others opted out of the work force completely as their men could demand higher wages from an employment market suddenly short of labour.

Overall, women were as directly affected by war as men. In the past their role was seen as passive although the actions of individuals such as Elsie Inglis and Ethel St Clair Grimmond proved that women were quite capable of assertiveness even in military matters. Since the late 20th century, the service world has expanded for women, so now they can fill nearly every military position and rise to high rank. A Scotswoman has even passed the extremely rigorous course for entry to the Royal Marines. The future role of women with the military could be very different to that of the past.

Chapter 20

Women in Medicine and Education

> Education is a leading out of what is already in the pupils soul
> Muriel Spark

Until comparatively modern times, a lack of scientific knowledge meant that medicine depended on traditional remedies, luck and a strong constitution for success. There were some specialists, such as the Beatons of the Western Isles, whose knowledge was prodigal, and whose recommendation of a combination of healthy living with a good diet was well ahead of its time. Others medical workers included bone-setters who worked only on broken or dislocated bones and female masseurs who eased aches and pains.

In the 17th century, surgeons normally served an apprenticeship, like any other tradesmen. Working without any anaesthetic other than strong spirits, they would set bones, haul out aching teeth, attempt to kill intestinal worms and amputate the occasional arm or leg. Often the patient survived, although not surprisingly most delayed the surgery until there was no alternative. Although all surgeons were officially men, in 1641 the Edinburgh surgeons were so alarmed that women had been infiltrating their occupation that they complained to parliament.

Physicians, however, were altogether different. They attended either the Faculty of Physicians and Surgeons at Glasgow, founded in 1599, or the 1681 Edinburgh College of Physicians, afterward often completing their studies at Paris or Leyden. Only men could become physicians.

With minimal birth control measures, many women were either pregnant or nursing babies for upwards of twenty years. Some historians suggest that two out of three women would die during their childbearing years, often during childbirth or of puerperal fever in the immediate aftermath. It was not until the 17th century that British university medical schools taught midwifery, and from that time, male midwives or doctors took over the management of these pregnant women who could afford their fees. The poor majority had to resort to the granny-woman, their mother or a female relative, but some of the untrained women who acted as midwives had vast experience.

Perhaps the pregnant poor were not so unfortunate, for Buchan's acclaimed *Domestic Medicine* of 1739 recommended taking 'half a pound' of blood from the arm of a woman who was believed to be in danger of a miscarriage. The infertile, apparently, could be cured by a diet of milk and vegetables. Nonetheless, Buchan also gave some sound advice: mothers should suckle their own children rather than handing them to a wet-nurse, and the poor should live in dry houses. Unfortunately, many thousands of poor women lived in shocking conditions and could not afford the time off work to feed yet another of their brood of children.

Even after they emigrated, many Scotswomen seemed to have a vocation in midwifery. Annie McKinnon emigrated from Glenshee in 1869 and shortly after her arrival in New Zealand married the manager of a sheep station. When he died she moved to the South Island town of Fairlie and worked as a midwife. The locals soon learned that 'Granny' McKinnon would overcome any obstacle to help deliver babies, often travelling miles over terrible roads and in bad weather. Mary MacGregor from Lanarkshire was already a midwife before she immigrated to New Zealand. Settling at Stockton in the South Island, she became known as 'Doctor' MacGregor as she travelled on horseback or foot to see to the pregnant women of the district.

Edinburgh University gained its first professor of midwifery in 1781, and began to teach obstetrics in 1825, while Glasgow initiated a lying-in hospital for women in labour in 1792. While some admitted any pregnant women, others allowed only respectable married women and barred single mothers. Naturally, doctors used the patients as teaching aids for the students. Equally naturally, many women preferred to have their babies at home, among familiar surroundings and faces. Unqualified female midwives continued to operate until at least 1902, when the Midwives Act demanded that all midwives should pass an examination. Forty-four years later the National Health Service Act at last gave universal care to women during and immediately after pregnancy.

Scotswomen, however, did not sit back and wait for men to doctor them. As well as the midwives and the wise women who used herbs and potions, there were women who hoped to become scientifically trained doctors. It was an Englishwoman, Sophia Jex-Blake who cracked open the door of formal medicine and allowed women to peer through. She entered Edinburgh University in 1869, to great hostility from some of her male colleagues and teachers. Many men honestly believed that it was indecent for young women to study anatomy. Jex-Blake obtained her degree abroad, later returning to Edinburgh to open a medical school of her own. Her Bruntsfield Hospital was solely for women and children, while other women, notably Alice Jane Shannon Ker and Jessie MacLaren MacGregor, followed her thrusting footsteps. In 1876 the Russell Gurney Enabling Act allowed women to study medicine and in 1894 Scotland saw her first female medical graduates in Marion Gilchrist and Lily Cumming. Perhaps better remembered was Elsie Inglis.

Born in Naina Tal, India, in 1864, Elsie Inglis became one of the first woman medical students at both Edinburgh and Glasgow Universities. Like Jex-Blake, she found that the male students did not take their women colleagues seriously, while on graduating, male doctors revealed a staggering level of prejudice. In 1891 Elsie Inglis founded Edinburgh's second medical school for women, but was well aware that much more was required. For a city the size of Edinburgh, maternity facilities were both limited and primitive. Childbirth was one of the most dangerous periods in a woman's life, turning what should have been the culminating experience of creation into an agony of fear and pain. One reason, Inglis believed, was the lack of understanding shown by some male doctors and midwives for their female patients.

Accordingly in 1901 Inglis founded a maternity hospital in Edinburgh with an all-female staff. A supporter of women's suffrage, in 1906 Inglis created the Scottish Women's Suffrage Federation, but she was a doctor first and set up ambulance services and hospitals to help wounded soldiers during the First World War.

By the 1920s, woman doctors were not the rarity they had been, although they were still in a minority. Indeed it was not until the Second World War that most hospitals admitted female doctors. One of the finest of these doctors, and a woman who left a trail for others to follow, was Margaret Fairlie.

Born in 1891, the daughter of an Arbroath farmer, Margaret Fairlie graduated from St Andrews University in 1915 as Bachelor of Medicine and Bachelor of Surgery. Seven years later she became a Master of Surgery and Doctor of Medicine. The Hospital for Sick Children appointed her as House Physician. Fairlie also worked at Perth Royal Infirmary and used her surgical skills as Resident Surgical Officer in Manchester's St Mary's Hospital before moving to Dundee Royal Infirmary.

It was in Dundee that Fairlie made her reputation and spent most of her professional life. After establishing a high grade Gynaecological and Obstetrical practice, Fairlie operated as an obstetrician over an area that encompassed Dundee and Angus. Fairlie added to her expertise at the Marie Curie Foundation in Paris, after which she became a pioneer in the use of radium therapy. With radium scarce, Fairlie used her influence to obtain all that she could for the Dundee Royal Infirmary and for the private practice that she also ran. In 1936 the Royal College of Obstetricians and Gynaecologists elected her a Fellow, but further honours were to come.

Right from its inception, the University of Dundee had been a progressive institution that taught women in equality with men. Now, in 1940 it became the first Scottish University to appoint a female professor. Margaret Fairlie was to hold the chair of Professor of Gynaecology and Midwifery from 1940 until 1956. Her students regarded her with a mixture of awe and affection, recognising her innate sympathy but also her obvious scholarship. While some called her 'Maggie', the majority referred to her as 'The Madam' and treated her with respect.

Once the war was over, Professor Fairlie continued to seek new challenges. While retaining her chair, she also became Warden of the West Park Hall of Residence for women students at Dundee University. The professor travelled widely, both as a medical practitioner and in her professorial role. Her expertise as a surgeon was renowned and in her spare time she painted in watercolours. Even after her retirement in 1956 the honours kept on coming. In 1957 St Andrews University graced her with the honorary degree of Doctor of Letters, while Dundee Royal Infirmary made her Consultant Emeritus. Overall, Professor Fairlie combined the skill of a surgeon with the patience of a teacher. In many ways she was the culmination of years of pushing by women to gain equality in medicine and education.

Women such as Caroline Doig of Forfar, who became the first woman member of the Council of the Royal College of Surgeons of Edinburgh, have followed her lead. Of them all perhaps Marie Stopes is among the best examples of a female Scottish scientist. Born in Edinburgh in 1880, she was an amazing woman who pioneered the world's first birth control clinic as well as being an expert on coal and fossils. She was also the first female scientist to be appointed at Manchester University and they were lucky to have her. But all these women have benefited from the sacrifices and endeavour of the early educational pioneers. Without basic schooling, there would have been no woman doctors.

There had been formal schooling in Scotland in the Dark Ages, but details are unknown, as the earliest existent records relate to the 12th century. The Church was involved in mediaeval education, mainly to create a class of learned priests although there was also a need for clerks to help the lords administer their lands. Girls of gentle blood were usually taught at home, but some were sent away to nunneries such as Haddington and Elcho for formal education. By the later middle ages, a few secular schools were accepting girls, where women were already breaking into the teaching profession. Women such as Katherine Bra, who signed the Dunfermline Burgh Court in 1493, were certainly literate.

Even before the Reformation, Scotland had around 100 schools, but during the 16th century this number multiplied. Most of the pupils were boys, but there were schools that catered for girls, much to the dismay of the Kirk. Not that the ministers were against the principle of female education; they encouraged everybody to be sufficiently learned to read the Bible, but they worried that schools outwith the control of the Kirk may slide into Catholicism.

The 1560 Book of Discipline outlined Scotland's education policy, allowing funding for schools to teach both genders. Only males, however, might go onto university education. By the later 17th century, there were schools specifically for girls, as well as sewing schools. Women ran many of these schools, although it is doubtful if the money-strapped spinsters or desperate widows were much better educated than their pupils were. Ignorance was rife, so in 1700 one Glasgow female teacher was accused of being a witch. Nevertheless, some landowners encouraged their tenants toward education. In 1688 the Baron of Stitchill fined any of his tenants whose children did not attend school, and insisted that girls should have at least two years education before going to a sewing school. In 1696 an Education Act spurred parishes to continue their educational duties despite the wide spread social and economic distress of the period. This Act fixed the salaries of schoolmasters at between 100 and 200 merks (between £5 11/1d and £11 2/2d) a year.

The Old Statistical Account of the 1790s confirms that most Scots, women as well as men could read and a fair proportion could also write. In some schools, such as in Ardchattan parish in Argyll, the wife of the schoolmaster was paid £3 by the Society for Propagating Christian Knowledge to teach 'young girls to spin and knit stockings'. There were, however, few women who could read and write with any fluency. Schoolmasters' wages rose in 1803, and houses of at least two rooms were to be built for them. Such was their low standing that many MPs and landlords protested at these 'palaces for dominies.' Not everybody agreed, and when the New Lanark Mills became operational, equal educational facilities were offered for boys and girls. Despite this bright note, however, most females enjoyed only basic education.

Some women, however, could startle the world. Mary Somerville, born Mary Fairfax, was one of these Border women who constantly appear on the world stage. After a childhood in Jedburgh, she moved to London in 1816 and, rather than spend her life in balls and conspicuous expenditure, chose to move in scientific circles. She also corresponded with eminent scientists from other countries, often in their native language. Recognised her as a talented mathematician, in 1827 Lord Brougham, the Reform politician, encouraged her to write and publish.

In her *Personal Recollections of Mary Somerville*, she wrote that this 'letter surprised me beyond expression. I thought Lord Brougham must have been mistaken with regard to my acquirements and naturally concluded that my self-acquired knowledge was so far inferior to that of the men who had been educated in our universities, that it would be the height of presumption to attempt to write on such a subject or, indeed, on any other.'

However, Somerville did write, squeezing in time between the demands of her family. 'A man can always command his time under the plea of business, a woman is not allowed any such excuse. I was sometimes annoyed when, in the midst of a difficult problem, someone would enter and say 'I have come to spend a few hours with you.' Frequently I hid my papers as soon as the bell announced a visitor lest anyone should discover my secret.'

She analysed Pierre Somin Laplace's *Mecanique Celeste* and in 1831 published a simplified account for the general reader, named *The mechanism of the Heavens*. A keen and vociferous supporter of women's emancipation, Somerville College in Oxford was named in her honour.

In general though, many authorities believed that educating women was a waste of time. The working classes required only sufficient schooling to make them useful employees who were used to time and work discipline, while too much education ruined middle class girls for marriage. According to contemporary wisdom, men wanted an amiable, inoffensive and ornamental wife to look at him with respect. What passed for feminine education was often only knowledge of painting and needlework, a superficial grasp of unconnected facts and the ability to play a musical instrument.

Nonetheless, some Scottish girls were sent to one of the growing number of girls' schools in England. These schools prepared young women for their station in life, with writing, reading and arithmetic, with 'lace making, plain needlework, raising pastry, sauces and cookery.' The girl's lives were unbelievably regimented, with no recreational exercise except a stiffly controlled walk. A great deal of emphasis was on learning, deportment and manners. There were also schools in Scotland; in 1848 the Newington Academy in Edinburgh had a 'Young Ladies Department that operated between 10 Am and noon, and from two PM until half past three. More impressively, the Scottish Institution for the Education of Young Ladies at Moray Place included book keeping and astronomy as well as maths, languages and science.

The next major step in schooling was the 1872 Education (Scotland) Act, which again confirmed mass education for all, but this time under the watchful eye of elected school boards. By the end of the century some female teachers such as Lila Clunas an elementary teacher in Dundee were also suffragettes. Others suffragettes such as Agnes

Husband of Tayport, were members of school boards and struggled to change matters from within. Even those fortunate women who managed to achieve an education were restricted in their choice of career.

However some private colleges did an excellent job. Arbroath Museum holds an Album with various pieces of poetry written by the women aged between 16 and 18 who attended one such Edinburgh school in the late Victorian period. Some of these words of teenage wisdom and dreams, mostly written in verse, show a healthy respect for themselves:

> 'A man's a fool who tries by force or skill
> To stay the torrent of a woman's will
> For when she will, she will, you may depend on't
> And when she won't, she won't, so there's an end on't'

Others reveal an equally healthy and attractively innocent interest in men:

> '16 nods make one wink
> 16 winks make one smile
> 28 smiles make one kiss
> 4 kisses make one moonlight meeting
> 20 moonlight meetings make one match'

There is still an attempt to retain a modicum of Scots:

> 'Some say that kissing's a sin
> But I think its nane ava
> For kissing has been in this warld
> Since ever there was twa'

And there was an occasional more daring piece:

> 'The lady's waist is 22 inches round

A gentleman's arm is 22 inches long
How admirable are thy ways, o nature.'

The 1918 Education (Scotland) Act ensured that secondary education became free for every child in Scotland. The 20th century saw a movement from selective to comprehensive schools and a new focus on an inclusive University education.

Frustrated Scotswomen had long been hammering at the brass-bound doors of Higher Education, with Mary MacLean founding the Edinburgh Ladies Education Society in 1867. Lecturers from Edinburgh University frequently taught the women of this society, who were not however permitted to graduate. It was quite appropriate that St Andrews, site of Scotland's oldest university, should also be the home of the 1876 Association to Promote the Higher Education of Women. Unlike most other universities, St Andrews allowed women to attend classes, but only to diploma level. That same year the Russell Gurney Enabling Act permitted universities to grant degrees to women, while in 1889 the Universities (Scotland) Act finally allowed women to attend higher education on complete equality with men.

Shortly after the end of the First World War, those women who had been able to obtain a university education benefited from the Sex Discrimination (Removal) Act. With the professions no longer closed, Scotland should have experienced a flood of eager young women into the professions. Instead there was a slight trickle, as if the tap was in place, but a malignant plumber controlled the flow of water. However, the women who did unravel the Gordian knot of old school ties from the doorways of misogyny and tradition revealed how much talent had been lying latent. One such was Margaret Henderson, who in 1926 became Scotland's first female advocate.

While 20th century women could attend university, only one Scotswoman actually founded a university. Miss Mary Ann Baxter of Balgavies had been born in 1801 into one of Dundee's most important textile families. The Baxter family was renowned as benefactors, giving money to buy Baxter Park and founding a trust that eventually resulted in the creation of the Dundee Technical Institute, since promoted to Dundee Abertay University. When David Baxter died in 1872, most of his fortune passed to his sister, Mary Ann Baxter, a devout Christian with a genuine interest in education. Mary had assisted in creating Baxter Park and now continued the family tradition of benevolence by giving over £3000 to the London Missionary Society for a steam yacht. The Society named the yacht *Ellengowan* after Mary's Broughty Ferry home, and in 1875 even named a river in Mary's honour. A few years later Mary bought another boat for the Missionary Society, as well providing funds toward a tender for *Mars*, the training ship for wayward and orphaned boys.

Mary Ann Baxter also gave £5000 for a convalescent hospital at Barnhill and helped found a very necessary Sailor's Home opposite the Custom House in Dundee. At that time seamen often haunted the most disreputable quarters of ports, spending their time and money in brothels and low public houses. A Sailors Home provided a clean and often Christian environment where they would be safe from exploitation and the notorious Boarding Masters that often doped the unwary before dumping them onto some hell ship. Mary Ann Baxter ensured that moneys were available for Dundee's Albert Institute and the YMCA, and helped found Panmure Church.

However, missionary work was not Mary's prime concern. At one time Sir David had been presented with the idea of establishing a university college within Dundee. He had not pursued the plan, but his sister was more determined. Mary Ann Baxter knew that nearby St Andrews University was experiencing a diminishing number of students and limited courses, and realised that the expanding town of Dundee had the funds and population to help. Recognised as a 'clever and far seeing lady,' Mary suggested that Dundee house a college of St Andrews University, to which she was willing to contribute £120,000.

After much discussion, the deed to found the University was signed at the end of December 1881. University College Dundee was bound to promote 'the education of persons of both sexes and the study of science, literature and fine arts.' Mary had ensured that no religious subjects were taught, and nobody had to announce his or her religion as a condition of entry. The college opened in October 1883, but unfortunately Mary was too ill to attend the ceremony. Dundee was the first university in Scotland whose foundation charter insisted that women and men were taught with complete equality.

Although women could now attend university, there were still limited openings for them, especially if they came from a working class background. Most graduated to become teachers, better paid than the majority of working men and women, but there must have been potential for much more. Even when they became teachers, women faced discrimination, as they had to leave their position if they dared to marry. Despite acceptance into Higher Education, women still had not achieved equal opportunities.

By the early 1950s, the number of women teaching in Scottish schools rose to well over 25,000, although few reached the apex of their profession. However, things changed dramatically in the latter decades of the 20th century. Women at last managed to smash through the glass ceiling, becoming head teachers in primary and secondary schools, as well as doctors and professors at the expanding Scottish universities. By the end of the 20th century girls, who for so long had been marginalized, were outperforming boys in virtually every subject. Educational success has certainly been achieved, but the 21st century poses different challenges. Educated women now balance the stresses and achievements of carving out careers with the joys and sheer graft of keeping a marriage and raising a family.

Chapter 21

Women of Literature

> Some write, confin'd by physic; some by debt;
> Some, for 'tis Sunday; some, because 'tis wet
> Edward Young

If Scottish literature is mentioned, most people will be able to respond with a handful of names, mostly from the 19th century and possibly all males. Walter Scott and Robert Burns will be confidently quoted, with the possible inclusion of Stevenson and Barry, and an occasional mention of Irvine Walsh. However, Scotland has produced an amazing number of women novelists, poets and serious writers. Even to list them would take many pages of text, so a few samples will be selected.

The Gaelic culture of the Highlands and Islands was oral rather than written, with great emphasis on long stories, songs and music. Martin Martin, a Skye factor who toured the Western Isles at the end of the seventeenth century, mentioned that both men and women could be poets. One female poet was Mairearad Nigheah Lachlainn, who wrote for the MacLeans, and another was Mairi Nighean Alasdair Ruaidh, whose name is often anglicised to Mary MacLeod. Born in Rodel, Harris, she was the Bard to Sir Norman Macleod of Bernera, a position that revealed both her talent and her high status. Her poetry, a mixture of paeans of praise and laments, mainly relate to the MacLeod clan of the 17th century, the period in which she lived. She wrote formal court poetry in a style that linked the classical Gaelic of the middle ages with the more informal vernacular language that was taking its place.

What is perhaps even more noteworthy is her age, for Mary MacLeod peaked when she was upward of seventy, and lived for a further thirty years. At a time when most Lowland women died young, longevity was not unknown in the Highlands.

Mary MacDonald was a much later Gaelic poet. Born in Bunessan in Mull, her Gaelic air, *Child in the Manger* was noted during her lifetime, but achieved worldwide fame a century after her death when the title was altered to *Morning has Broken* and the words set to a sea shanty.

The Borders was another area of literary talent. Alison Rutherford was born in Selkirkshire in 1713, but became better known in Edinburgh under her married name of Cockburn. In common with many Scots, she wrote about her home area, with her 1765 version of 'Flowers of the Forest' so haunting that it can twist the understanding heart. She wrote in Fairmilee Tower, with the River Tweed a melodious background that can nearly be ascertained within her words. For the best effect, the listener should be at the field of Flodden or in one of the lonely Border valleys with a soft wind soughing through stark spring trees. Cockburn, however, was not the only woman to write of Flodden, for Jean Elliot, another Borderer and daughter of Gilbert Elliot of Minto House, also composed the words of 'Flowers of the Forest.'

Despite such interest in long gone battles, Alison Cockburn, was not inclined to dwell in the past. Much preferring the mixture of elegance and joviality that was social life in Edinburgh, she mixed with the elite and presided over balls and assemblies for more than six decades. At a time when the literary world was close knit, she thought that the young Walter Scott was a 'most extraordinary genius' long before he became famous, and exchanged flattery with Robert Burns.

The late 18th and early 19th century saw an interest in Romanticism, possibly as a reaction to the preceding Age of Reason. Walter Scott was arguably the greatest Scottish Romantic, but others also weaved their spell of words to create a false, if fascinating picture of Scottish history. Carolina Oliphant was a songwriter rather than a novelist, but her treatment of the Jacobite Risings helped create the romantic myths that are still partially believed today. Born only twenty years after the battle of Culloden, Carolina grew up through a childhood of Jacobite reminiscences. Both her father and grandfather had been out for the Stuart cause, with her father reputedly the last man to speak with Charles Stuart at Culloden. In reprisal, the Hanoverians had torched their house of Gask and sent Carolina's father into exile. Carolina wrote her famous song 'The Auld Hoose' to commemorate this event:

> 'The auld hoose, the auld hoose, deserted tho' ye be
> There can ne'er be a new hoose will seem sae fair tae me.'

There is also the possibility that the term 'auld hoose' refers to the House of Stuart, and the 'new hoose' is the House of Hanover. All his life, Carolina's father refused to recognise the Hanoverians as the King and Queen of Scotland or Britain. The Oliphant family jealously guarded the spurs, bonnet and white cockade that Charles had worn during the 1745 rising, so it was perhaps no wonder that Carolina's best remembered songs have Jacobite themes. 'Charlie is my Darling' is a bright, cheerful song of praise to the handsome young prince while 'Wi a hundred pipers' related to the actual Jacobite invasion of England. The melancholy 'Will ye no come back again?' is a desperate request to the departed prince to return to Scotland after the failure of the rising.

Carolina did not start writing until she was 30 years old, and, despite living at a time when polite society was becoming more anglicised, she wrote in Scots. The sad deterioration that had already set into the old Scots culture is shown by the imperfections of her language, into which many English words and phrases creep, but the attempt was genuine. Possibly many Scots female writers used their mother tongue in preference to English as a form of defiant cultural nationalism, a reminder that 1707 had seen a Union, not a conquest. Writing in Scots was also a reminder of the essentially classless spirit of Scotland at that time. Much of Scottish society remained vertically rather than horizontally divided, with place and name of birth as important as money or class. There was, however, still a gulf between those of gentle birth and the remainder, even though they spoke a similar language.

Perhaps there were literary Scotswomen from lower down the social scale, but it was the work of women such as Lady Lindsay, Lady Wardlaw, Alison Cockburn and Carolina Oliphant that has survived. Oliphant wrote as Mrs Bogan of Bogan and even after she married her second cousin, Major Nairne in 1806, she used a false name so that not even her husband knew of her talent. This self-imposed anonymity encouraged the public to credit other writers with the songs that Caroline, later Lady, Nairne wrote. Robert Burns was accepted as the author of her 'Land of the Leal,' which she had borrowed from an ancient song, 'How Now the Day Daws.'

Lady Nairne wrote an amazing number of songs that were popular throughout the nineteenth and much of the twentieth century. Her 'Caller Herrin' is often accepted as a genuine song of the Scottish fisherwomen, for its accurate depiction of a people and period that is now past. Her 'The Rowan Tree' is perhaps too sentimental to be sung now, despite the rowan being a tree of vast importance to our ancestors. Another of her songs, 'The Laird o' Cockpen' with its allusions to Midlothian, was a rewrite of a 17th century ballad whose bawdy verses 'When she cam ben, she bobbit' were bawled out in drinking howffs across Scotland. The original version related to an un-named Laird of Cockpen who 'kist the collier lass.' It is possible that the laird was Mark Carse who the Kirk Session rebuked in 1702 for his 'scandalous convers with Isabella Hall.' Knowing of the free sexuality of many of Scotland's women, it is to be hoped that Isabella Hall enjoyed her wanton behaviour.

It is very unlikely that Queen Victoria, or any of her ladies in waiting who also enjoyed Lady Nairne's work, would know the original words.

In a romantic, sentimental age, her songs of sanitised Jacobitism and respectable working people sounded sweet in the drawing rooms of polite society. Even Lady Nairne herself allowed her Jacobite past to slide away as she grew older. Rather than dream of a return of a departed dynasty, she became a religious writer and did charitable work for the poor in Edinburgh. Lady Nairne died at Gask in 1845, hopefully to be remembered as one of the great writers of Scottish songs.

Another Highland woman who wrote for a political cause was Mary MacPherson. Born in Skye in 1821, MacPherson was a nurse by profession, and turned to writing when she was falsely imprisoned in Inverness for theft. Initially her poetry protested her innocence, but gradually she widened her scope, fighting to support the crofters in their struggle for land reforms.

While these women poets worked within Scotland, Marjory Kennedy-Fraser took Scottish poetry to the world, before dredging half-forgotten songs from her own country. Marjory was born into a musical family, with one ancestor being the conductor of choirs in Perth while her father David Kennedy was a popular singer. As well as bearing her husband a brood of musical children, Marjory's mother was a talented pianist. As the children grew, David Kennedy trained four of them into a musical quartet, and when Marjory, the youngest was 15, he took them on the first stage of what would be a travelling life. In 1871 they performed in Edinburgh, singing Scottish songs at a time when Queen Victoria ensured that everything Scottish was in vogue. Pleased with their success, David Kennedy embarked on an ambitious Empire-wide tour.

Perhaps the life of a singer may sound peaceful, but the Kennedy's faced gales on their voyage to Australia, then sandstorms and a Biblical plague of locusts during their 18-month tour of the continent. Their songs appealed to the many exiles as they visited the cities and the small outback towns before crossing the Tasman Sea. The Kennedys found an equally enthusiastic audience among the Scots of Otago Province in New Zealand. Then it was across the Pacific to North America, where they faced frostbite while singing to the

Scottish communities in Canada. After a brief respite in Britain, the Kennedy's toured South Africa at a time when the country was ablaze with news of the Zulu War, before Marjory spent some time studying classical music in Italy.

Back in Edinburgh, Marjory married Alexander Fraser, but rather than change her name, hyphenated the surnames to become Marjory Kennedy-Fraser. The couple produced two children but, tragically, Alexander died in 1890. With the Kennedy family quartet broken up, Marjory began a new career as a music teacher, lecturing on classical composers, and Celtic music from Cornwall, Brittany and Ireland. In her spare time, she wrote a music column for the Edinburgh Evening News.

It was the painter John Duncan who encouraged Marjory into the next stage of her life. As the professor of Celtic Art at Chicago University, he travelled to Scotland to 'steep himself in Celticism.' In the summer of 1905, Marjory and John Duncan left the staid atmosphere of classical Edinburgh to visit the more remote of the Western Isles.

At one time mercenary soldiering had been the main career for the men of the Uists and Benbecula, now it was crofting and fishing. At the height of the herring season the bays were filled with fishing boats, while island woman gutted and packed fish. However, there were few facilities for the visitor and Marjory felt as if she had sailed 'out of the 20th century back at least to the 1600s.' There were no hotels on the island, no proper roads, no fences or even carts. Women carried peats on creels, lived with their men in black houses whose unmortared walls were topped with heather thatch. All the same, Marjory, in her biography *A Life of Song* wrote: 'I awoke the next morning and looked from my window out to the sea; I seemed to be on an enchanted island.'

While Walter Scott had been the first to take a wheeled vehicle into Liddesdale in his search for material, Marjory Kennedy-Fraser was the first professional lowland musical to tap the raw sources of Gaelic culture. On her first day in the Isles she met 'a little girl, Mary McInnes, who sat on my knee and sang island songs to me.' Marjory wrote down all that she heard, both from the people that she interviewed and those she heard singing at the island ceilidhs. As Martin Martin had discovered two centuries previously, both men and women sang with grace and untutored skill.

Some songs, such as *The Eriskay Lullaby, The Mermaids Croon* and *The Hebridean Mothers Song* had probably been sung for many centuries, while others, such as *The Skye Fishers Song* and *The Mull Fishers Song* were relatively modern. While there were long ballads, many songs illustrated the working life of the islanders and were sung at the milking and churning, reaping and waulking, or when the men were rowing the boats on the wild Atlantic. Delighted with what she had found, Marjory returned to the islands with a recording gramophone, complete with large horn. With most of the young people working, the older folk monopolised the theatre and performed the songs with which they had grown up, while Marjory recorded faithfully and played back to them. In her own way, Marjory was a pioneer of aural history as well as a musician, for without her work many of the correct tunes and Gaelic intonations may have been lost.

Barra, the southernmost large island of the Outer Hebrides, was a goldmine. Marjory recorded the 'Ballad of MacNeil of Barra', the 'Fairy Planet' and the ranting, incomparable 'Kismuil's Galley' that became a mainstay of folk singers throughout the 20th century. Working with the Reverent Kenneth MacLeod of Gigha, Marjory continued to collect songs. Where only a fragment remained, Marjory and MacLeod would fill in the gaps with suitable words, and on her return to Edinburgh, she would translate the words into English and work the aural music into print. Using her extensive musical knowledge, Marjorie also turned the songs into music that could be played on the piano or the more traditional harp. In 1909 Marjory Kennedy-Fraser came to what was the peak of her career when she had her *Songs of the Hebrides* published. It was the culmination of a lifetime of work with Scottish and classical music and it is unlikely that anybody else had the range and depth of skills necessary to locate, translate and arrange the Gaelic songs.

As a contrast to the Gaelic of Marjory Kennedy-Fraser, Marion Angus was an East Coast poet who wrote in Scots. Born in Aberdeen in 1866, Angus grew up in an Arbroath manse, as well as Aberdeen, Edinburgh and Helensburgh. Her books of verse include *Sun and Candlelight* of 1927 and *Lost Country* of 1937. Her best remembered work is *Alas Poor Queen*, a lament for Mary Queen of Scots.

Until the 19th century, women novelists were a novelty. Even at the beginning of that century, many of those women who did write masked their gender behind a male nom-de-plume. As the years rolled by and women recovered their collective self-confidence, female writers penned their own names on work that matched anything their male colleagues could produce. One of the most notable of the early 19th century writers was Lady Charlotte Susan Maria Bury.

With the lack of education among even middle class women, only the upper classes had the skill, as well as the spare time, to allow their ideas to flow from the sliced point of a quill. As the youngest daughter of the 5th Duke of Argyll, Lady Charlotte was one of these privileged women, but the quality of her work shines above any idea of class. Married twice, firstly to Colonel John Campbell in 1796, and again to the Reverent John Bury, Lady Charlotte had time to write sixteen novels, of which *Flirtation* and *Separation* are perhaps the best. As an antidote to the contemporary view of wives as sexless creatures to be worshipped on a pedestal, Lady Charlotte has also been credited with authorship of the 1838 *Diary Illustrative of the Times of George IV*, which is as risqué as anything written in the period.

Almost contemporary with Lady Charlotte, was Susan Edmonstone Ferrier. She was the tenth and youngest child of an Edinburgh solicitor who knew Walter Scott as a friend. Ferrier was thirty-five when her first novel, *Marriage,* was published. Like her later works, *The Inheritance* and *Destiny* the style and content were similar to Jane Austen's work, but written with a Scottish accent. Perhaps if she had lived a more outgoing life, Ferrier would be as well known as her work deserves, but she spent the best part of her life running her father's home. Walter Scott, however, rated her work very highly, terming her his 'sister shadow.' Much contemporary opinion believed that a woman could never have written books of such quality; they gave the honour to Scott. Possibly because the dialogue was in Scots, Ferrier's books never receive the attention they undoubtedly deserve.

Jane Welsh Carlyle is remembered for her letters, but perhaps should be admired for her fortitude in remaining married to the difficult Thomas Carlyle. As Samuel Butler acidly pointed out 'it was very good of God to let Carlyle and Mrs Carlyle marry one another and so make only two people miserable instead of four.' Jane Welsh Carlyle freely admitted marrying Carlyle from ambition, but surely paid for it with a relationship that was stormy at best. Her refusal to become a writer irritated her husband, they were not sexually compatible and Carlyle was a morbid recluse, but despite all these problems Carlyle missed her terribly when she died. The publication of her diaries and letters after his death reveals a writer of immense skill.

Less known and possibly of less talent, Clementina Graham had other claims to fame apart from her literary success with the novel *Mistification*. All her life she was proud of her descent from Graham of Claverhouse, while she also spoke of her friendship with Admiral Duncan, the victor of Camperdown. More unusually, and surely uniquely, when she was aged 95, Clementina Graham modelled for the figurehead of *Duntrune*, the Dundee Clipper Line vessel that was named after her house. She also launched and named the ship.

Of all the 19th century female novelists, Margaret Oliphant was perhaps the most prolific as well as the woman who write with most width and vision. Her fiction portrayed women in a realistic setting, not as mere helpmates of men, but as thinking creatures of experience in their own right. Oliphant was born in Wallyford, just outside Musselburgh, in 1828 as Margaret Wilson and in 1852 married Francis Wilson Oliphant, her artist cousin. When Francis died seven years later, Oliphant wrote professionally to pay back the £1000 debt he had left her and to support her children and those of her brother. Writing out of necessity, not as a hobby, possibly explains the sense of realism that adds backbone to even *A Beleaguered City* (1880), a superb tale of the supernatural.

She wrote her first novel at the age of 16 and her first published work, *Passages in the Life of Mrs Margaret Maitland* at the age of 21. Oliphant produced an amazing 100 novels and over 200 articles for Blackwood's Magazine, a notable literary publication. Her best books include *The Ministers Wife* of 1886, and *The Chronicles of Carlingford*, 1861 - 1876, studies of manners that include *The Rector and the Doctor's Family* [1863] and *Miss Marjoribanks* [1866]. Her superb *The Library Window* of 1895 possibly best reveals the width of her talent. Awarded a Civil List pension in 1868, Oliphant is surely one of the most professional of the 19th century female writers, earning the sobriquet, 'a feminist Trollop' for her application. To read a true picture of the reality of literary life for a Victorian woman, her posthumously published *Autobiography,* 1899, is priceless.

The sheer number of quality women authors in the Victorian period is fascinating. Perhaps the increase in education, coupled with a lack of alternative employment opportunities encouraged women to take up the pen, but the volume of their literary output is astonishing. The 20th century, however, saw only an increase in the number and influence of female authors.

Born in 1863, Violet Jacob was another woman born to a landed family. She was the daughter of the Laird of Dun beside Montrose. She was also a traveller, as she married Major Jacob and lived for some time in India, but her best-known works are her poems in the language of her native Angus. Her *Songs of Angus* (1915) and *More Songs of Angus* (1918) perhaps belong more to the fading Scotticism of the Victorian period than to the brutal realities of the 20th century, but they are still worth reading. Interestingly, her *Lairds of Dun,* a history of the area in which she grew up, is academically accurate and perhaps better reveals her talent as a historian.

Although she wrote neither poetry nor novels, Florence Marian McNeill should never be left out of any collection of Scottish writers. Born in Orkney in 1885 and raised in a manse, McNeill was educated locally, in Glasgow and in Europe, returning to Scotland to graduate in Glasgow University. She worked in London and Aberdeen, but her true vocation shone through in 1920 when her *History of Iona* was published. Her interest in folk culture became apparent nine years later when her *Scots Kitchen*, came out. With this book, McNeill reveals that Scotland possessed a vibrant culinary culture of her own. However, it was not until 1969 that the magnificent *The Silver Bough*, a four-volume collection of work on Scottish folklore and folk festivals was published. Standard reading for anybody with an interest in the subject, or as a general background to Scottish culture, *The Silver Bough* complemented the interest in folk music that has since spread around the globe.

Scotswomen naturally made their mark in the folk revival. One of the best was Jean Redpath, of Edinburgh, who also lectured in music in the United States. Isla St Clair, whose clear voice is surely unique, sings of farming and the sea with particular knowledge as she comes from a northeast fishing family. Alan Lomax once described Jeannie Robertson, the Aberdeen born singer as 'a monumental figure of world folk-song.' Her family were travelling folk, these wandering natives of Scotland who have for generations acted as a storehouse of traditional knowledge and tunes, so Robertson had a unique insight into her ancient culture.

Writing as Marie Corelli, Mary Mackay wrote romantic novels whose melodramatic content would not be successful today, but which were popular in the late 19th century. Sensational titles such as *The Mighty Atom* and *The Sorrows of Satan* gave some levels of the reading public an escape from their humdrum lives that is today provided by the television and cinema.

Annie Swan is remembered as a writer of light romantic novels, but she also helped raise morale during the First World War. At one important meeting in the immediate aftermath of the slaughter, she listened to delegates from a host of nations lauding the part their countries had played in defeating the menace of the Kaiser. Well aware that Scotland had actually given a higher percentage of her manhood to the war than any other nation, Swan stood up to talk. After she thanked the assembled men for helping Scotland to win the war, she received the loudest cheer of the day. Sometimes it takes a Scotswoman to appreciate the contribution that the men of her country have made to the world.

Elizabeth Mackintosh, the Inverness born playwright and novelist is possibly best remembered by her pen name of Gordon Daviot. Her *Richard of Bordeaux* was published under that name, as was her biography of Graham of *Claverhouse*. However, some of her other writings, such as The *Franchise Affair*, were written under the name of Josephine Tey. Mackintosh was one of the earliest Scotswomen to write detective fiction, and surely one of the few Scottish writers who also taught physical education. Her main character, the detective Alan Grant, appeared in several successful and highly crafted stories. As a sign of changing times, Mackintosh also wrote dramas for the new media of radio.

Mackintosh was only one of many splendid women writers of the 20th century, among whom Naomi Mitchison shines out as a startling talent. Edinburgh born but educated in Oxford, Mitchison's novels on Sparta and Greece perhaps reveals a classical education, but certainly show a skill in clarity and detail. Her *Bough Breaks* and *Black Sparta* cannot really be matched as a literary picture of early Greece. Mitchison also wrote of Egypt in *Corn King and Spring Queen*. Writing, however, was only part of Mitchison's life. Married to the Labour MP and minister of land Gilbert Mitchison, she travelled extensively and in 1963 the Bakgatla people of Botswana made her Tribal Adviser and Mother, which is surely a unique honour for any Edinburgh writer. Even after viewing all the beauties of the world, however, Mitchison settled at Carradale in Kintyre.

Other early 20th century women included Nan Shepherd, whose *The Weatherhouse* is an amazingly skilful work. Catherine Carswell and Willa Muir are other women whose work has all but been relegated to the forgotten shelves of local libraries in favour of English and foreign writers. Hardly known outside a limited circle, Mary Brooksbank was an Aberdeen born poet who always spoke her own mind. She joined the Communist Party when she was aged 21 and received a 40-day sentence in jail for starting a riot in Dundee. In the 20s and

30s, communism was rife in a Dundee where unemployment was high and many people lived as poorly as any Dickensian character. Some families lived in houses where orange crates were the only furniture and employment only a dim memory. Brooksbank campaigned in person and in words against such conditions. In 1930 she founded the Working Woman's Guild and next year was the only woman among 23 people who were charged with mobbing and rioting. The battles between police and communists were fierce, but when Brooksbank realised that Stalin was as big a tyrant as any capitalist, she made her feelings known and the Communist Party got rid of her. Shorn of its politics, her poetry is earthy, vibrant and genuine.

The literary work of Muriel Spark, the daughter of a Suffragette who wrote the famous *Prime of Miss Jean Brodie* is well known. Fewer people realise that she also worked in Central Africa and in British Intelligence during the Second World War. Many of her works appear humorous, but contain an unsettling, often-sinister twist that often leaves the reader slightly disturbed. Toward the end of the 20th century, women writers overtook men both in numbers and in popular impact. Possibly this trend reflected a growing number of female publishers, or a new image of manhood that was derived from a diminishing number of traditionally male jobs. Men had to emphasise their masculinity by 'macho' toughness where reading and education did not play a large part. Women such as Muriel Spark, Jessie Kesson, Janice Galloway and Liz Lochead are major players on the Scottish literary scene. It would not, of course, be possible to write any chapter on literature without including that 21st century phenomenon, *Harry Potter*, by J. K. Rowling, with her Edinburgh and Perthshire connections.

As the 21st century rolls on, the outlook is healthy for women who like to write. As well as the traditional book and magazine market, women also contribute to radio and television writing, so there is ample scope for their talents. Females will continue to adorn the future of Scottish literature.

Chapter 22

L'envoi

A small book such as this cannot tell the story of Scottish womanhood. It can only scrape a small part of the surface. For every woman mentioned, many thousands have been omitted. For example: women such as Mary Garden the Aberdeen born soprano who sang in Chicago and Paris and Ann Grant who wrote *Letters from the Mountains*. There were women such as Jesse King the designer and internationally acclaimed book illustrator, Thea Musgrave the composer and Madeleine Smith the murderess. There were women such as Helen Smellie from Glasgow, the first woman to be accepted as a member of the Stock Exchange, Margaret Kidd, the first woman Sheriff-Principal. Most contemporary women have not been mentioned, women such as Lorraine Kelly, Carol Smiley and Lesley Riddoch of television and broadcasting fame.

However, this book is intended as an introduction to a surprisingly varied and endlessly talented nation of women. The past is gone, but their fame frequently remains to be found; perhaps because she has so many, Scotland tends to neglect her heroines. Although many battles have been won and the future appears to be secure, there are still glass ceilings preventing the advancement of women to some positions. There remain a few professions where women seem unable to progress as their talent demands, but given their character and past achievements, Scotswomen certainly have the ability to shatter a few panes of glass.

In February 2004, a report highlighted the fact that businesses started by women in Scotland have a better chance of achieving success than those founded by men. The impact of women on business since the 1960s has been immense; where once women were a minority in banks and financial houses, now they outnumber men. There are far more female than male teachers, women dominate the human resources, clerical and administrative departments of most Scottish companies. There are Scotswomen managing large businesses, women run hotels and retail stores, work in the legal and political field and as engineers, environmentalists, archaeologists; some also work offshore on oil rigs. Indeed, Scotland has a higher percentage of women in senior management positions than any other part of the United Kingdom, with Dundee the city where women have the best chance or rising to the top.

Even in the field of sport, Scotswomen have made a major impact in the closing stages of the 20th and the early 21st centuries. It was a woman's curling team that brought home a gold medal from the 2002 Olympics, and a Lossiemouth rower who won Gold in 2012, while Ellen MacArthur and Emma Richardson, with strong Scottish connections proved that even long distance yachting is not closed to Scotswomen. As the only woman and youngest ever person to complete the solo Round the World Race in 2003, Richardson deserves a mention. On her return her only complaint was that her muscular arms might frighten off her boyfriend. Her Scottishness was confirmed when she visited Helensburgh Yacht Club, where she first learned her skills. There are a growing number of Scottish sports women, so that while athletes such as Liz McColgan who have raced around the track, women play golf at most Scottish courses and women's football and rugby are expanding sports.

There is also a darker side. While most women have gladly accepted the mantle of responsibility and progress, there are disquieting reports of rising numbers of women that indulge in law breaking. Scotswomen

L'envoi

have also taken part in major crime, with a woman matriarch of a Fife drug operation jailed early in 2004. The problems of success have also affected businesswomen, with a higher proportion of female senior managers resorting to the bottle than is the case among their male colleagues.

The majority of Scotswomen, however, do not choose such paths. There has always been a strong pragmatic streak through Scotswoman, which matches the sincerity, romanticism, financial acumen and bloody-minded stubbornness that has seen them through great trials and tribulations. Now at last the way ahead is clear and they can carve out a new Scotland free of prejudice and false barriers.

Chapter 23

Selected Bibliography

Primary Sources: University of Dundee Archives

Census Report 1881 MF/2 (2) 1881 89/282 (Lochee)
Cock, James, *Diary of James Cock* MS 6
Cock, James, *Diary of James Cock, 1834 and Up* MS 6
Cock, James, *Diary of James Cock*; 1866 MS 6
Letter from James Cock, 17th November 1838 (MS 66 11/10/10)
Letter from Edward Cox to Father Van de Rydt, 8th July 1891 MS 66/II/10/59 (1)
Letter from James Cox to Father Van de Rydt, 1891 MS 66/II/10/59/2

Primary Sources: Printed

Baillie, Lady Grisell; *The Household Book, 1692 – 1733* (Scottish Historical Society, Edinburgh 1911)
Cannon, R, *Historical Records of the Royal Regiment of Scots Dragoons* (Longman Orme and William Clowes, London, 1840)

Selected Bibliography

Census of Scotland 1871 (Tables of the Number of the Population of the Families, of Children receiving Education, of houses, and rooms with windows in Scotland and its islands on 3rd April 1871) (Edinburgh 1871)
Census of Scotland 1891 (Tables of the number of the Population, of the Families, and of rooms with windows in Scotland and its islands on 5th April 1891 (Edinburgh 1891)
Dundee Social Union (Dundee 1905)
Dundee Social Union: Report on Housing, Industrial Conditions and the Medical Inspection of School Children (Dundee 1905)

Engels, Frederick; *The Condition of the Working Class in England*; (Grenada, London 1969)
Factories Inquiry Commission, Supplementary Report: Employment of Children in Factories, Part Two – session 4th February 1834 (Shannon & Southampton 1968)
Grant, Elizabeth, *Memoirs of a Highland Lady*, (Canongate, Edinburgh, 1988)
Magnusson, Magnus, (Editor); *Laxdaela Saga* (Penguin Books, Harmondsworth, 1969)
Minutes of Evidence Taken Before the Royal Commission on the housing of the Working Classes: Scotland 1884/5 (Shannon 1970)
Parliamentary List of Voters for Dundee 1868-69
Parliamentary Register of Voters, Burgh of Dundee 1884-85
Parliamentary Register of Female Voters, Burgh of Dundee 1884-85
'Reports of Assistant Commissioners on hand-loom weaving in Several Districts of
England, Scotland, Ireland and Continental Europe 1839-40' in Irish University
Press Series, *British Parliamentary Papers: Industrial Relations: Textiles* (Shannon, Ireland 1970)
The Dundee Directory (Dundee, various dates from 1850 – 1889)
Withrington, Donald J., & Grant, Ian (Editors), *The Statistical Account of Scotland 1791-1799, Volume XVIII Angus*, (Wakefield 1976)

Secondary Sources, Books

Archibald, Malcolm; *Sixpence for the Wind: A knot of Nautical Folklore* (Whittles, Latheronwheel, 1999)
Archibald, Malcolm; *The Whalehunters*, (Mercat, Edinburgh 2004)
Barrow, G.W.S.; *Robert Bruce and the Community of the Realm of Scotland* (Edinburgh University Press, Edinburgh, 1976)
Black, J. L. *Penicuik and neighbourhood*, (Edinburgh, ND)
Brown, Hamish; *The Fife Coast*; (Mainstream, Edinburgh, 1994)
Cameron, David Kerr; *The Ballad and the Plough*; (Futura, London 1979)
Cameron, A. D.; *Living in Scotland 1760 – 1820;* (Oliver & Boyd, Edinburgh 1969)
Chadwick, Nora & Dillon, Myles; *The Celtic Realms*; (Sphere Books, London 1973)
Clark, G. Kitson, *The Making of Victorian England* (London 1985)
Davidson, James D. G. *Scots and the Sea* (Mainstream, Edinburgh, 2003)
Dickinson, W. Croft et al; *A Source Book of Scottish History 1424 – 1567* (Thomas Nelson, London & Edinburgh, 1958)
Dorward, David; *Dundee, Names, People and Places* (Mercat Press, Edinburgh 1998)
Evans, Eric J. *The Forging of the Modern State: Early Industrial Britain 1783-1870* (Harlow 1996)
Farwell, Byron; *Queen Victoria's Little Wars*, (Wordsworth, Ware, 1999)
Featherstone, Donald; *Victorian Colonial Warfare: India* (Blandford, London, 1992)
Fischer, Thomas A.; *The Scots in Germany* (Otto Schulze & Co, Edinburgh, 1902)
Fischer, Thomas A.; *The Scots in Sweden* (Otto Schulze & Co, Edinburgh, 1907)
Fraser, George MacDonald; *The Steel Bonnets* (Barrie & Jenkins, London, 1971)

Selected Bibliography

Gordon, Eleanor, *Women and the Labour Movement in Scotland 1850-1914* (Oxford 1991)

Grimble, Ian; *Clans and Chiefs*; (Blond & Briggs, London, 1980)

Harris, Pat, *Scotching the Myths of Lochee: Cox Bros., Lochee and the Irish* (Dundee 1994)

Haley, Arthur H.; *Our Davey: General Sir David Baird* (1757 – 1829), (Bullfinch Publications, ND)

Hewitson, Jim; *Far off In Sunlit Places*, (Canongate, Edinburgh, 1998)

Hope, Annette; *A Caledonian Feast* (Grafton, London & Glasgow, 1989)

Johnson, Paul: *20th Century Britain*; (Longman, London & New York, 1994)

Kelsall, Helen and Keith; *Scottish Lifestyle 300 Years Ago*; (Scottish Cultural Press, Aberdeen, 1986)

Leneman, L; *In the service of life: the story of Elsie Inglis and the Scottish Women's Hospitals* (Mercat Press, Edinburgh 1994)

Linklater, Magnus & Hesketh, Christian; *John Graham of Dundee: Bonnie Dundee For King and Conscience* (Canongate, Edinburgh, 1992)

Lochhead, Marion; *The Scots Household in the 18th Century* (Edinburgh 1948)

Lynch, Michael (Editor); *The Oxford Companion to Scottish History* (Oxford University Press, Oxford, 2001)

Mackie, R. L. *A Short History of Scotland*; (Oliver & Boyd, Edinburgh 1952)

McCorry, Helen; *The Thistle at War* (National Museums of Scotland Publishing, Edinburgh, 1997)

MacGregor, Forbes, *Famous Scots: The Pride of a Small Nation* (Gordon Wright Publishing, Edinburgh, 1984)

MacDougall, L; *The Prisoners at Penicuik* (Midlothian District Council, Dalkeith, 1989)

MacDougall, Ian; *Hard Work ye ken: Midlothian Women Farmworkers*; (Tuckwell, East Linton 1996)

McKean, Charles; *Edinburgh: Portrait of a City* (Century, London 1991)

McKean, Charles, & Walker, David, *Dundee: An Illustrated Introduction* (Edinburgh 1984)

Mackintosh, W. R.; *Around the Orkney Peat-Fires*; (Kirkwall Press, 1967)
McGowran, Tom, *Newhaven-on-Forth Port of Grace;* (John Donald, Edinburgh 1985)
Miller, James; *Salt in the Blood: Scotland's Fishing Communities Past and Present* (Canongate, Edinburgh, 1999)
Mitchelson, Rosalind; *Lordship to Patronage, Scotland 1603 – 1745*; (Edinburgh University Press 1981)
Munro, Ian S.; *The Island of Bute* (David and Charles, Newton Abbot, 1973)
Nicholson, Ranald; *Scotland: The Later Middle Ages,* (Oliver and Boyd, Edinburgh, 1974)
Paterson, Raymond Campbell; *For the Lion: A History of the Scottish Wars of Independence 1296 – 1357*; (John Donald, Edinburgh, 1996)
Paz D.G. *The Politics of Working –Class Education in Britain 1830-50* (Manchester 1980)
Phillips, Douglas and Thomson, Ron; *Dundee, People and Places to Remember* (David Winter and Sons, Dundee, 1992)
Prebble, John; *The Highland Clearances*, (Penguin Books, Harmondsworth, 1963)
Prebble, John, *The Lion in the North: One Thousand Years of Scotland's History* (BCA, London, 1974)
Robertson, Elizabeth; *Mary Slessor* (NMS, Edinburgh, 2001)
Scott, Sir Walter; *Letters on Demonology and Witchcraft*, (Wordsworth, Ware, 2001)
Shafe, Michael (Compiler); *University Education in Dundee 1881 – 1981* (University of Dundee, Dundee, 1982)
Smout. T. C.; *A History of the Scottish People, 1560 – 1830*; (Fontana, London, 1969)
Smout, T. C.; *A Century of the Scottish People 1830 – 1950*; (Fontana, London 1987)
Smyth, Alfred P.; *Warlords and Holy Men: Scotland AD 80-1000* (Edinburgh University Press, Edinburgh, 1984)
Szasz, Ferenc Morton: *Scots in the North American West 1790 – 1917* (University of Oklahoma Press, Norman, 2000)

Selected Bibliography

The History of the Revolt in India, (Chambers, Edinburgh, 1859)
That Land of Exiles: Scots in Australia (HMSO Edinburgh 1988)
Torrie, Elizabeth P.D.; *Mediaeval Dundee: A Town and its People* (Abertay Historical Society, Dundee, 1990)
Walker, David, *Dundee Architecture & Architects 1750-1914* (Dundee 1955, 1964)
Walker, William, *Juteopolis: Dundee and its Textile Workers 1885-1968* (Edinburgh 1979)
Warden, Alexander J., *The Linen Trade: Ancient and Modern* (London 1864)
Watson, Norman, *Daughters of Dundee*; (Linda McGill, Dundee, 1997)
Watson, Mark, *Jute and Flax Mills of Dundee* (Tayport 1990)
Whatley, Christopher; *The Scottish Salt Industry 1570 – 1850: An Economic and Social History* (Aberdeen University Press, Aberdeen, 1987)
Whatley, Christopher A., Swinfen, David B., Smith, Annette M., *The Life and Times of Dundee* (Edinburgh 1993)
Wormwald, Jenny; *Court Kirk and Community: Scotland 1470 – 1625* (Edinburgh University Press, Edinburgh, 1981)
Young, G.M. *Portrait of an Age: Victorian England* (London 1977)

Secondary Sources: Articles in Books

Kemp, John, 'Red Tayside – Political Change in Early Twentieth Century Dundee' in Miskell, Louise, Whatley, Christopher and Harris, Bob (Editors), *Victorian Dundee – Image and Realities* (East Linton 2001)
Lenman, B. P., 'The Industrial History of the Dundee Region from the 18th to the early 20th Century' in Jones, S. J. (Editor) *Dundee and District* (Dundee 1968)

Printed in Great Britain
by Amazon